FEATURING YVON PREHN
DESKTOP PUBLISHING COLUMNIST FOR CHRISTIAN COMPUTING MAGAZINE

How to Use Your Computer to Create

BETTER BULLETINS NEWSLETTERS AND MORE!

A STEP-BY-STEP GUIDE to Creating Better Communications Through Desktop Publishing

Gospel Light

Gospel Light is an evangelical Christian publisher dedicated to serving the local church. We believe God's vision for Gospel Light is to provide church leaders with biblical, user-friendly materials that will help them evangelize, disciple and minister to children, youth and families.

We hope this Gospel Light resource will help you discover biblical truth for your own life and help you minister to your church. God bless you in your work.

For a free catalog from Gospel Light please contact your Christian supplier or call 1-800-4-GOSPEL.

PUBLISHING STAFF

William T. Greig, Publisher
Dr. Elmer L. Towns, Senior Consulting Publisher
Dr. Gary S. Greig, Senior Consulting Editor
Jean Daly, Managing Editor
Pam Weston, Editorial Assistant
Kyle Duncan, Editorial Director
Bayard Taylor, M.Div., Editor, Theological and Biblical Issues

ISBN 0-8307-1827-3

Printed in U.S. A.

How to Make Clean Copies from This Book

YOU MAY MAKE COPIES OF PORTIONS OF THIS BOOK WITH A CLEAN CONSCIENCE IF:
- you (or someone in your organization) are the original purchaser;
- you are using the copies you make for a noncommercial purpose (such as teaching or promoting your ministry) within your church or organization;
- you follow the instructions provided in this book.

HOWEVER, IT IS ILLEGAL FOR YOU TO MAKE COPIES IF:
- you are using the material to promote, advertise or sell a product or service other than for ministry fund-raising;
- you are using the material in or on a product for sale;
- you or your organization are **not** the original purchaser of this book.

By following these guidelines you help us keep our products affordable.
Thank you,
Gospel Light

This book is dedicated with love
to Paul,
my partner in life and ministry.

A Note About the Examples in the Resource

There are numerous examples of desktop produced publications in the book. A few notes apply:

- None of the names, phone numbers, or addresses are real. Nor are the churches or ministries illustrated.
- The examples are based on the many actual church and ministry publications I have received from my desktop publishing seminar participants. They represent real projects being produced by people in ministries and churches across the U.S.
- Some of the examples are adapted from actual material from the First United Methodist Church in Colorado Springs. These examples include "Adapted from FUMC" and are used with permission.
- Many of these examples use "dummy text" which starts out, "Loren ipsum. . . ." These are random letters grouped to look like words.
- All of the photos were scanned in. Some were scanned as realistic photos, some were scanned as a high-contrast illustration. The quality is not as good as it would be if they were traditionally produced but typical of a lot of scanners. The photos are used to illustrate design principles only.

Book Misc.

- Clip art: The clip art used in the book is from a variety of sources. Please see the resource section for how to reach the various suppliers.
- Trademarks: Rather than put a trademark in every occurrence of the trademarked names used throughout this book, the names are used only in an editorial way and benefit the trademark owner with no intention of infringement of the trademark intended.
- Notice of Liability: The information in this book is offered without warranty. While every precaution was taken in preparing this book, neither the author nor publisher shall have any liability to any person or entity with respect to any liability, loss or damage caused or alleged to be caused directly or indirectly by the instructions contained in this book or by the computer hardware and software products described or mentioned herein.
- The book was previously published under the title, *The Desktop Publishing Remedy, Making the Computer Work for Your Ministry* in 1993 by David C. Cook Publishing. It was also published under the title, *Tap the Power of Desktop Publishing for Your Church or Ministry* in 1995 by Yvon Prehn.

Table of Contents

People in churches and ministries all over America are using desktop publishing to powerfully and economically communicate their message in the Information Age. You can too!

chapter 1

Introduction

You've joined a great army of Christian communicators when you decided to tackle producing ministry publications with your computer! Let me introduce you to some of the folks I've had the privilege of working with as I've taught my seminars around the country on desktop publishing (DTP) for ministry, for example:

- Church secretaries like Marti, Sally, and Gretchen who have a computer and are working hard to produce the church bulletin, newsletter, flyers and ads.
- Pastors like Robert who want to make the publications he sends to his youth group readable and fun. He started out with a newsletter, now he does calendars and flyers as well.
- Parachurch staff like Grace who wants to produce cost-effective donor letters and updates that inform and inspire.
- Lay people like Hugh, a volunteer with a church-related counseling center, who wants to use his retirement time to produce brochures explaining how the center can help hurting folks.

"The Word became flesh and made his dwelling among us" (John 1:14).

Jesus took on human form so He could speak the language of His people and communicate to them what God was like.

Our continuing opportunity and challenge in desktop publishing is to follow that example—to make the words of the gospel flesh and blood in the lives of people today.

From teaching these and hundreds of folks around the country from groups as varied as international ministries to tiny churches, I've observed the same struggles with this new technology.

You start out assigned to do the bulletin or newsletter and that's exciting, but it doesn't take long until you realize you have so much to learn about computers and publications. Nobody told you when you got started you'd have to learn to be an editor, designer, typesetter, layout artist and publication production manager.

But you do have to learn all these skills. I've seen all the folks I mentioned grow in their skills and confidence with computers and watched them produce desktop-published projects that surprised them. I've seen computer-generated frustration turn to fun; confusion turn to confidence. You will too.

What you do is important!

Do you realize that your church bulletin or newsletter might be the only piece of Christian literature a non-Christian might ever see?

If a stranger wanders into your church, what do your pieces say to them? This book will help you create welcoming, professional pieces that reflect the caring of your church and the gospel of Jesus—trusting that the first pieces of Christian literature they see won't be their last!

More important though than learning these technology skills, as you read this book remember at the core all of this really isn't about computers or desktop publishing. It's about ministry.

Desktop publishing is a ministry-tool not just new technology. It can be used to flesh out the words of Jesus Christ and the works of His kingdom to our generation. The computer and DTP is simply the latest means we can use to tell the old and ever new story.

I commend you for your courage to try new things, for the patience to learn the skills required. It isn't easy and it isn't magic, but the results are well worth the effort involved. Know that my prayers are with you, for grace and peace, wisdom and courage as you enter this new arena of ministry.

What desktop publishing (DTP) can do for your ministry

"When technology . . . is introduced, new ways to express your work are suddenly discovered and your church's ministry is strengthened as a result."

William R. Johnson
The Pastor and the Personal Computer

If DTP is primarily a tool for ministry, how does it accomplish ministry goals? A few of the ways are listed below. You'll discover many of your own as you work with DTP.

DTP can satisfy people's need for information.

The bulletin, newsletters, calendars and prayer letters are a necessity in the Information Age. People want to know what is going on in a way that answers their questions and is easy to comprehend. This is one of the greatest benefits of DTP.

DTP can produce professional-looking pieces that communicate to today's audience.

Professional doesn't mean expensive. DTP brings the tools of publication professionals: typesetting, the ability to put text in columns, and to use charts and illustrations, into the hands of any sized church or ministry.

DTP can be a cost-effective and time-saving way to produce communication pieces.

Though the initial investment in time and money for DTP can be considerable, it costs far less and takes much less time to produce publications using DTP than it does with traditional publishing.

How this book can help you

If you're new at DTP or still considering it , read through the entire book to get a good overview of the DTP process.

After you understand the basic process, refer back to individual chapters for specific training in the various areas.

The Internet and how this book applies:

Though a later section comments directly about going online, all of the DTP and design principles you learn in this publication will help you create quality publications for the Internet. The tools and communication principles are basically the same.

This book will take you step by step through the entire desktop publishing process and will give you the skills to make DTP a successful tool in your ministry. In the book you'll learn:

- An overview of computer hardware and software. That you don't have to be a computer genius to create DTP projects.
- How to plan your DTP projects. How to evaluate your audience, your communication goals, resources and time limitations.
- How to write for desktop publishing to effectively combine written and visual communication. Tips to create powerful headlines, captions and body copy that will inform and inspire.
- All about type—how to select, use and adapt it to your communication needs.
- Ways to flesh out your basic message by integrating graphics and photos into your publications.
- Specific guidelines for layouts of church and ministry logos, stationery, bulletins, newsletters and many other communication pieces that you can copy and modify for your own projects. You'll also see a gallery of what other folks have produced.
- Finally, tips on proofing, selecting the right paper, getting it produced and managing DTP—for now and the future.

You don't have to know how to tune up your engine to drive a car. In the same way, you don't have to know much about computer hardware to be able to produce good desktop published communications.

chapter 2

Computer Hardware

Your computer hardware knowledge isn't what makes great DTP communications.

Technology is just a tool—your skills, your heart for ministry, and your desire to communicate your message is what is most important.

The most important hardware is you!

If you already know how to use your desktop publishing software, there are really only two things you need to know about computer hardware to do desktop publishing. The first is how to turn on the computer to access the program and the second is how to turn on the printer to print it.

Though there is much you can learn about computer hardware, most of it isn't critical for you to understand to be able to produce fantastic DTP documents.

I was producing a national newsletter using desktop publishing before I knew what a single computer term meant. The same is true with many successful desktop publishers.

In many churches, often a volunteer who works in high tech takes care of all of the hardware concerns. Just make sure you know how to contact yours when you need him or her.

In numerous Christian organizations the information systems department takes care of the hardware and the communications people do the projects. Teamwork gets the job done.

You don't have to understand computers to do DTP

It's not that computer hardware knowledge isn't useful to learn. It is. If you run into problems with your computer, the more you know about it the easier it is to take care of it and get back to your project without waiting for someone else to bail you out. You'll make more knowledgeable buying decisions the more you know about computer hardware.

But as useful as these things are to know, don't let the computer intimidate you and don't feel you have to master knowledge of the hardware before you can begin to produce excellent DTP pieces.

Where to learn more

"A computer. . . does not require in-depth mathematical knowledge and, contrary to popular belief, the computer does not think for itself."

William R. Johnson,
The Pastor and the Personal Computer

Information about computer hardware could fill the whole book. What follows is simply an overview, but it will define the most common terms you'll encounter and apply them to your work. If you want to learn more about computer hardware, there are numerous sources including:

Computer user groups

These are one of the best ways to learn about computers. They consist of groups of people who own a similar brand of computers.

The overall user groups also usually have novice or beginner meetings and classes. Go to these groups to ask questions and you'll learn lots. User groups also usually have people available

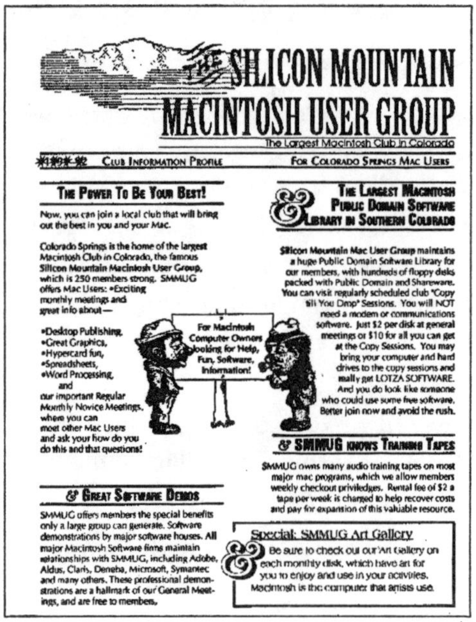

THE SILICON MOUNTAIN MACINTOSH USER GROUP

The Largest Macintosh Club in Colorado

Club Information Profile — For Colorado Springs Mac Users

The Power To Be Your Best!

Now, you can join a local club that will bring out the best in you and your Mac.

Colorado Springs is the home of the largest Macintosh Club in Colorado, the famous Silicon Mountain Macintosh User Group, which is 250 members strong. SMMUG offers Mac Users: •Exciting monthly meetings and great info about—

•Desktop Publishing,
•Great Graphics,
•Hypercard fun,
•Spreadsheets,
•Word Processing,
and
our important Regular Monthly Novice Meetings, where you can meet other Mac Users and ask your how do you do this and that questions!

& The Largest Macintosh Public Domain Software Library in Southern Colorado

Silicon Mountain Mac User Group maintains a huge Public Domain Software Library for our members, with hundreds of floppy disks packed with Public Domain and Shareware. You can visit regularly scheduled club "Copy till You Drop" Sessions. You will NOT need a modem or communications software. Just $2 per disk at general meetings or $10 for all you can get at the Copy Sessions. You may bring your computer and hard drives to the copy sessions and really get LOTZA SOFTWARE. And you do look like someone who could use some free software. Better join now and avoid the rush.

& SMMUG knows Training Tapes

SMMUG owns many audio training tapes on most major mac programs, which we allow members weekly checkout priviledges. Rental fee of $2 a tape per week is charged to help recover costs and pay for expansion of this valuable resource.

& Great Software Demos

SMMUG offers members the special benefits only a large group can generate. Software demonstrations by major software houses. All major Macintosh Software firms maintain relationships with SMMUG, including Adobe, Aldus, Claris, Deneba, Microsoft, Symantec and many others. These professional demonstrations are a hallmark of our General Meetings, and are free to members.

Special: SMMUG Art Gallery

& Be sure to check out our Art Gallery on each monthly disk, which have art for you to enjoy and use in your activities. Macintosh is the computer that artists use.

A computer user group newsletter.

User groups are a great way to learn about computer hardware, software, systems and desktop publishing production tips.

*So are **SIGS,** which are "special interest groups" within the larger group. There is usually a desktop publisher's SIG within most groups and it is an invaluable place to learn about desktop publishing.*

who are able to answer your questions. They are great to get to know and their expertise is usually free or much less expensive than hiring a consultant.

Become an active member of a computer user's group if possible—you'll receive a great return in knowledge on the time you invest.

Other folks doing the same kind of DTP work

For years I met once a week with a friend who was doing the same kind of DTP work I was. Doing DTP in ministry is challenging and quite different than doing it in the corporate world—find a friend who has the same struggles.

Nothing beats being able to swap ideas of what works, what doesn't, and what are the latest tips and tricks you've learned in the middle of a project.

Computer publications

There are a multitude of computer magazines and books on the topic of computer hardware. Fortunately most libraries carry the more popular magazines and many of the books. Look there first—you'll probably find most of the information you need.

There are two publications that are especially useful for people just getting started in computers.

For IBM compatibles: *PC Novice* is fantastic. It is a magazine that explains how a computer works in plain language. For subscription information for *PC Novice* call 1-800-848-1478. After you master that publication, there are a huge number of PC related magazines that can help—go to your newsstand for ideas.

For Macintosh user: *The Macintosh Bible* (not to be confused with the Holy Bible on disk, which is an entirely different product) is a book that will tell you everything you want to know about your machine. It's in very understandable language and keeps coming out with updates that get better all the time. *The Macintosh Bible* is available from Peachpit Press, 1-800-283-9444.

Software and hardware manuals and tutorials

It's a common assumption that nobody reads the computer manuals or tries the tutorials that come with the computer or software.

That's too bad because there is a lot of useful information in them. But to get the most out of them don't sit down and try to read the manual through or perform the entire tutorial when you first get your computer or new software. Read the bare minimum and try enough of the tutorial to get you working on your system. Then put them aside for awhile and just work on your computer.

After a few months, go back to your manual and read a little section at a time. Try the tutorial again. They will now make much more sense to you. Just because they didn't make sense to you when you first got your system, doesn't mean you should toss them forever—you need a frame of reference first.

Videos are a good investment for training because you can watch them again and again and use them for training volunteers.

We've got a great video that goes along with this book— *Eight half-hour training sessions for anyone doing DTP in ministry. Call Gospel Light Publications at 1-800-4-GOSPEL to order a copy.*

Computer training and classes

There is a vast selection of computer training resources available: classes at junior colleges, adult education, seminars and the computer store where you purchased your computer. If you don't want to take a class in person, training is available on video or cassette tape. Many computer groups have them for you to borrow. There are also personal trainers available.

No matter what methods you use, there comes a time when you need to stop researching and jump into learning about and trying a computer itself. And that's what we'll do next.

Mac or PC, what's the difference?

You can do desktop publishing on any brand of computer, Mac or PC or a large networked computer system running UNIX.

As long as you have DTP software and minimum hardware requirements, DTP production is possible.

In the past the Mac was definitely better at DTP, but with the introduction of Windows 95 that's no longer true.

There are primarily two separate worlds of computers—the computers that are IBM compatible often referred to as PCs and the computers made by Apple. The IBM compatible computers include not only computers that are made by IBM, but computers made by a variety of other manufacturers such as Zenith, Packard Bell and Compaq. IBM compatible means they have an operating system that is similar to the one IBM uses and that they can operate the same software programs. We'll call all of these "PC" for short in the rest of the book. Although a PC, which actually means "personal computer" theoretically could be an IBM compatible or a Mac, it has become common jargon to refer to the IBM compatibles primarily as "PCs."

The Apple Computer Corporation makes the Macintosh and they have an operating system that is primarily unique to that one company. There are a large variety of Macintosh computers, including Performas, PowerBooks, the new Power Macintoshes and all the older models that still work well for DTP. We will refer to all of them in the rest of the book as "Mac."

First, the differences between the two will be explained. Then the discussion on hard drives, floppy disks, monitors, keyboards, printers and scanners will be similar for both.

CPU or central processing unit

"Prolonged computer happiness is more a matter of personality than of hardware and software."

John Bear, Ph.D., Computer Wimp

The central processing unit is often referred to as the brains of the computer. It is the part of the computer that actually does the computing work. In Mac computers the CPU is a 68000-family microprocessor chip made primarily by Motorola. In an IBM compatible it is an 80000-family chip made by Intel initially and now made by several other companies.

The actual number of the chip determines in part how fast your computer will operate and the complexity of operations it can perform. In addition to the number of the chip, you will also have a number that tells the speed of your computer. In the past, 66 MHz was considered blazing speed, now it is adequate, but not exceptional. Speeds of 150 MHz are possible with some Pentiums and Power Macs.

For publications such as the average church newsletter or bulletin you don't need a super fast computer, but if you start doing color work, sound, video or complex image editing with the computer, the additional speed, along with extra RAM is very helpful.

In IBM compatibles, some of the older models will have an 80386 chip; the newer, faster and more powerful models, a 80486 or Pentium chip. In computer ads they will simply refer to the machine as a "486 computer" or a "Pentium computer." It is extremely difficult to do desktop publishing with an IBM on anything less powerful than a 386 computer with 8 MB of RAM. If you want to use Windows 95 and a program like Pagemaker, you need at least 16 MB of RAM and at least a 486.

For Macs, a Performa would be the base machine recommended. If possible, a PowerMac with 16-24 MB of RAM is better.

As I travel around teaching, I see too little RAM as one of the biggest reasons folks doing DTP in ministry have problems with their computers. Too little RAM will cause your system to lock up, go slow and crash. In addition, you won't be able to run many programs well.

The operating system or user interface

Think of the operating system or user interface as the translator between the computer chip and you. The computer chip sits there with its tremendous computing power, but it needs a way to tell you what is going on and you need a way to tell it what you want it to do. You communicate through the user interface.

This used to be where there was a tremendous difference between Mac and PCs. This was because the Mac first used what is called an intuitive, graphical user interface (sometimes abbreviated as GUI and pronounced "gooey"). What that means is that things on the computer screen make sense to the average person even if they haven't learned computer commands. For example, to delete something you put it into the trash can. It looked like this:

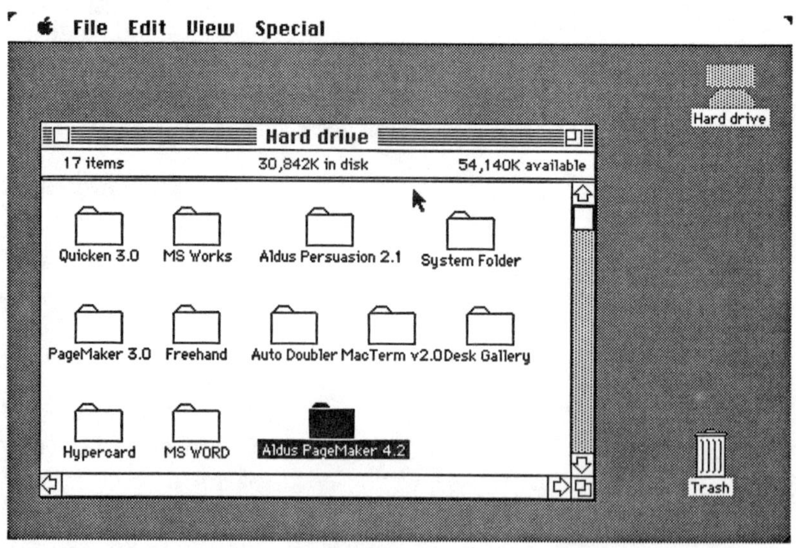

This is what the Mac user interface looks like. Until Windows was invented, this easy-to-understand interface was often the choice of desktop publishers. However, with the invention of Windows and especially Windows 95, PCs now have a graphical interface that is also intuitive and easy to use.

Hardware recommendations for DTP:

Though some of the low-end DTP software will run on less-powerful systems, the configurations below would be the minimum requirements for the current versions of Pagemaker for both PCs and Mac.

If you will be doing extensive graphics manipulation, color work, or photo-editing, your RAM requirements will be significantly higher.

Mac

Minimum: You can do DTP on older Macs if you have a compatible program. For someone buying a new Mac, go with at least a Performa. The new Power Macs are excellent.
16-24 MB RAM
500 MB hard drive

IBM

Any compatible 486 or Pentium
Windows 95
16-24 MB RAM
500 MB Hard Drive-note: the gigabyte hard drives have come down so much in price on PCs, you might as well get one.

Initially PC computers didn't have a graphical interface. They had DOS as an operating system, a system which required you to type in commands that were often difficult to remember.

Windows, giving IBM a Mac face

Windows is a user interface software that makes the DOS operating system look like a Mac by providing pictures or icons of the programs and tasks you want to do. Instead of requiring you to type in commands, you select the icon as you do with a Mac. You have to have Windows if you are going to run Pagemaker and many other DTP programs on a PC. It makes a PC much easier to use and allows users to quickly become more productive on the computer. Especially with the introduction of Windows 95, the PC is as easy to use as the Mac.

Mac or IBM, what is best for DTP?

You can do DTP on either system. Both are very good computer systems—arguing about which is the best computer is meaningless because they are both extremely powerful.

What often determines which system will be used for DTP is that whatever system is currently in use in the church office for everything else is what will be used for DTP. In many cases this will be a PC. In the past, the Mac had a strong advantage over the PC in ease of use and its ability to do good DTP. That has changed significantly and there is little reason today to buy a Mac if the rest of the office has PCs to do your desktop publishing.

The importance of training

Regardless of what system you get, count on plenty of training and practice time. None of us were born with an innate ability to use the computer. To say a Mac is easier to use than a PC is like saying an automatic transmission is easier to learn than a stick shift. That may be true, but for either one, learning to drive a car takes lots of time, training and practice. Like driving a car, once you learn to use a computer to accomplish various communication tasks, it becomes second nature and you can't imagine ever being without one.

Computer memory—hard, RAM and floppy

Your computer has several ways it handles and stores the tasks you give it to do. They consist of:

Hard drives

The hard drive is a metal disk located inside the computer case. It can store large amounts of data.

It helps to think of this storage section of the computer as being similar to a filing cabinet where you store things you aren't presently using but that you need access to on a regular basis. The programs that enable you to do various tasks, the projects you've completed and want to save on the computer, all of these are stored on the hard drive. Once you have saved it, the data on the hard drive doesn't change when you turn the computer off.

RAM or the Random Access Memory of the computer is located in here on RAM chips.

ROM or the Read Only Memory of the computer is located here on an inaccessible chip.

The hard drive is also located in the computer case on a metal disk.

RAM—Random access memory

If the hard drive is the computer's filing cabinet, the RAM is like your desktop. You take programs and files you are working on out of the hard drive (your file cabinet) and load them into the RAM (your desktop) where you can work with them.

RAM is also the computer's short-term memory. Whatever you put in it is erased when you turn the computer off unless you've saved it to either your hard drive or a floppy disk.

Desktop publishing is just like traditional publishing in that lots of space is needed to do it. In traditional publishing you had to set the type and create the graphics, lay them out on a drafting table, work with T-squares, ink, and scissors. It took up a lot of space in an office for all that equipment and the more complex the project, the more space it took.

DTP on the computer is similar in that it takes up quite a bit of space, but here the space is in the RAM. Computers usually come with 8 or more megabytes (MB) of RAM. The minimum amount is adequate if you are only going to do word processing. If you are going to use the graphics and layout capabilities of DTP you need at least 16-24 MB of RAM for them to run well and quite a bit more if you get into large color graphics or photo-manipulation.

It is important to remember that the RAM is only working space. You always have to save your work to your hard drive or floppy drive or you will lose it when you turn off the computer.

Floppy disks

Floppy disks are the portable storage system for your computer, similar to file folders for your work. On floppy disks you can store the projects created in the computer, make an extra copy or carry them to another computer.

Floppy disks enable you to store and transport projects you've created in your computer. Treat them gently to avoid damaging data. Be sure to use them frequently to back up your work.

Floppy disks come in two sizes: 3.5 inch and 5.25 inch, though the 5.25 are rapidly becoming obsolete. They fit into disk drives of the same size in computers.

Even though the 3.5 floppy drives are encased in a hard plastic coating, all floppy drives should be treated with care.

One of the most important uses of floppy disks is to back up your work so that if anything happens to the copy that is on the hard drive (hard drives can crash and erase all your work) you have a copy. Get in the habit of making backup copies of your work often. Store a copy at another location for extra protection.

Many of the files with which you end up when doing DTP will no longer fit on a floppy disk. There are a large number of back-up systems available now: One older favorite that you can also use to back up your work is a Syquest drive. It is an external drive that can handle platters of 44MB up to 250 MB. The newer Zip and Jaz drives are also very popular if you have very large files. The Zip drive in particular is inexpensive and handles 100 MB backup disks. These disks look like a fat 3.5 floppy disk.

Whatever system you get, just be sure you use some system for back up of important work. As folks in the computer world always say, "It isn't a question of *if* your hard drive will crash, only a question of *when*."

Monitors—the computer's window to the world

A color monitor looks nice, but remember in most instances you'll be printing your work in black and white. One useful DTP trick with a color monitor however is to select either type or graphic images, color them, and then when printed out, they'll be a shade of gray.

The monitor is the part of the computer that looks like a TV screen where you can see what you are doing. Some come as part of the computer; some you can purchase separately. They come in a variety of types and sizes and all of them are useful for DTP.

Most monitors come in color today and most have a fairly good resolution. The numbers mean little if you don't like that particular monitor, so take time playing with it before you purchase one.

Monitors come in a variety of sizes, but cost can more than double for a large-size screen and it's often difficult for ministries to justify the extra cost. You can do any project with any size of screen, it just might take a bit longer because you have to move your image around a little more.

Keyboards

To prevent some of the repetitive strain injuries try the new ergonomic shaped keyboards—once you try them, you may not want to go back to a standard one.

Try wrist rests and various typing positions—take care of yourself so your DTP work brings you satisfaction, not injuries.

Don't forget overuse of the mouse can also cause repetitive strain injuries, so get a comfortable one and take frequent rests from using it.

Computer keyboards are similar to the keys of a typewriter, with the addition of a numeric keyboard and a top row of keys called function keys.

There are also all sorts of fancy keyboards: extended keyboards and now various split and ergonomically designed keyboards that are supposed to cut down on the stress of hours of typing.

Try out different keyboards and see what feels right for you. Some people use the standard keyboard and love it. Others prefer the extended version. Research is being done to find new shapes for keyboards and ways of using them that will cut down on repetitive motion injuries that can be the result of hours spent at the keyboard. If you haven't tried one of the new keyboards, take time to do it. They are much more natural feeling and comfortable.

I use one of the new ergonomic ones and it makes a world of difference on lengthy typing projects.

No matter what keyboard you use, be sure to take frequent breaks, stretch, flex your fingers, do back and neck stretches to keep yourself from injury. A good shoulder massage is recommended also.

The mouse, trackball and other input devices

"Learning to use a computer is the most complex mental activity most people will engage in between school and death."

John Bear, Ph.D., Computer Wimp

The mouse is a small palm-size device that is used to manipulate objects on the computer screen. It moves on a roller across a mouse pad and controls the moving cursor on the screen. A trackball is a mouse turned on its back. Instead of moving the mouse, you move a ball in the plastic square.

Either you love them or you hate them, but whatever your feelings, you've got to learn to use one if you're going to do DTP.

It works well to leave someone totally alone when they first encounter the mouse. Even the person with the greatest eye-hand coordination in the world will feel very awkward using one at first. Eventually however, you won't be able to imagine working without a mouse.

There are also digitizing tablets that you can draw on with a stylus that inputs the image directly into your computer program. You need to have a high-end drawing program to make these really useful, but for artists they are great.

Advances are being made all the time to improve voice input to computers, but it doesn't work very well at this time for desktop publishing.

Printers

You need a laser printer to produce professional-quality DTP masters that can be used for reproduction.

An ink-jet printer works well for individual copies. But a master made on an ink-jet printer will not be as sharp and clear for reproduction as one made with a laser printer.

The printer is the output device for your system. No matter how great your design skills or how good you are at laying out your DTP publication, if you don't print it with a good printer it won't look professional.

Your old dot matrix printer won't work for DTP. The letters and art work are too rough for all but the most casual of publications.

Ink-jet printers may be fine for text only and for first generation copies, but you can't reproduce copies from them at the quality you need to do true DTP work.

Laser printers are what made DTP possible. They enable you to produce a master that can then be used to print many copies of your document from a photocopier or printer. A laser printer is what makes your work look typeset. In the past 300 dpi used to be the resolution was considered fantastic for DTP. Now 600 dpi is the minimum for professional-looking work.

There are now many laser printers available in a wide range of prices. A printer that would do great quality 600 dpi printing used to be several thousand dollars, now Hewlett/Packard makes excellent ones for under $600.

At minimum you need a printer that will allow you to print graphics and type in a variety of sizes. Also, make sure your printer will allow you to take full advantage of the software you

A page description language, of which Postscript is one of the best known, is a type of programimg built into printers that places a majority of the work of processing the shape of graphics and type in the printer rather than in the computer. It makes the printer work faster and look better in its final output.

have purchased. Today, this usually means getting a Postscript printer. Postscript is a page description language built into the printer that will allow your printer to print type and many kinds of graphics at their best quality.

About color printers

Color is fun, but it is still very expensive to produce in quantity. Again, most affordable color printers are ink-jets and to reproduce the masters from them does not give you very good print quality.

Scanner

A scanner is similar to a miniature photocopy machine and is used in exactly the same way. It can either be a hand-held one or a flatbed scanner. Both types of scanners pass a beam of light over an image to copy it like the photocopy machine. Instead of the image coming out on paper it is stored digitally on the hard drive or computer disk.

You can copy clip art, photographs, textures, other documents, signatures, hand-drawn materials—all sorts of things with scanners. Once you've scanned these images onto a disk, you can access them and use them in any of your DTP projects.

CD-ROM drive

The huge demand for computer games—for more realistic action, for more video, color, sound and all the multimedia tricks is one of the forces that has developed CDs and had brought their production cost down.

Even if you aren't a game player, you can take advantage of the huge amount of data available on these low-cost, but very efficient storage devices.

One of the newer additions to most computers, a CD-ROM drive allows your computer to read the information stored on CDs. What makes CDs so useful is that they can store huge amounts of information very inexpensively. One CD can hold 650 MB of data or what can be stored on 430 of the highest density floppy drives. Because of the cost savings involved in this (one CD costs only about fifty cents to produce in quantity, about the same as one floppy and it stores 450 times more material), more and more software will be coming on these in the future.

CDs are also the only way to cost-effectively store sound, video and complex graphic images. They started out as a medium for distributing complex games, but are now being used for a variety of ministry purposes including Bible software, games, and educational works.

Most new computers come with CD drives built in. Get at least a 4x speed to be able to access the currently complex images.

Modem

You've got to have a modem to hook up with the Internet—just attach a phone line to your computer and with the proper software, you're ready to go.

The modem is what allows your computer to connect to the phone lines and gives your computer access to the outside world via the various online service providers such as CompuServe, America Online and Prodigy and the Internet. If you aren't already using one of these, you will want to learn how. They are great sources for all sorts of DTP resources and information. They also provide an entirely new arena for you to publish your work.

Most new computers come with modems built in. Be sure to get one with at least a 28.8 speed modem. Anything less than that will not allow you to access graphic images at more than a crawl.

Suggestions for getting the hardware you need for ministry

It is difficult to do good desktop publishing with outdated hardware. In addition to the mechanical problems, if you have an old, slow system it may not even allow you to run some of the newer and very useful programs.

At the same time, for many ministries, it is very difficult to put money for computer hardware into the general operating budget. In light of that, below are some suggestions for getting the hardware you need:

Before you begin to raise money for a computer project, do enough research to know what you need to do the work you envision. One suggestion is to find someone in a similar ministry situation. Find out what they have, how they like it, what other or additional equipment they'd get.

1. Determine what you need.

Talk to the computer savvy people in your church. Shop around. You often will get the best buys on systems that aren't the newest, but are still being sold.

2. Come up with a budget and what you will do with the machines.

Don't forget to include costs for software and adequate training for three areas: learning how to use the computer itself, learning the specific software programs and learning how to do your specific tasks such as desktop publishing.

Don't forget to budget for extra RAM! Almost no machine is sold with adequate RAM to run today's programs. Remember, no matter what the system, you need 16 to 24 MB to do desktop publishing well.

3. Make it a special giving project.

Often a special giving project with measurable goals works well with this kind of project. It appeals to business people in a congregation who know you can't do current DTP on an old Tandy 286. They also know you can't do professional DTP without training.

If your congregation wants you to be producing professional publications you need the hardware, software and training to do it.

4. Politely refuse offers of used hardware.

You can get some nightmares of incompatible systems. Ask folks to sell it elsewhere if you are offered some and to bring the proceeds to you.

5. Pray lots.

The Lord cares about you and that you have adequate equipment to do your work. "Give us today our daily bread," I think applies quite well to computer needs. We'll never have every computer gadget or software we want, but the Lord promises to supply our *needs* in ministry if we ask Him.

Desktop publishing software is what makes desktop publishing possible. The same computer that manages your church finances can also produce publications with the right software.

chapter 3

Computer Software

The terms "software" and "program" mean the same thing and are used interchangeably. You can refer to either DTP software or a DTP program.

As complex and expensive as the computer hardware might be, it can't do a thing without software. Software is the programming or instructions that tell your computer what to do. There are numerous kinds of software that instruct your computer to do a variety of tasks. DTP software is only one of them.

To understand DTP software, it might be helpful to look at other kinds of software you may already be familiar with. In addition, it is important to see how each kind of software you already have can be used in your DTP ministry.

Word processing software

Word processing software allows you to create and manipulate text. With it you can write, edit, move, add or delete words and spell check your work. Word processing software is a great way to learn to use a computer because it is simply the electronic version of something you are already familiar with—typing.

If you already have a computer, you probably have some kind of word processing software. WordPerfect and Microsoft Word are the two most popular products, though there are many less expensive programs that work quite well.

Most text for newsletters, brochures and many other DTP projects is first created using word processing software.

Some of the current upgrades of the high-end programs, such as Pagemaker, have very powerful word processing in the DTP program itself, but in some cases it is still easiest to create your text in a word processing program and then bring it into your DTP program.

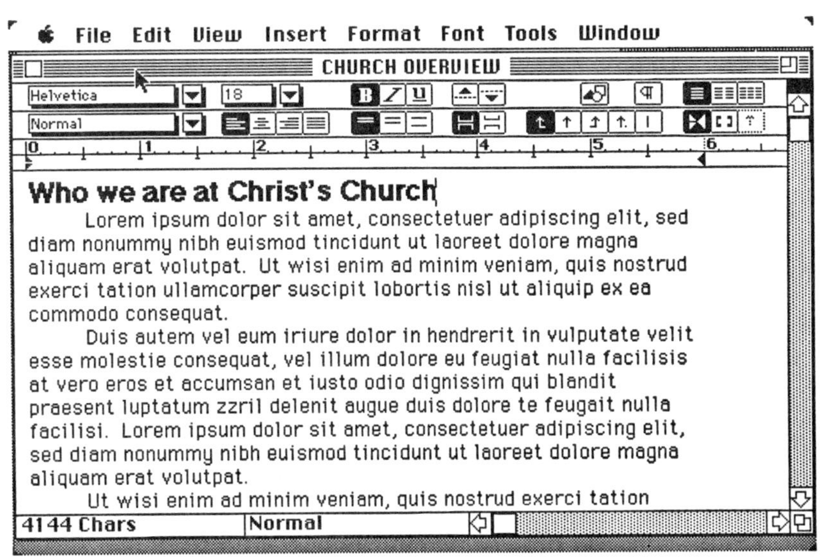

This is an example of word processing software, in this case a file from Microsoft Word. This file could then be placed into a DTP program, formatted into a type size and style, and become part of a newsletter.

Word processing software is the computerized version of typing and correcting written communication. Other software is similar in that it takes an activity previously done by hand and has the computer do the hard, repetitive parts of the job.

Database software

Database software allows you to create, organize, store, recall and sort records of related data. Many church management programs are primarily database programs. They are the electronic substitutes for Rolodexes® and index cards.

In databases you can store lists of church members, their addresses, phone numbers, birthdays, children and ages, and their areas of volunteer interest.

With desktop publishing you can create a variety of publications targeted to various segments of your congregation or ministry. After you have created the various publications you then use your database to sort your mailing list and print out labels to a specific group. For example, you might do a mailing to the youth of the church or to business donors for a ministry using presorted and printed database lists.

Using database software wisely can be a way for ministries to use technology to respond to individualized interests and needs.

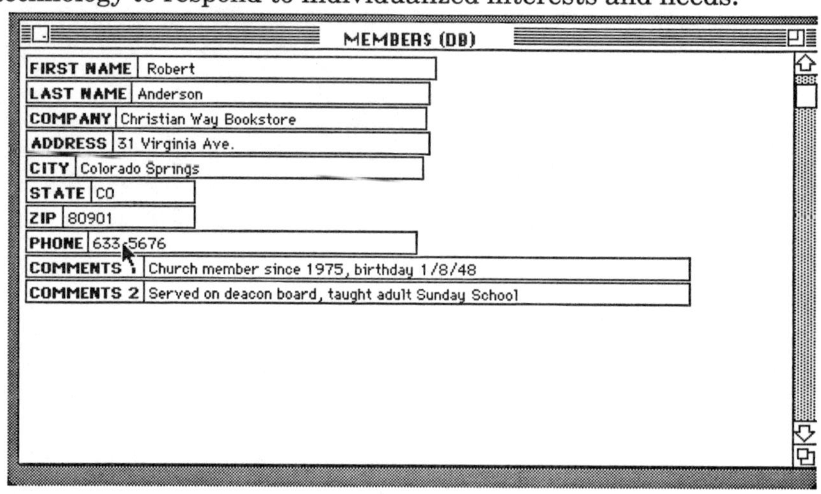

This is what a typical record looks like in a database program. You can look up, sort, organize and print out lists of people depending upon how you organize your records and the capabilities of your program.

Database programs allow you to compile and sort mailing lists based on specific areas of interest. For example, you could send a DTP-created brochure to all the Sunday School teachers of the church or the parents of high school students.

Spreadsheet software

Spreadsheet software looks like an accountant's work sheet and it is used for keeping track of financial or other numerical data. Spreadsheet software is frequently found in church and ministry management packages.

Most spreadsheet programs have a great function where you can simply hit a key to turn a column of figures into an easy-to-understand chart for use in a document such as a mission report. This chart-drawing ability enables you to take material created in various spreadsheets and turn it into easy-to-understand charts and graphs for illustrating various aspects of your ministry.

Depending upon the program, you can create a variety of charts including pie charts, bar charts, line graphs and scatter graphs.

Once the chart is created it can then be placed into DTP publications such as newsletters, overheads and brochures.

This is how a typical computer spreadsheet looks.

Ages at church (SS)

	A	B	C	D	E	F
1	Age 0-11	15				
2	Age 12-17	28				
3	Age 18-29	47				
4	Age 30-45	40				
5	Age 46-60	35				
6	Age 60+	18				
7						
8						
9						
10						

With the click of a mouse, the table above is automatically converted to this chart. It could then be placed in any DTP document and used to illustrate the ages of church members.

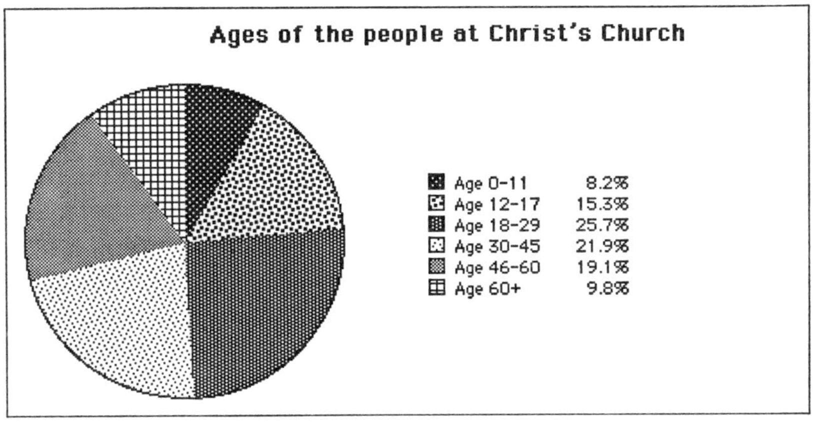

Communications software

Communications software allows your computer to talk to other computers through a modem, which is a device that hooks computers to telephone lines. You can use the modem to access computerized databases or to leave messages with other people who are hooked to the same computer bulletin board or on-line service.

There are numerous on-line services where you can look up topics in an encyclopedia, research statistics, scan the latest information on important topics or ask advice of experts. Some on-line services charge and you pay as you go by typing in your credit card number or are billed monthly; others are free.

After you find the information you want, you can then use it for background research or copy it into your document and pass it along to the people receiving your DTP publications.

This is a typical list of books from the library when a request was made for a copy of what they had on church growth. Using the computer modem and communications software, this list was available in seconds on the computer screen.

It could easily be copied into a DTP program as a list of resources to give to a study group.

MacTerm

```
1                                               PPLD                1989
   The western tradition.  programs 11-12  [videore 937. W5272
2 Callahan Kennon L                             PPLD                1983
   Twelve keys to an effective church :  strategic 254.5    C156T
3 Wagner C Peter                                PPLD                1981
   Church growth and the whole Gospel :  a biblical 254.5   W132C
4 Mylander Charles                              PPLD                1979
   Secrets for growing churches                 254.5    M997S
5 DuBose Francis M                              PPLD                1978
   How churches grow in an urban world          254.5    D817H
6 McGavran Donald Ande                          PPLD                1977
   Ten steps for church growth                  254.5    M145S
7 Larson Martin Alfred                          PPLD                1976
   The religious empire :  the growth and danger of 336.22  L334R
<RETURN> TO CONTINUE DISPLAY
ENTER <LINE NUMBER(S)> TO DISPLAY FULL RECORDS (Number +  B  for Brief)
<P>REVIOUS FOR PREVIOUS PAGE OR <Q>UIT FOR NEW SEARCH
```

Illustration or graphic software

Illustration or graphic software allows you to create images that range from simple lines and filled shapes in some of the basic programs to extremely complex 3-D illustrations in the high-end packages. You create or modify illustrations with these programs and then import them into your DTP layout. This software also allows you to alter or crop images you scan into your computer.

Though you don't have to have an additional graphics program to do DTP, they are useful if you do complex drawings or manipulation of scanned images.

Toolbox

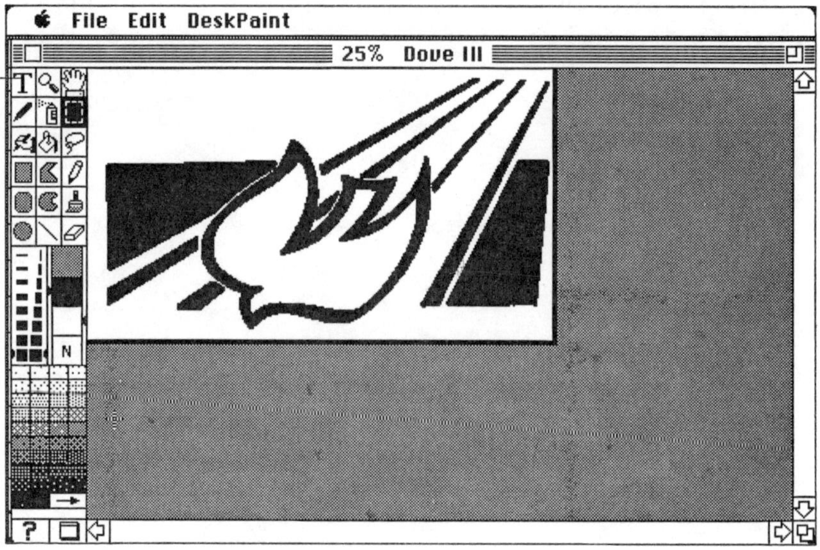

In this illustration program the image of the dove was scanned in and can now be manipulated with any of the tools in the toolbox to the left of the window.

The toolbox contains tools to draw lines, paint textures, erase, spatter paint and many other drawing tasks.

Integrated software

Integrated software packages usually combine a word processor, spreadsheet, graphics, database and communications software all in one package. They are cost-effective ways for a church, ministry or small business to get started in computers.

The DTP capabilities they offer are limited, but they can be a good way to get started. Many features they offer are useful to small churches and ministries. They also work well on laptop computers.

Two popular programs are Microsoft Works and Claris Works.

Desktop publishing software

DTP software allows you to lay out graphics and text on computer-generated pages to create professional-looking, typeset documents. All DTP programs have these features.

There are many DTP software packages available. Great-looking pieces can be created with any of these packages and the how-tos in this book can be used with all of them.

Mail order bargains

Software can be purchased through the mail at significant discounts. For example, a DTP package listed in the $800 range can be found for approximately $500 by mail order. A package listed for $250 will cost approximately $100 ordered by mail.

For a listing of mail order software sources see the resource section.

The more expensive and fully-featured programs are Pagemaker and QuarkXPress. Pagemaker and QuarkXPress are available in versions for both the Mac and PCs.

In addition there are DTP programs that cost about half as much. For the Mac, these include Aldus Personal Press, Ready, Set, Go! and Clerygcal Publisher.

For PCs the most popular and highly recommended is Microsoft Publisher.

One of the best ways to determine which DTP software package is best for you is to talk to people using DTP for the same tasks you want to use it for. Spend some time if possible actually seeing the program in use before making your purchase. If that is impossible, look up the software reviews in computer magazines in the library for a detailed discussion of features.

How DTP software works

For desktop publishing in a ministry setting, I especially recommend two programs:

On the introductory end, it's hard to beat Microsoft Publisher. Available for around $70 or less, and it comes with great templates, artwork, fonts and instructions.

If you find you want to do more advanced DTP, my program of choice is Pagemaker. This book was created with Pagemaker. I also like it because lots of folks use it and there are numerous classes and third party support books and resources for learning it.

As the example below illustrates, in many DTP programs all of the elements for your publication are placed on what is called a pasteboard, similar to a drawing table in real life.

By pointing with the mouse, you can take the elements, such as the graphic of the people and the additional text at the left of the screen, off the pasteboard and move them into the newsletter.

In the square box labeled "toolbox" to the right of the newsletter you can select tools to draw boxes, lines, squares, and circles on your page in addition to entering text and cropping graphics.

In the box labeled "styles" you can select pre-determined type sizes and type styles for your headlines, body text, and any other selections of text you specify.

Instead of wondering what things will look like, many DTP programs have a feature called WYSIWYG. It is pronounced "wizzy-wig." It stands for "what you see is what you get."

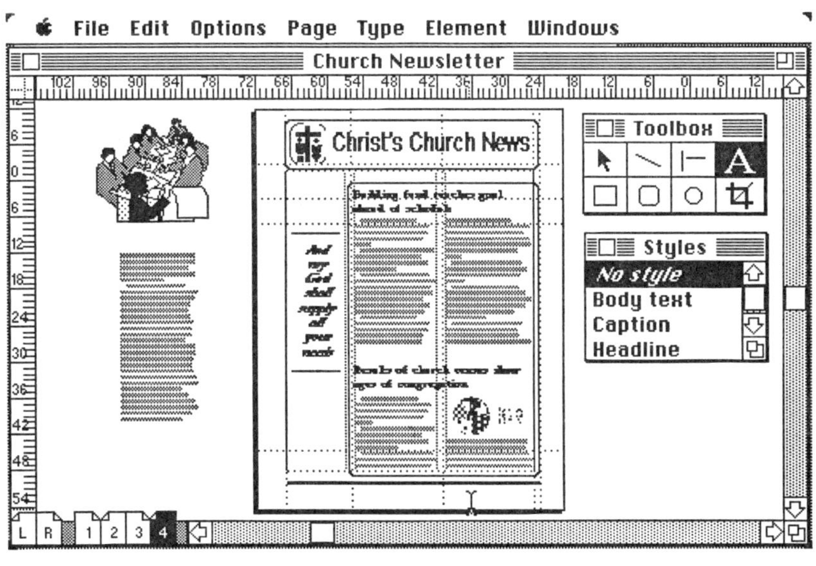

This is a screen capture from Pagemaker. Not only can you see what the newsletter in the center will look like when it is printed, but you can edit text, move graphics around, and make any changes you want in this view.

Utilities software

All of the types of software discussed so far are what are known as application software. They allow you to perform specific tasks.

There is another kind of software that has the potential of making work you perform on your computer run more smoothly. This software falls under the general category of utilities software. This software can keep your hard drive running at top performance, prevent crashes, help diagnose problems and recover lost data. Other utilities programs can protect your computer from viruses, compress files, and perform many other tasks. Norton Utilities is one of the best-known utilities programs.

"Drop that mouse and come out with your hands up!"

—or what can happen when the SPA discovers you are using pirated software

Moral of the story—as SPA says, "Don't copy that floppy."

More information on setting up legal software guidelines and systems for your church or ministry is available from the Software Publishers Association hot line number, 1-800-388-7478.

But no matter what your rules and controls, nothing beats a system check on your personal integrity software.

When you purchase software, the licensing agreement, unless it specifically states otherwise, is one copy for one machine. Anything else—to copy somebody's software, to try it out, to lend it to someone because they don't have money for their own—is illegal.

Scenarios of federal marshals bursting into corporations and searching hard disks, fines of up to $300,000, various public apologies, and assorted humiliations have been the response of the Software Publishers Association (SPA) who has gotten tired of asking nicely that people not illegally copy their software.

Here's why: in 1990 the total *income* for the software industry was $4 billion while the estimated income loss due to piracy was $2.4 billion. That was in the U.S. alone. Losses worldwide, where pirated software is sold openly, far exceeded their income.

To counter this loss, the SPA "investigates cases of copyright infringement involving corporations, educational and nonprofit institutions, commercial dealers, pirate bulletin boards and software rental operations." Some of their tactics include:

- Anti-piracy hot line—This is where the action begins. People call to report suspected unauthorized use of software.
- *Ex Parte* seizure orders—The federal marshals really do come in, hard drives are searched and the software on them compared to what has been paid for.
- Audit Letters—Prior to a seizure, the SPA usually attempts to work with a potential offender by sending him or her a letter asking for a formal software audit, destruction of illegal copies, purchase of legal copies and implementation of new policies.
- Litigation—If matters are not handled happily with letters, the SPA legal staff starts action. They are currently litigating an average of two cases a week with a high success rate. Fines up to $100,000 per infringement are allowed by federal law.

The most important work you do in desktop publishing takes place before you turn on the computer—it is in how well you plan your message and production.

chapter 4

Planning

The multitude of choices available with desktop publishing can be both a blessing and a problem. It is a blessing not to be tied to typing everything out, to be able to use bold or italic type at different sizes, to be able to put materials in two and three column formats, to add pictures and photos.

Though many things are possible in DTP, not every possibility is right for every audience. The typeface and illustrations that might be perfect for a mission committee report would not work for a flyer describing a children's program. The key to successful DTP design is matching your design to your audience.

The cover for the mission committee report below uses the contemporary Avant Garde typeface, clean square lines, and a traditional map of the world. These elements combine to give a clear, professional message.

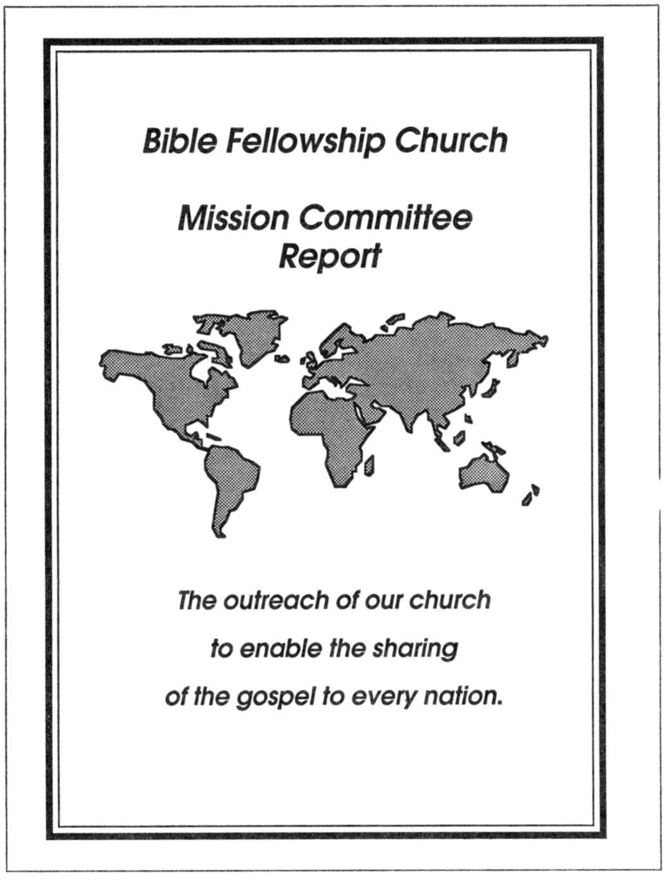

Even if we aren't aware of it, our minds have an extensive graphic vocabulary.

We might comment, "That's a great ad!" or "That one was really dumb." We know if a printed piece communicates its message or if it doesn't work.

When you plan your DTP projects, use that vocabulary you already know to create pieces that communicate your message precisely and clearly.

This flyer for the children's fair uses the Bookman typeface, a playful graphic of children, and the large headline to give a message of a fun, casual event.

Plan before you turn on the computer

Once you sit down to the computer to actually produce your project, it's very difficult to keep the big picture in mind. It's easy to get so tied up in just trying to get the computer to do what you want to, you often don't have the time to think through the goals of your communication piece.

If your piece is to accomplish the ministry goals you've set for it, you need to plan ahead. Planning ahead will also save you lots of actual production time.

Desktop Publishing Project Planning Sheet

"If you've ever worked on a well-thought-through project, you know what a pleasure it is. And if you've worked on one that's been poorly planned, you know how frustrating it can get. Careful planning makes everyone's job easier."

Elizabeth W. Adler,
Print that Works

Planning can take anywhere from a few minutes by yourself to lengthy planning meetings with the entire staff. Whatever time you schedule to plan, please take time to do it. The planning guide on the next page will help you. Make copies of it and use it for all your projects.

There are two parts to the planning sheet. On the left hand side you fill in basic factual information about your publication. On the right is a column labeled "Design, graphics, text ideas." Use this column to brainstorm ways to translate your project plans into tasks on the computer.

We'll go through an example of how you would use this sheet. Let's say you want to create a four-page newsletter for your church.

When you plan your DTP project, don't forget to account for mailing times, if you are sending dated material out in bulk mailing. In addition, if you have volunteers do the labeling or stuffing, they often only come in once a week.

Project name

Name the project the same on the sheet as you do on your computer file, so you can easily find it. If you must abbreviate the name for the computer file (as some computers limit the number of characters that can be in a file name) have both the full name and the computer file name on the planning sheet.

Example: Project name: Church Newsletter

Computer name: CHNLET

Also, remember the printer may not be able to get to your project immediately. You'll have a much better relationship with your printer if you only ask for a rush job in a real emergency.

Date needed

The important date to record is when it actually needs to be in people's hands. Once you know that, work your production schedule backwards from it. Be sure to take into consideration mailing times.

Production considerations

DTP isn't magic. Constantly setting unrealistic deadlines for yourself is one of the fastest ways I know to make you hate it. DTP gives you the ability to do lots of things, but at first, while you are learning your system and software, you won't do them quickly.

Desktop Publishing Project Planning Sheet

	Design, graphics, text ideas
Project name:	
Date needed:	
Production considerations:	
Budget:	
Purpose: Why are we doing this?	
Goal: What do we want to accomplish with it?	
Audience: Who are they?	
Where are they: Physically?	
Emotionally?	
Spiritually?	
Our identity: Overall?	
In this piece?	

Desktop publishing deadlines don't have to make you a nervous wreck!

The secret to peaceful DTP success is being realistic in your scheduling.

If you want to do a project well, keep up with other work demands, maintain your sanity and a good relationship with the people you work with, be realistic about the time it takes to schedule desktop-published projects.

If you're new at DTP or are doing a totally new project and don't have any idea how much time a project will take:

1. Be honest about that and plan for flexibility.

2. Keep a log of how long projects take as you learn and you'll have a basis for future estimates.

At first it is hard to estimate how long projects will take. Give it your best guess and then record how long it actually took. After a few months you'll have a more realistic picture. At that time you can enter a production schedule for the year in your calendar.

In the example, by taking into consideration the people involved in the project and their present responsibilities, the newsletter needs to be started on the first of the month to mail on the 25th.

Budget

You can do wonderful things on a low budget, but knowing what limitations you have or what extra money you can spend up front will help you schedule your time wisely.

In our example, we decide we want to use a nice recycled paper instead of the inexpensive, colored bond paper we use to run off projects in-house. We make a note to ask the printer if he has it on hand or if it needs to be ordered.

Purpose

Why are we doing this?

How you answer this question has a direct bearing on how you put together your DTP piece.

For the newsletter example, the answer might be to increase involvement of our members in church activities.

Goal

What do we want this piece to accomplish?

No piece can accomplish everything. You can't tell the entire story of your ministry in each piece you produce. For example, the goal for the newsletter might be to promote Sunday School classes.

Audience

Who are they?

This question isn't as simple as it first appears. Especially today in our information-overloaded world, publications need to be carefully targeted to individual needs. People expect that because that is what they get in other communication areas of life.

Remember when there were only three primary television networks? Cable telvision now offers a network for every taste from education to sports, from science fiction to religion.

Remember *Life* and *Look* magazines, the publications the entire nation used to read? Now there is a publication for every narrow interest.

There was a great fear when computers first came out that they would make everything the same. The opposite has happened. People now have the option of producing a nearly infinite variety of publications.

The changing American family:

Parade *Magazine reported the following information based on a Census Bureau comparison of data between 1970-1991:*

In 1970 "married couples with at least one child under 18 living at home," made up 40 percent of all households; today they make up 26 percent.

In 1970 there were 3.8 million single-parent families or 12.9 percent of the population. Today there are 10.1 million single-parent families. They make up 29 percent of families with children. Mothers head almost 90 percent of single-parent families.

In 1970, almost 400,000 babies or 11 percent of all children were born to single mothers. Now one million babies and 27 percent of all births are to single mothers.

The number of unmarried couples rose from 523,000 in 1970 to 3 million now. Forty percent of these couples have children.

The number of people living alone has increased from 20 percent of all households in 1970 to 30 percent today.

The more carefully you know your audience and target your publication specifically to their interests and needs the more it will serve them and accomplish your purpose.

In the newsletter example, the most basic answer to "who is our audience?" would be: They are members of our church, both sexes, all ages. The answer becomes more specific as the following questions are answered.

Where are they?

Physically

It is difficult to divorce your publications from the context of twentieth-century life.

People's lives today are extremely busy. Physically, they are full of crammed schedules and conflicting demands. Mentally, people are often on overload.

To get some control, many people have taken time management classes where they are told that to get through the volume of material that bombards them each day, they need to skim the headlines, read the subheads and captions, look at the pictures, and only read articles that will be of benefit to them. Studies show most people do that to the materials they receive—skim through them to see if there is anything of interest. Many materials are tossed even before they are opened.

If we want people to read our message, we have to structure it in such a way that people can comprehend what we want them to know without much effort. As the book continues you'll get specific ways to do that, but it's important to remember this principle while planning.

Emotionally

Contemporary life hurts. Publications don't need to remind people of their pain. Publications need to provide messages that promise healing.

A great way to find out about the emotional situation of your audience is to ask them, "What do you see as the great emotional needs of your fellow church members today?" By asking them about their friends they won't personally feel put on the spot, but they will usually answer you from their experience.

Keep that in mind as you create your publication.

In our example, suppose that we asked several of our members what they saw as people's greatest emotional needs. If the most common answer was that people are lonely we might want to feature the fellowship of people with Christian beliefs.

Spiritually

Is your target audience presently involved in your church or ministry? If it is for a totally in-house group such as a Sunday School teacher's committee, you don't need to define the meaning of salvation or baptism. Jargon is acceptable if everybody understands the meaning. It becomes a kind of shorthand way of communicating. But if your audience doesn't understand your jargon and the terms that are meaningful to you, you'll lose them.

Answers to the acronyms quiz :

ASM means All-City Social Ministries. A visitor wouldn't have a clue what this meant.

FUMC means First United Methodist Church. When first attending there, visitors heard the church referred to as simply "First Church." For months they wondered what a "FUMC" was.

H.U.G.S. is a Sunday School class that means "helping us grow as singles." At first this sounds like some sort of emotional, social group. Newcomers might fear they will have to hug everybody!

None of these acronyms are self-explanatory. Always remember what it means to be a stranger and communicate in a way that is welcoming and clear.

Quiz:

Do you know the meaning of the following terms? Answers are at the side of this page along with visitors' responses to them.

ASM

FUMC

H.U.G.S.

These are all acronyms used as abbreviations and familiar to the church staff that uses them but they can be confusing to newcomers and visitors.

Be very careful about abbreviating terms in your publications. Be sure to spell them out on first reference. Try not to use abbreviations at all in material that visitors will read. If you spell out terms they will feel more at home.

The Bible can be just as confusing for those who grew up without church training, as is the case with many people today. Remember to spell out books of the Bible. In bulletins or similar material, such as Bible study guides, include a page number by the verse references for people who use pew Bibles.

In our example publication, we can assume most of the people receiving it are Christians, so we can use Bible verses and Scripture references in the newsletter. We still want to avoid abbreviations everyone may not know.

Our identity

Who are we, overall?

Each of our churches are all *only parts* of the body of Christ, not the whole thing. No one is able and shouldn't even try to be all things to all people. Your publications need to reflect your uniqueness.

When you put together your messages, it's easy to lose your identity by trying to be all things to all people in every publication. Practically you can't do that. A good ministry publication shouldn't try to deliver too many messages in one piece.

Theologically it doesn't work too well either. A good inspiration of the importance of communicating your particular focus comes from the book of Nehemiah.

In this book the Israelites were rebuilding the wall after returning from the Babylonian captivity. The wall was their national security system, an essential part of the safety of the nation. To rebuild it each family was assigned one specific part of the wall. With each family working on their part and knowing they could call for help if they needed it, the entire wall got built, they were protected from their enemies, and Israel was restored as a nation

Imagine what would have happened if instead of attending to their assigned part, each family ran around the city laying a brick here and there, trying to be part of rebuilding the entire wall?

Not only would they have been exhausted, the job as a whole probably wouldn't have gotten done. Fortunately, they trusted their leader Nehemiah, did their part, and the wall was built.

We each need to work on building up our part of the kingdom of God. Every church and ministry has a different part of the wall to work on.

What is your unique identity and message?

- Are you primarily interested in outreach to non-Christians or in helping believers grow in their walk with the Lord?
- Does your church have an active singles' ministry? Do you focus on social concerns?
- Is your church liturgical and traditional?
- Is your ministry targeted to business men or teenagers?
- Do you emphasize Bible study or missions involvement?

This picture of a family makes up only 26 percent of the population today.

Be sensitive in publication planning. Don't assume that all your audience fits in this picture.

Take time to decide your distinctive identity and allow it to guide your publications. Communicate your identity clearly. Work on your part of the wall with joy.

Our church for the newsletter example could be described as a 150-member church in a suburban neighborhood that emphasizes outreach to the unchurched in our community, growth in our walk with God and fellowship with each other.

Our identity—in this piece

Always keep in mind the overall mission and purpose of your church and ministry, then specifically state what part of that message you want to emphasize in the particular communication piece you are working on.

For our example project, let's say we emphasize our fellowship with each other and opportunities for Christian growth.

Turning goals to graphics

Now that you know who you are and what you want to accomplish, you can work on translating those goals into the nuts and bolts of the newsletter you'll produce.

Desktop Publishing Project Planning Sheet

	Design, graphics, text ideas
Project name: *Church newsletter, CNLET*	
Date needed: *Send out 25th of each month.*	
Production considerations: *Need to begin on the first to mail 25th, earlier if work allows.*	*Consistent template, length, format, to make production easier.*
Budget: Can we afford better paper?	*Tan recycled would be nice.*
Purpose: Why are we doing this? *To increase involvement of members in church activities.*	*Make information easy to read, layout clear, schedule printed inside.*
Goal: What do we want to accomplish with it? *To increase Sunday School class attendance.*	*Include descriptions of classes. Show teachers' pictures. Describe activities of classes.*
Audience: Who are they? *Church members, both sexes, all ages.*	*Fairly conservative design so it will appeal to everybody. No wild graphics or colors.*
Where are they: Physically ? *Busy lives.*	*Make articles short and to the point. Show why it is worth their time. No fluff.*
Emotionally? *Lonely, needing friends of similar beliefs.*	*Stress fellowship with Christians. Excellent teaching. Print small group schedule.*
Spiritually? *Christians mostly.*	*OK to use Bible verses and scriptural references.*
Our identity: Overall? *We are a church that emphasizes outreach, growth in our walk with God and fellowship.*	*Use church logo, keep address and phone number easy to find.*
In this piece? *We want to emphasize our fellowship with each other and opportunities for Christian growth.*	*Clearly state goals of fellowship and growth in upbeat, fun ways. Use photos.*

Grids and templates are the desktop publisher's design security blanket and the graphic ground rules for putting together publications.

chapter 5

Grids and Templates

In the previous chapter you learned how to plan the basic purpose and production schedule of your publication. Now you'll decide its basic form.

Microsoft Publisher has taken the use of grids and templates to a new level with the creation of its PageWizards. Not only do they come in a variety of styles, but they ask you questions as you set them up so they can be customized to your particular needs.

The easiest and most efficient way to do this in DTP is by creating and using a grid. A grid is the underlying structure made up of nonprinting lines that tells you where to put things on a page. It makes design decisions for you and saves an immense amount of time as you assemble your publication.

In the past, grids were printed in non-reproducing blue ink on white paper and designers would paste up their publications using these lines. In today's computer programs, the grids are dotted lines you see on your computer screen, but they don't print out on your actual projects. You place text and illustrations using these lines as guides. This is what one looks like:

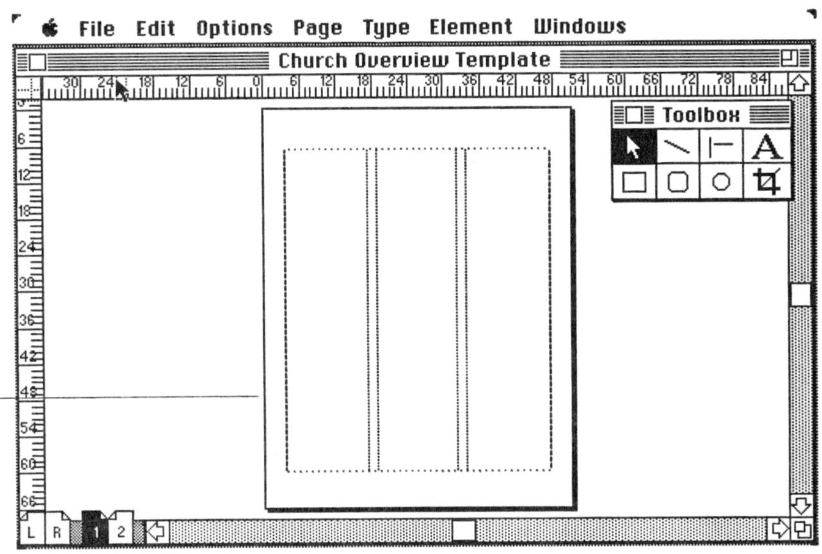

This is what a grid can look like on your computer screen. The dotted lines will not show up when your publication is printed out, but they define the columns and margins of your publication.

There are few skills that are more useful when you are using DTP than learning to use grids. Grids will:

- Identify margins and columns.
- Provide consistent placement of graphic elements such as page numbers, headers and footers.
- Provide a professional, consistent look for recurrent publications. You don't need to and shouldn't create a different design for every issue of the church newsletter you put out.
- Provide discipline and security in making design decisions for nonprofessional DTP designers.
- Decrease production time in recurrent publications, because overall design decisions do not need to be made for each issue.

How grids and templates are created

Many grids are pre-drawn as templates in DTP programs. A template is a combination of the layout grid and a style guide that forms an electronic prototype of a publication. The layout grid is like the illustration on the previous page and shows where to place blocks of text and graphics. The style guide tells you what type specifications will be used in the publication.

A template for a newsletter. The column measurements, type size, style and spacing between lines of text have all been predetermined.

To use a template in a DTP project, simply replace any of the items in the template with new text or illustration.

Recurrent or periodic publications, such as a monthly newsletter, may be saved as a template. If this is done, a new one does not need to be created for each issue.

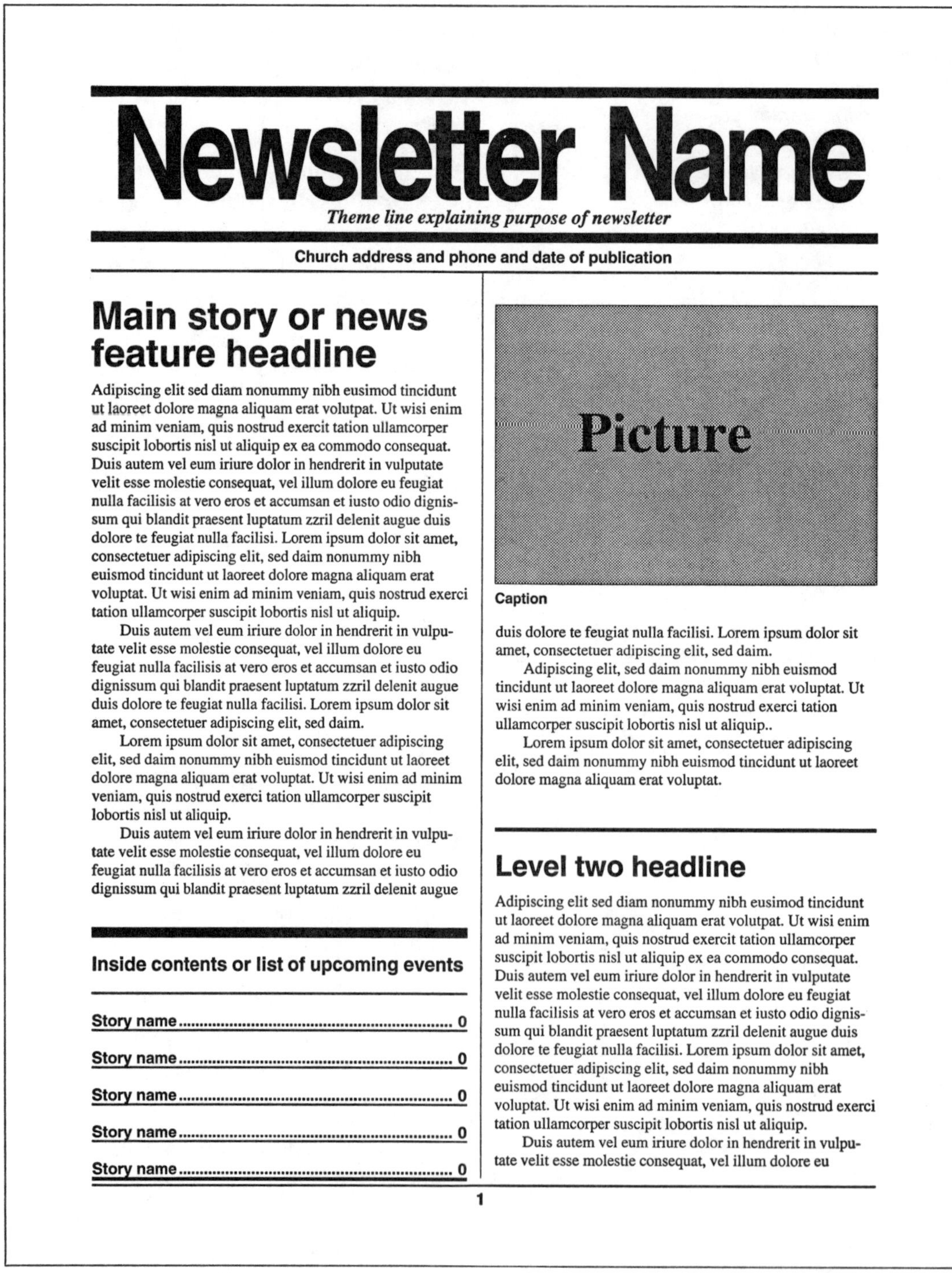

Newsletter Name

Theme line explaining purpose of newsletter

Church address and phone and date of publication

Main story or news feature headline

Adipiscing elit sed diam nonummy nibh eusimod tincidunt ut laoreet dolore magna aliquam erat volutpat. Ut wisi enim ad minim veniam, quis nostrud exercit tation ullamcorper suscipit lobortis nisl ut aliquip ex ea commodo consequat. Duis autem vel eum iriure dolor in hendrerit in vulputate velit esse molestie consequat, vel illum dolore eu feugiat nulla facilisis at vero eros et accumsan et iusto odio dignissum qui blandit praesent luptatum zzril delenit augue duis dolore te feugiat nulla facilisi. Lorem ipsum dolor sit amet, consectetuer adipiscing elit, sed daim nonummy nibh euismod tincidunt ut laoreet dolore magna aliquam erat voluptat. Ut wisi enim ad minim veniam, quis nostrud exerci tation ullamcorper suscipit lobortis nisl ut aliquip.

Duis autem vel eum iriure dolor in hendrerit in vulputate velit esse molestie consequat, vel illum dolore eu feugiat nulla facilisis at vero eros et accumsan et iusto odio dignissum qui blandit praesent luptatum zzril delenit augue duis dolore te feugiat nulla facilisi. Lorem ipsum dolor sit amet, consectetuer adipiscing elit, sed daim.

Lorem ipsum dolor sit amet, consectetuer adipiscing elit, sed daim nonummy nibh euismod tincidunt ut laoreet dolore magna aliquam erat voluptat. Ut wisi enim ad minim veniam, quis nostrud exerci tation ullamcorper suscipit lobortis nisl ut aliquip.

Duis autem vel eum iriure dolor in hendrerit in vulputate velit esse molestie consequat, vel illum dolore eu feugiat nulla facilisis at vero eros et accumsan et iusto odio dignissum qui blandit praesent luptatum zzril delenit augue

Inside contents or list of upcoming events

Picture

Caption

duis dolore te feugiat nulla facilisi. Lorem ipsum dolor sit amet, consectetuer adipiscing elit, sed daim.

Adipiscing elit, sed daim nonummy nibh euismod tincidunt ut laoreet dolore magna aliquam erat voluptat. Ut wisi enim ad minim veniam, quis nostrud exerci tation ullamcorper suscipit lobortis nisl ut aliquip..

Lorem ipsum dolor sit amet, consectetuer adipiscing elit, sed daim nonummy nibh euismod tincidunt ut laoreet dolore magna aliquam erat voluptat.

Level two headline

Adipiscing elit sed diam nonummy nibh eusimod tincidunt ut laoreet dolore magna aliquam erat volutpat. Ut wisi enim ad minim veniam, quis nostrud exercit tation ullamcorper suscipit lobortis nisl ut aliquip ex ea commodo consequat. Duis autem vel eum iriure dolor in hendrerit in vulputate velit esse molestie consequat, vel illum dolore eu feugiat nulla facilisis at vero eros et accumsan et iusto odio dignissum qui blandit praesent luptatum zzril delenit augue duis dolore te feugiat nulla facilisi. Lorem ipsum dolor sit amet, consectetuer adipiscing elit, sed daim nonummy nibh euismod tincidunt ut laoreet dolore magna aliquam erat voluptat. Ut wisi enim ad minim veniam, quis nostrud exerci tation ullamcorper suscipit lobortis nisl ut aliquip.

Duis autem vel eum iriure dolor in hendrerit in vulputate velit esse molestie consequat, vel illum dolore eu

1

You can also create your own templates

Though many DTP programs come with templates, many times you will want to create one of your own. To do so you will need to learn the typographic way to measure and find sources for generating graphic design ideas.

Measurements the typographic way

Measuring in inches is very awkward when you are doing any kind of page layout or when you are working with type. The fractions of inches are confusing. Long ago a system was developed to measure type using points and picas and it has been used in the typographic and graphic arts fields ever since.

There are six picas to an inch. Because picas are much smaller than inches the measurements can be stated as whole numbers. For example, 4 picas instead of 2/3 of an inch. This makes measuring in picas much easier than measuring in inches for your DTP work.

Points are primarily used for vertical measurements and will be discussed in more detail in the chapter on typography.

This illustration shows the difference between inches, points and picas.

It is much easier to measure in your DTP work if you learn to use picas because you don't have to deal with fractions of inches.

Measuring with picas is also the standard method of measurement in the graphic arts and printing world.

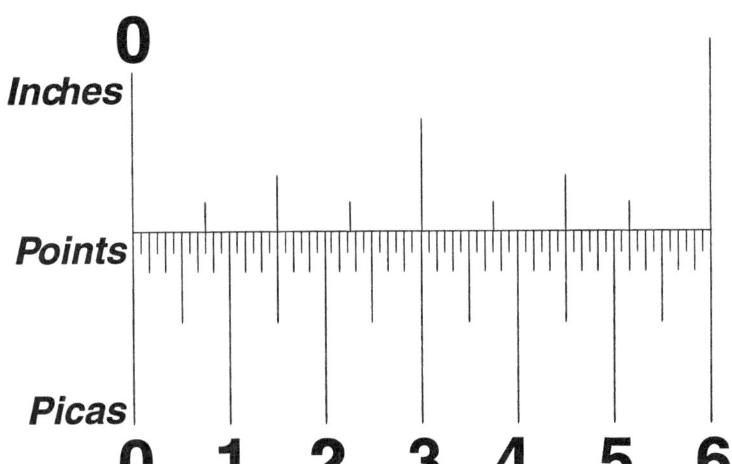

There are:

- ***6 picas to an inch***
- ***12 points to a pica***
- ***72 points to an inch***

You can purchase a pica ruler at an art supply store. DTP software will have a setting where you can change your rules to picas. This is the system graphic artists, typographers, and printers use. Once you become used to it, measuring with picas will make your desktop publishing life much easier.

How to come up with design ideas

Before you can create design ideas it helps to have an accurate definition of design. Most people think of designing for publications means a decorative, interesting, highly artistic creative act—a process out of the reach of ordinary people.

Webster's definition of design presents a different picture.

By definition, a good design has much more to do with a clear, well-thought out plan than it does with innovative, artistic creation.

Your design should reinforce your message, not detract from it.

The definition of design:

de•sign (di zin) *vt.* 1. to sketch an outline for; plan 2. to contrive 3. to plan to do; intend. *n.* 1. a plan; scheme 2. purpose; aim 3. a working plan; pattern 4. arrangement of parts, form, color, etc; artistic invention.

Note that only the very last part of the definition has anything to do with the artistic aspect often associated with design. The rest of the definition emphasizes the heart of good design—it is a plan, an arrangement of parts chosen that will accomplish your purpose and clearly communicate your message.

The limits of design

"The purpose of graphic design is to make it as easy as possible for readers to understand your message. Because graphic design is a tool, not an end in itself, it should be unobstrusive, almost transparent."

Roger C. Parker, The Aldus Guide to Basic Design

Design is the messenger, not the message. That is why it is so important to plan your message before you begin designing.

In evaluating many DTP publications, one of the biggest reasons they don't accomplish their purpose is not because of "bad" design, but because the design wasn't appropriate to the message. It is an ever present temptation to put something into your publication just because "it looks pretty" or because you have the ability to do so in your desktop program.

Before you put anything into the design of your publication, always ask, "How does this line or graphic or box or whatever contribute to the message?" Sometimes the most simple grids and designs are the most effective. Look at some of the most popular and well-read publications in America today—the *Wall Street Journal, Readers Digest, TV Guide,* or the news magazines. You can create "fancier" designs than the templates for those publications on the most basic of DTP programs. But why do that?

Creators of these magazines don't do the fancy designs for a reason. The clean, clear organization makes the information—the message—primary. Good design enables readers to always know where to find information they want, in what order, and in what section.

This is not to say you can't ever add graphic interest and excitement to your publications. You can, but be sure that you have a basic design that communicates.

How do you know what will work? Look around and evaluate the communications that you think work well for others. In addition to the publications mentioned, look at the newsletters you read and the ads you respond to, then copy and adapt what you see into your publications.

Copy and adapt

Once you have collected a number of publication samples, it is a good idea to file them for easy retrieval.

Some categories that may be useful are:

Types of publications:
- *Brochures*
- *Bulletins*
- *Calendars*
- *Direct Mail*
- *Flyers*
- *Forms*
- *Logos and stationery*
- *Newsletters*

Miscellaneous design ideas:
- *Graphic treatments*
- *Illustrations*
- *Folds*
- *Layouts*
- *Paper*
- *Photography*

Solomon told us long ago in Ecclesiastes 1:9, "there is nothing new under the sun."

That statement was never more true than in the area of publication design. However, there is little that is original in this area—most good designs are merely adaptations of other good designs.

It is against copyright law to copy the text of what someone writes without permission. However, there is nothing wrong with copying the measurements of a newsletter that you like or using type in the same size on your captions or headlines.

Learning the proportions of designing publications is one of the hardest things for beginning designers. Most people who get into DTP haven't studied the golden mean and proper classical proportions in design school. They just need to know what kind of margin measurements will work in their Sunday School brochure.

Get out the pica ruler and measure

If you see something you like, get out your pica ruler and measure. Make notes of the measurements on the piece and when you need to design something similar you'll have a reference.

Look carefully at some of the national, highly-circulated publications. Look at the little things—column size, placement of headlines, picture captions. Notice how your eye travels through the publication. Ask yourself: what did I want to read first and why? what did I skip?

By looking at other publications, measuring them and recording their specifications, you can quickly create a grid for your publication. Your text, your graphics and arrangement will make it a completely new publication.

Learn to improve your work by studying other pieces in this way and comparing them with your own. For example, maybe three or four newsletters that you like have a 12-pica top margin before the text starts—since yours have a top margin of only eight picas, now you know why the top of yours looked cramped. From looking at other newsletters and measuring them, you realize adding four additional picas to the size of your top margin will give you the look you want.

Create a sample file

A sample file is invaluable when you need ideas. I have my sample file organized by types of material—newsletters, brochures, donor appeals, etc. I also have sample files of parts of publications such as ways to do call-outs or captions.

Even the greatest designers need help in coming up with ideas.

This is the method used by Nigel Holmes, who designs graphics for Time magazine and has written extensively about desktop publishing:

"Whenever you see an image in a magazine or newspaper or even on a packet of cereal . . ., cut it out and keep it in a scrapbook. . . .When searching for an idea. . ., all sorts of images can be viewed that will start the mind working—perhaps along different lines from the preconceived. . . .The brain has a great capacity for putting odd images together that it might not have thought up without this visual stimulus."

Nigel Holmes,
Designer's Guide to Creating Charts and Diagrams

In addition to the direct mail you receive, listed below are some more ways to get material for your sample file:

- Go to the library and look at the graphic arts magazines. Photocopy ideas that you like.
- Go to mission fairs and trade shows to pick up promotional material. It's always helpful to pick up material of a ministry you know nothing about.
- In addition to the graphic arts magazines, look at the decorating magazines, fashion magazines and gardening magazines for visual ideas. Decorating and fashion magazines will tell you what colors are popular. Gardening magazines will give you great ideas for combining colors and shapes.
- Write notes on your samples of what you liked about them and what you didn't. Sometimes an unusual fold works well, sometimes the placement of a headline gives added impact to the message.

In addition to noting what you liked, ask questions and note them on the sample. Note errors to remind yourself not to make the same mistakes. For example, in some of my files I've got:

- A direct mail package—complete with personalized letter, catalog of addresses of service centers, and other fancy pieces—that doesn't name the product they sell.
- A church newsletter and newcomers' information mailer with two different addresses for the church. I later found out one was the business office, but the publication never said that.
- A "personalized" letter about Christian education addressed to the "parents of Yvon Prehn." It also contained pictures of 18-year-olds that I could look forward to going to school with in the fall. Good example of a mail list gone bad.

I keep these examples, not to be critical, but to remind me of the many, many mistakes I can so easily make. So much can be done with DTP and it helps to remember that publishing power isn't infallible.

- Swap publications with fellow desktop publishing people. Talk about what worked and what didn't.

You've got your plan and you've got your template—now what do you put into them?

In the coming chapters you'll learn how to write for your DTP publications and then how to illustrate your ideas.

DTP writing combines the skills of journalism, advertising and direct mail in a form that communicates visually as well as verbally.

chapter 6

Writing for DTP

"Christians owe it to themselves to be conscious of their words; they are full of history and power and spiritual significance."

Bob Hudson and Shelley Townsend, ed., A Christian Writer's Manual of Style

Writing for desktop publishing puts a new twist to the old skill of written communication. To communicate successfully with today's audience you need to learn to take your writing skills and add to them the skills of publication design, journalism, advertising and direct mail.

People today are busy. To save time when they receive a printed piece, whether it is their evening paper or your church newsletter, they skim it quickly. They look at the pictures and captions, read the headlines, and take in as much information as they can without having to work too hard or take too much time. If the articles are too long or the basic message can't be grasped immediately, they will put it aside—probably never to be read.

If you want to minister to people today, your challenge is to communicate in a form that is manageable for them.

A writing formula that works—the big three

Please note: if someone else or a group of people in your church or ministry do most of the writing for your publications, please have them read this section.

Keeping in mind how people take in information today, how can communication pieces be structured to appeal to them? There is an easy and effective way to do this. Once you grasp the following principles and apply them, your DTP projects will effectively communicate your message.

This chapter contains a summary of research about what works in direct mail and advertising. Researchers in these areas have the advantage of being able to measure the results of their work with precision and many of their findings have proven to apply well in the field of DTP materials.

The research shows that people take in information and respond to it in basically three levels in a fairly predictable pattern. Below is an overview of the levels. Following the overview, there is an example of how these principles apply in an actual article written by a minister for a church newsletter. The remainder of the chapter includes tips on effective writing for each level.

Level one

Consists of:

- Headlines and subtitles
- Subheads and call-outs
- Graphics and photos
- Captions that go with them

Time spent per page: 3-5 seconds

Percentage of readers: 80 percent

In direct mail studies, 20 percent of the folks who receive an unsolicited piece won't even open it.

Challenge:
- Be relevant here—give people a reason to continue reading.
- Give enough information so the reader learns enough to understand the key points or to make a desired response.

"On the average, five times as many people read the headlines as read the body copy. It follows that unless your headline sells your product, you have wasted 90 percent of your money."

David Ogilvy,
Ogilvy on Advertising

Level two

Consists of:
- Short sections of body copy
- Information inside boxes
- Charts, tables, diagrams
- Captions with them

Time spent per page: 30-90 seconds

Percentage of readers: 10-60 percent are still with you

Challenge:
- Expand key points.
- Provide another level of information.

Level three

Consists of:
- Body copy

"Four times as many people read captions as read body copy."

David Ogilvy,
Ogilvy on Advertising

Time spent: depends upon amount of remaining material

Percentage of readers: 1-10 percent

Note: You will have a higher percentage of readers of the body copy from people who are expecting a publication, or if the publication is of great benefit or interest to them. Probably less of our materials fit into that category than we'd like to think.

Challenge:
- Complete your message.

Communicate your message on all three levels

"Readers want what is important to be clearly laid out; they will not read anything that is trouble-some to read."

Jan Tschichold,
Thirty Centuries of Graphic Design

People process information and make decisions on all three levels. If you get your message out through each of them, the favorable responses to your message and the participation rates in your ministry events will increase dramatically.

You can use the graphic and typographic tools available to you in DTP: changing the type size and style, using columns, graphics and pictures to break your message into the three levels.

The article on the next two pages illustrates how this can be done. The purpose of the article is to get people involved in the various volunteer ministries of the church. In the first example the material is presented as it might be in a typed or word-processed newsletter or flyer. The second is the same material organized in the three level format in a desktop-published church newsletter.

This is the same article as the one on the next page. But because it has no typographic clues, subheads, or other graphic devices for the reader to skim, it's much harder to read.

This is the kind of piece that is all too easy to "put aside to read later"— which means it will most likely never get read.

On the other hand, if you only read the subheads and the boxed material on the next page, even though you may not get the full message, you know enough to respond.

CLAIM YOUR OWN MINISTRY NOW
by Rev. Darrell E. Mount

In my 11 years of ministry here at First Church, I have never been so excited about our church! Why? Because we are on the threshold of a tremendous shift in our understanding of ministry. Below I'd like to share with you three reasons for my excitement about our program "Claiming My Ministry."

First, I'm excited about "Claiming My Ministry" because I know how significant my call to ministry is.

"Sure," you say, "You're a pastor, called by God to give himself to others in a special role." Well, yes, that's true, and it is a very special feeling to know that what I do every day is closely tied to Christ's ministry in our church. My calling to the ordained ministry came when I was 30, following careers in the military and in engineering. But I feel that God called me to ministry long before I became a pastor. And this special calling to ministry is one I claim every Sunday when I enter my Sunday School class to teach.

This ministry which I claim helps make sense of my daily activities. I know I am called by God to do it. There is purpose in my life.

Second, I'm excited about "Claiming My Ministry" because I'm sure many of you are going to experience the joy I know, as you claim your ministry.

One of the most joyful aspects of being a pastor in our church working with volunteers in all areas of the church's life is seeing the enrichment that occurs when someone claims his or her ministry for Christ.

Dr. Trigg, our senior minister, has a vision shared by the staff. This vision is: "Every member in ministry." I know you will enjoy the added meaning in your life which will come to you, too, as you claim your ministry. Faith takes on an added dimension when you give yourself to a specific ministry. You're in for a treat.

Third, I'm excited about "Claiming My Ministry" because our community has never needed your ministry more than now.

Children, youth, singles, elderly—really, all of us—have a tremendous need for acceptance, understanding and caring. Only Christ can provide this. As you join your hands with His, you can make an awesome difference not only in our church, but also within our community when you claim your ministry. The goals of our church are basically five-fold: to be involved in mission, to pursue spiritual and personal growth, to engage in meaningful worship, to embrace the diversity of our work and to provide a supportive church community. I am confident that you too are called by God to claim your ministry in one or more of these areas. What a difference you can make in our community as you claim God's call on your life.

This is a window of opportunity. Come on, let go and let God. God is calling. Claim your part of God's ministry. You'll be glad you did!

Adapted from FUMC

Above is an article presented as it would be if created on a word processor or typewriter and printed either as a handout or page of a simple newsletter.

Because the type and spacing are all the same, there are no visual clues for the reader and no way for the reader to scan the content.

It is all or nothing reading. If the reader doesn't have time to sit down and read the entire piece he will put it away to read it later, which means it probably won't be read at all.

This is the same article as is on the ***previous page.***

Subtitle below the headline explains the program—remember not everyone is as familiar with your program as the staff is!

People will always look at pictures and read the caption below them. A great way to summarize your message is to restate it in your caption.

The first sentence of each section was increased in size, made bold, and printed in a different type style than the text. This turns the sentence into a subhead. The subheads lead readers through the article and allow for easy skimming.

the Encounter First United Methodist Church

Claim your own ministry now!

"Claiming My Ministry" is a volunteer program at First Church that seeks to enable and encourage every person in the congregation to discover and practice their spiritual gifts.

This next week you will receive a special letter from Dr. Trigg along with a very important commitment card. On the card, you will find many areas of ministry waiting for your commitment.

This issue of the Encounter contains a special section which describes most of the areas.

I encourage you to look it over and prayerfully consider God's call to you.

This Sunday you will have the opportunity to personally to claim your ministry for this next year.

by Rev. Darrell E. Mount

In my 11 years of ministry here at First Church, I have never been so excited about our church! Why? Because we are on the threshold of a tremendous shift in our understanding of ministry. Below I'd like to share with you three reasons for my excitement about our program "Claiming My Ministry."

First, I'm excited about "Claiming My Ministry" because I know how significant my call to ministry is.

"Sure," you say, "You're a pastor, called by God to give himself to others in a special role." Well, yes, that's true, and it is a very special feeling to know that what I do every day is closely tied to Christ's ministry in our church. My calling to the ordained ministry came when I was 30, following careers in the military and in engineering. But I feel that God called me to ministry long before I became a pastor. And this special calling to ministry is one I claim every Sunday when I enter my Sunday School class to teach.

This ministry which I claim helps make sense of my daily activities. I know I am called by God to do it. There is purpose in my life.

Second, I'm excited about "Claiming My Ministry" because I'm sure many of you are going to experience the joy I know, as you claim your ministry.

One of the most joyful aspects of being a pastor in our church working with volunteers in all areas of the church's life is seeing the enrichment that occurs when someone claims his or her ministry for Christ.

Dr. Trigg, our senior minister, has a vision shared by the staff. This vision is: "every member in ministry." I know you will enjoy the added meaning in your life which will come to you, too, as you claim your ministry. Faith takes on an added dimension when you give yourself to a specific ministry. You're in for a treat.

Third, I'm excited about "Claiming My Ministry" because our community has never needed your ministry more than now.

Children, youth, singles, elderly—really, all of us—have a tremendous need for acceptance, understanding and caring. Only Christ can provide this. As you join your hands with His, you can make an awesome difference not only in our church, but also within our community when you claim your ministry. The goals of our church are basically five-fold: to be involved in mission, to pursue spiritual and personal growth, to engage in meaningful worship, to embrace the diversity of our work, and to provide a supportive church community. I am confident that you too are called by God to claim your ministry in one or more of these areas. What a difference you can make in our community as you claim God's call on your life.

This is a window of opportunity. Come on, let go and let God. God is calling. Claim your part of God's ministry. You'll be glad you did!

Adapted from FUMC

Using the same material as on the previous page, this page has been laid out using the three-level approach by making the lead sentence in each section bold and larger than the text. In addition, a subtitle below the headline, subheads throughout the text, a picture and caption and section of boxed text (pulled from the article) have been added.

The reader now has a way to quickly skim the page to find out the essential facts of the article. Even if they spend only five to ten seconds skimming the page, they will know enough to respond.

Successful level one writing

Level one consists of:

- *Headlines and subtitles*
- *Subheads and call-outs*
- *Graphics and photos*
- *Captions that go with them*

Remember these categories of writing are what 80 percent of your readers will read. If you want to get your message across to the greatest number of people, you need to do it here. Following are guidelines and examples on each category.

Headlines

To make an effective headline, you need to do more than simply label. Tell a story; give some information; ask for action.

For example, most church newsletters have a column that is entitled something like:

These column headers are labels only.

The reader has no idea of the content of what follows or if it's worth the time to read.

Pastor's column

Message from Rev. Smith

This type of headline is a useful label, but it doesn't tell you anything about the contents. If people are in a hurry and don't know what the article contains or why they should read it, a large percentage will skip it.

It is much more likely people will read the column if the headlines intrigue the reader or give them an idea of the content of the article that follows. You don't need to do away with the title "Pastor's column" or similar labels. Just typeset them as a section head and then put the headline below it.

This treatment works well. You can label the column, but also provide a headline that informs the reader of the contents that follow.

Pastor's column

Church Relief Committee giving aid just hours after hurricane's devastation

Additional headline tips:

Consider using downstyle

Traditionally headlines have been written with the first letter of each word capitalized.

A more contemporary way of writing headlines is to write in what is called downstyle. USA TODAY pioneered this style in journalism. Downstyle is when the headline is written as a sentence without a period. When a headline is written downstyle, proper names and acronyms stand out and are easier to identify.

Though both methods are still used, downstyle is preferred for contemporary publications.

A headline written downstyle—written as a sentence without a period. Do headlines this way for contemporary publications.

A headline written in the traditional manner of capitalizing the first letter of every word—Jan White, premier publication designer, calls these "headlines with hiccoughs."

Joy Smith challenges HUGS singles' group to develop a theology of self-care

Joy Smith Challenges HUGS Singles' Group To Develop A Theology Of Self-Care

Use a verb

Think of your headlines as a sentence with a period. Sentences need verbs. Headlines that stop at simply labeling are boring—no action takes place. Adding a verb is not only more informative, but it adds action and life to your headline.

Without a verb this headline merely lables the event

Using verbs in this headline adds power to the message. It turns the label into a story.

Promise Keepers Men's Conference

Promise Keepers Men's Conference expects 50,000 men to pack CU stadium to hear challenge for godly living

Longer headlines work well

After reading a headline like the one above, people often ask, "But isn't that too long for a headline?"

It isn't if you want to communicate your message. Effective direct mail and popular journalism all have headlines that are sometimes quite lengthy. People will say, "But they'll find out all the facts when they read the story."

True. And remember, on average only one to five percent of your readers will read the entire story, but 80 percent will read the headline. Give your readers a key part of your message in the headline if you want the greatest number to get your point.

Promise a benefit in your headline

This is one of the primary rules for writing effective advertising and direct mail copy. Though you may not often think of it in this way, when you are writing about your church or ministry, you are in some ways attempting to sell a product. To paraphrase a book title, it is in many ways the greatest product ever created, and one with many benefits.

Consider the following headlines for an article on giving:

Innumerable studies show that the number one question in peoples' minds when they read is "What's in it for me?"

Because not too many of us are looking to add additional guilt to our lives, guilt in the headline is not a powerful motivator to get a reader to look at your story. Promising a benefit works much better.

Headline without a benefit:

Can a man rob God?

Good news headline:

You can take it with you—giving as an investment of eternal value

What to avoid in headlines

Puns, inside jokes, acronyms that only an inside audience knows— all of these can make your headline harder to understand. Don't try to be cute or catchy in a headline. Strive to be clear and complete the first time your headline is read.

Subtitle or deck

Though these can clarify or expand a headline, don't use them as an excuse for an unclear headline.

Though decks or subtitles can be considered part of the headline because they are usually read along with it, these lines serve as a transition between the headline and the text. They explain or expand the meaning of the headline, show its significance and help encourage the reader to continue into the text.

Subtitles are especially useful in church and ministry publications as a place to explain the meaning of a term or program mentioned in the headline. The example below shows how:

Writing a descriptive subtitle like this is a great way to explain an unfamiliar program in your ministry and to set up the background of the upcoming article.

Youth find Christ in Chrysalis

Chrysalis is a three-day spiritual renewal retreat for youth patterned after Emmaus for adults. The term chrysalis is the name of the growth stage between caterpillars becoming butterflies. Spiritually it symbolizes that through the experience of dying to self, Christ can transform us into new beings.

Six First Church teens experienced this transformation on Chrysalis weekends this summer. Below two of them tell their stories.

Adapted from FUMC

Not only do subtitles get readers into the story, but they explain programs to long-term church attenders who may have forgotten their meaning. Decks also introduce newcomers to some of the programs of the church. Try to use them in more of your writing.

Subheads

These sections of text or labels notify readers of the subdivisions of text by labeling or summarizing what follows. After skimming subheads a reader can then go back and either read the entire article or select those sections that contain information they need.

In the previous article, "Claiming your ministry," skimming the subheads gives readers the main points of the article even if they don't have the time or interest to read the entire piece.

In the example below the subheads allow readers to select the areas they need to read and to find them quickly. The subtitles are clear, not cute or confusing.

Enjoy each other, outdoors and time with Jesus on retreat

What is it?
The entire Youth Sunday School of First United Methodist Church will gather together for a weekend at John Wesley Ranch. The weekend will give youth a chance to escape the pressure of school while they enjoy the outdoors, each other and Jesus.

Who is it for?
This is an All-Youth Sunday School Retreat. Every Youth in grades 7-12 is eligible to attend.

When is it?
The retreat is November 6-8. Transportation will leave First Church at 6:00 p.m. on Friday, and will return on Sunday.

How much does it cost?
The cost of the weekend is $39.00 if you register and pay by October 19, $44.00 by October 25 and $49.00 after that. Last day to register is November 4.

Remember: Scholarship money is always available to you if you have trouble coming up with the bucks. Contact Robert or Gary if you need financial help.

What to bring?
Yourself, sleeping bag or blankets, pillow, toiletries, towel, jeans or casual clothing, rain poncho, warm coat, flashlight, Bible, pen, notebook, tennis shoes or other comfortable shoes, a wacky costume for Saturday night, and don't forget your Jerry Trigg look alike dolls (available in the Youth department for $9.95 plus $15.95 for shipping and handling).

Where will we sleep?
Senior High, grades 9-12 will lodge at the John Wesley Ranch. Junior High grades 8-9 will lodge at the Golden Bell Retreat Center. (Golden Bell was Robert's great grandfather who established the camp in 1984).

What not to bring?
No boom boxes will be allowed. You may bring Walkmans.

Adapted from FUMC

The brief article above makes excellent use of subheads.

They clearly label the information that follows and make it easy to look up facts for future reference.

It's a well-written, brief article that has all the important information included, plus it has a bit of humor woven in (after all it is for Junior High and Senior High schoolers).

Visual tips for subheads

- Make subheads one size larger than the text below them.
- Use boldface type.
- Use either the same typeface as the text below them or a contrasting typeface.
- Make them flush left (not indented, but placed next to the margin) whether or not the text below them is indented.

Writing subheads

Think of the subheads as a layer of meaning or an outline sitting on top of your article that summarizes the main points of the message you want to get across.

You can either determine these main points first and then write the additional information under them, or write the sections of text and then summarize or label them with your subheads.

Call-outs

These can also be called pull quotes, breakouts or similar terms. In traditional magazine publishing they are a particularly interesting quote that is literally pulled from the main part of the text. Their purpose is to pull the reader into the text of the story.

Though you can use this method in your DTP publications, because of the limited space in these publications and the time constraints of your reader, a more powerful way to use them is to emphasize the point of your message or to add additional material to the subject being discussed as the example below illustrates.

Does success for the Christian mean a heavenly Disneyland?

Lorem ipsum dolor sit amet, consectetuer adipiscing elit, sed diam nonummy nibh euismod tincidunt ut laoreet dolore magna aliquam erat volutpat. Ut wisi enim ad minim veniam, quis nostrud exerci tation ullamcorper suscipit lobortis nisl ut aliquip ex ea commodo consequat. Duis autem vel eum iriure dolor in hendrerit in vulputate velit esse molestie consequat, vel illum dolore eu

"I climbed the ladder of success to the top, only to discover that my ladder was propped against the wrong wall." Jeb Stuart Magruder

feugiat nulla facilisis at vero eros et accumsan et iusto odio dignissim qui blandit praesent luptatum zzril delenit augue duis dolore te feugait nulla facilisi. Lorem ipsum dolor sit amet, consectetuer adipiscing elit, sed diam nonummy nibh euismod tincidunt ut laoreet dolore magna aliquam erat volutpat.

Ut wisi enim ad minim veniam, quis nostrud exerci tation ullamcorper suscipit lobortis nisl ut aliquip ex ea commodo consequat.

Lorem ipsum dolor sit amet, consectetuer adipiscing elit, sed diam nonummy nibh euismod tincidunt ut laoreet dolore magna aliquam erat volutpat.

Ut wisi enim ad minim veniam, quis nostrud exerci tation ullamcorper suscipit lobortis nisl ut aliquip ex ea commodo consequat. Duis autem vel eum iriure dolor in hendrerit in vulputate velit esse molestie consequat, vel illum dolore eu feugiat nulla facilisis at vero eros et accumsan et iusto odio dignissim qui blandit praesent luptatum.

Szril delenit augue duis dolore te feugait nulla facilisi. Lorem ipsum dolor sit amet, consectetuer adipiscing elit, sed diam nonummy nibh euismod tincidunt ut laoreet dolore magna aliquam erat volutpat. Ut wisi enim ad

"Nothing that you have not given away will ever be really yours. Nothing in you that has not died will ever be raised from the dead. Look for yourself, and you will find in the long run only hatred, loneliness, despair, rage, ruin, and decay. But look for Christ and you will find Him, and with Him everything else thrown in." C.S. Lewis

minim veniam, quis nostrud exerci tation ullamcorper suscipit lobortis nisl ut aliquip ex ea commodo consequat.

Too often in an effort to cram in more text than will actually fit, quotes are jammed in like this.

When they are this crowded they lose their impact.

Either edit your material to give them more room or leave them out.

Also remember to indent your text inside boxes.

Consectetuer adipiscing elit, sed diam nonummy nibh euismod tincidunt ut laoreet dolore magna aliquam erat volutpat.

Ut wisi enim ad minim veniam, quis nostrud exerci tation ullamcorper suscipit lobortis nisl ut aliquip ex ea commodo consequat.

Lorem ipsum dolor sit amet, consectetuer adipiscing elit, sed diam nonummy nibh euismod tincidunt ut laoreet dolore magna aliquam erat volutpat.

"What good is it for a man to gain the whole world, yet forfeit his soul?" Mark 8:36

Ut wisi enim ad minim veniam, quis nostrud exerci tation ullamcorper suscipit lobortis nisl ut aliquip ex ea commodo consequat. Duis autem vel

Captions

Tips on taking, cropping and reproducing photos for desktop publishing are in the chapter on photography.

People always look at the pictures on a page and if there is a caption beneath it, they will read it.

Captions provide a wonderful opportunity to get our message across, to summarize the main idea of an article to give essential information.

Consider the church newsletter on this page and the next. The only difference between them is one has captions and one doesn't.

Without captions the pictures on this page don't make any sense.

We know they are probably about the mission trip, but we aren't even sure what people are doing in them.

the Encounter First United Methodist Church

Youth Mission Team learns the language of love

"How can I speak to these people if I don't know their language?" Pondered a frustrated Susan Meider upon arrival of the Sr. High Mission Team to the orphanage in Cuidad Serdan, Mexico.

About two-thirds of the team did not know a lot of Spanish, but to the team's delight, they found that the love of Jesus is a universal language. As the team interacted with the residents of the orphanage, they found ways to express their care and compassion. The residents of the orphanage, likewise, were able to share their joy for life and love for the Lord.

The team spent four wonderful days at the orphanage teaching the Bible, playing games, singing songs, and sharing together with the residents. The Lord knit hearts together in spite of the language differences.

The team shared in a communion service with the residents of the orphanage in which the power of the Holy Spirit was evident. The residents and the team both knew the Hebrew song "alleluia" and could sing it together. As they lifted their hearts to the Lord in praise, the presence of Christ was manifested. The team learned that the language of love is compassion, mercy, empathy, and concern.

The Mexico Mission team will share their experiences at the 8:25 a.m. service on August 16. Come and hear the great things that God has done!

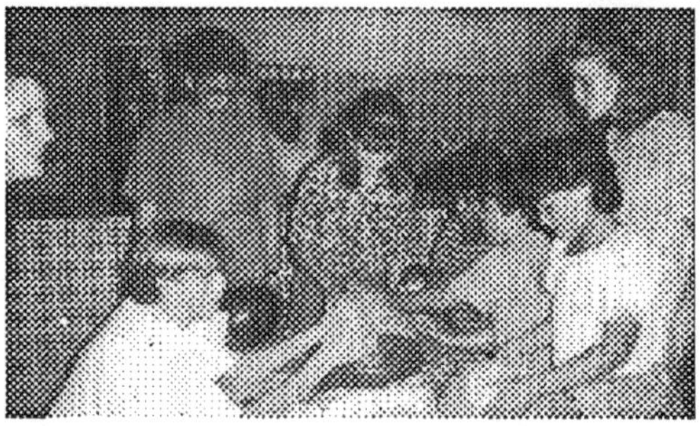

Adapted from FUMC

With the addition of captions, these photographs now tell a story, because the captions tell you what is going on in the pictures.

Unfortunately, people often don't take the time to caption photographs in their church or ministry newsletters, prayer letters, or other material that is sent out. It's so easy to assume everybody knows what is going on or that they will read the article and then figure out the picture. Both assumptions are seldom correct. Take the extra time to caption your photos and get maximum communication impact from them.

the Encounter First United Methodist Church

Youth Mission Team learns the language of love

"How can I speak to these people if I don't know their language?" Pondered a frustrated Susan Meider upon arrival of the Sr. High Mission Team to the orphanage in Cuidad Serdan, Mexico.

About two-thirds of the team did not know a lot of Spanish, but to the team's delight, they found that the love of Jesus is a universal language. As the team interacted with the residents of the orphanage, they found ways to express their care and compassion. The residents of the orphanage, likewise, were able to share their joy for life and love for the Lord.

The team spent four wonderful days at the orphanage teaching the Bible, playing games, singing songs, and sharing together with the residents. The Lord knit hearts together in spite of the language differences.

The team shared in a communion service with the residents of the orphanage in which the power of the Holy Spirit was evident. The residents and the team both knew the Hebrew song "alleluia" and could sing it together. As they lifted their hearts to the Lord in praise, the presence of Christ was manifested. The team learned that the language of love is compassion, mercy, empathy, and concern.

The Mexico Mission team will share their experiences at the 8:25 a.m. service on August 16. Come and hear the great things that God has done!

The language difference didn't stop these teens from sharing many fun activities.

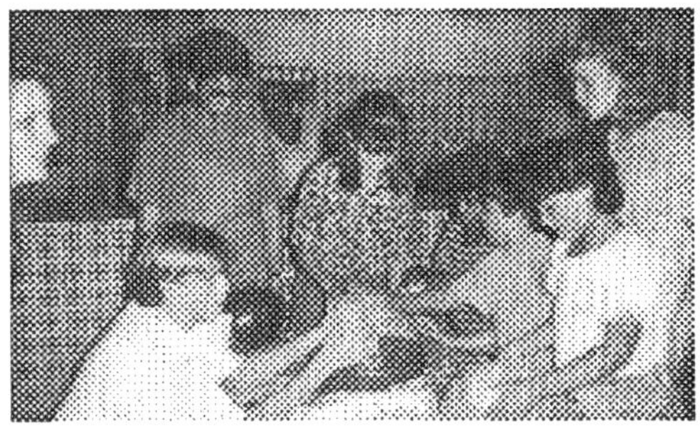

Team members and residents of the orphanage worked together on many projects.

On their last night together they celebrated with a traditional Mexican party. *Adapted from FUMC*

Not only are leaving out captions a missed opportunity to communicate, but think about what happens when you look at a photo album of a family you don't know. It can bring up lonely feelings. If you have lots of photos in your ministry publications, but don't tell people who is in them or what they are doing, that same feeling of loneliness can arise in the readers of your publications.

You want your ministry publications to not make anyone feel left out, to make people feel at home—writing clear explanatory captions can help do that.

Successful level two writing

Level two consists of:

- *Short sections of body copy*
- *Information inside boxes*
- *Charts, tables, diagrams*
- *The captions that go with them*

After your readers have looked at the headlines, pictures and captions, they will usually skim over this next level. If they find it useful and interesting, they may invest the time in reading the body copy, but you can't count on it. If your message is important, (and most ministry messages are) try to get at least enough of it in this level for your readers to take action or learn the most important facts that you want them to know even if they don't read the rest of the text.

Below are tips for creating successful level two communication.

Short sections of body copy

"I try to leave out the parts that people skip."

Elmore Leonard

Anything is easier to assimilate if it is in manageable parts. You don't put a whole pizza into your mouth at one time, a box of chocolates isn't a melted mass of sugar and fillings you consume with one gulp.

Cut up your article like dividing a pizza. Give people a piece they can hold on to. Arrange your suggestions with each thought complete like chocolates wrapped in their paper holders.

Creating bite-size sections of body copy is easy to do if you were careful in constructing your subheads—your body copy will naturally fall into easily digestible sections of text.

Information inside boxes

These sections of text are also known as sidebars.

If you have a list of items, tips, schedules, anything that can be arranged in a bulleted list—all of these can be communicated well in a sidebar. You can also use boxed text to point out a significant part of your message or to emphasize the date and time of a special meeting.

Not only are lists and summaries usually easier to read in such an arrangement, but boxed text and lists add visual interest to your desktop published page.

Charts, tables, diagrams, and the captions with them

The most important point to remember in placing charts and graphs in your publication is that not only are the charts and graphs themselves important, but even more important are the captions that go with them.

Just as with photographs, people will usually look at the graph or chart. If you don't have a caption with it, don't count on its message being understood. Few graphs or charts are self-explanatory.

Successful level three writing

Level three consists of:

- *Body copy*

Writing body copy for desktop publishing is like giving a three-minute speech. Three minutes doesn't seem like much time to make your point, but you can pack a lot into it and the results can be quite powerful.

The following tips will help you write effective body copy.

Get to the point

We must be powerful and concise in our writing. A captive audience for our communications does not exist. Americans are bombarded with:

- *500 commercial images per day*

If that is not distraction enough, they also have available:

- *10,000 magazines*
- *6,000 radio stations*
- *400 television stations*

There is no time in DTP material for rambling introductions, space to tell your personal history, the theories behind what you're writing or your feelings on why you think it is important.

Nor is there room for apologies, Please don't ever say, "This is such an important topic, I really can't do it justice in this small space."

No one piece ever said it all. John tells us that even all of the books in the world can't begin to tell the full story of Jesus. Think of your writing as a continuing dialog with your audience. Tell them one thing at a time, get right to the point, and then tell them something else another time.

The following example is an excellent illustration of this principle. It comes from a church newsletter and is part of a continuing series of articles on working with volunteers.

No wasted words here. The author gets directly to the point, tells the story and quits.

Make your meetings matter

by Gretchen Richardson, Director of Volunteers

Volunteers need to feel that their presence matters—that what they discuss and plan will result in decisive action and visible ministry. How you conduct your meetings sends a direct message to volunteers on how much they matter to you.

How are your meetings?

- Is your committee stuck in a reporting mode so that you can't decide where you're going?
- Do the staff chairs make the reports rather than leading an exploration of goals, making decisions and determining action?
- Are committee members slipping away?

Here are some meeting hints that may be helpful:

- Try skipping the reports.
- Try dealing with a clear agenda, making critical decisions and taking action.
- Let volunteers know that their opinions do matter. Wake everybody up and give them the chance to participate.
- If no action is required, decide whether the meeting is necessary. If not, call it off or postpone it.

Next week: How can business and fellowship be combined?

Adapted from FUMC

Write for the eye

Desktop writers can place words on a page, but unless they create a clear and vivid picture in another's mind, the message isn't communicated. A selection of words alone won't communicate. Our minds have to create a visual image to give our emotions and will something to respond to. Choose words that will fashion a specific and powerful image in your mind's eye. Make your audience touch, see, smell and experience exactly what you are writing about. The examples below show how to do it. First, try to picture this description of a ministry:

This first description does not give the mind's eye a concrete picture. "Wonderful" is a word without a specific meaning.

Description #1

I want to share with you how wonderful the Prison Fellowship pen pal program is.

What do you see in your mind's eye? You don't see anything specific do you?

Now try to visualize this:

In this description, the specific words enable the reader to seethe ministry.

Description #2

Mark had been in prison for two years. During that time he had never had a visitor, never received a letter or a phone call.

His first contact with anyone outside the prison came the day he got his first letter from his Prison Fellowship pen pal.

Do you see Mark? Of course you do.

Different readers might see a different Mark, but each one sees a person being helped in a concrete way. You see him in the second description and not the first because the second description contains concrete words that call up concrete images in your mind.

Generalities like "wonderful" call up completely different images in each person's mind. When some people think "wonderful," they think hot fudge sundae, not a prison ministry. Give people a concrete picture made up of specific people, places or events to give meaning to whatever you write about.

How to write for the eye

Tell stories about specific people

Jesus was a master at this. He didn't just tell us that God waits to forgive us, that He loves us no matter how far we fall. He told the story of the prodigal son.

The Bible is filled with stories of the experiences of individuals. When we think about the Bible what comes to mind is not the doctrine of the atonement or the theology of spiritual gifts. We think of Moses, Ruth and Peter. God used human lives to illustrate His eternal truths and our publications can do the same.

To illustrate a ministry, instead of using a dry description have somebody tell you his or her story. For example, imagine you want to get people to help in your youth program. You could place a notice like this in the church bulletin or newsletter:

Typical notice asking for help in a church newsletter.

Experience satisfaction in working with our youth—volunteer at the church office today!

Or you could tell the story about a couple who are working with youth like this youth department did in a recent newsletter:

This article not only asks for help, but it tells you what your involvement would be like, allows you to meet a couple already involved and puts the needs and rewards of the ministry in the terms of their life.

You may not have nor want to use this much space in your newsletter to write a story like this. You can still illustrate a ministry or lesson in the life of a person in a paragraph or two.

Look at the Gospels for examples of how to do this. In Luke 21:1-4, Jesus illustrates sacrificial giving by briefly telling the story of a widow who gave "all she had to live on."

The life you put into your story is more important than the length.

Why do two 50-year-olds spend 20 hours each week in youth ministry?

"The Van Normans are the coolest adults I know," says eleventh grader, Jessica Untener.

Jessica has known the Van Normans for two years through Disciple Bible Study, retreats and mission trips. She's not alone in her evaluation of the "cool" Van Normans.

Linn and Judy have been loving teenagers at First Church for the past five years. They've done everything from teach Sunday School to sweat on mission trips. Currently they lead 27 youth in Disciple Bible Study on Sunday nights. They are putting in about 20 hours per week in ministry.

"The more we put in, the more we get back," says 51-year-old Linn. "God has put us in a situation financially so that we can give a lot of our time to teens." The Van Normans believe God has blessed them, not so that they can travel the world, but so they can contribute to the lives of others.

The pay-off comes in the connectedness we feel to the kids in love, understanding and appreciation.

Judy and Linn feel their calling is to teenagers because they remember their own struggles as teens. "I remember my own adolescence clearly," says Judy. "There were a lot of conflicts. I wish I could have had a significant adult that I could have talked to. It would have made a difference for me."

So what makes a "cool" youth worker? The Van Normans didn't come equipped with boom boxes, but they've got one invaluable asset. "Love is the only way to live successfully," says Judy. "And God is love."

The difference that Christ's love has made in their lives is what the Van Normans are sharing with our teens.

If you've got some extra time and love to give, meet with us for one hour on Wednesday evening, June 6 at 6:00 p.m. in the youth meeting room. We'll be sharing an overview of the ministry of the youth department and ways you can help. Our needs range from volunteer prayer partners and cookie makers to active involvement with the kids. The time involved? From one hour a week to as much time as you can spare. Call us at 555-0000 for more info.

Adapted from FUMC

Illustrate a concept or theological idea with a real-life situation or picture.

Again, the Bible is masterful in doing this. In it we witness people living out the reality of God in their lives. Our challenge is to come up with illustrations from life today to change lives.

For example, say you want to motivate people to work with your youth program. You want people to see how difficult life has become for teenagers today and you decide teen suicide is the example you will use to illustrate it. You could say:

The facts are impressive amounts, but they don't communicate anything real.

> Too many kids are dying by their own hands each year. And though the number that commit suicide is in the thousands, even more attempt suicide.

Or you could say:

A word picture that makes the facts come alive.

> Think back to the last athletic event you attended at a high school gym. Envision the mass of kids, their enthusiasm and excitement. The average high school gym holds 1,000 kids. Last year the same number of students that would fill five high school gyms—5,000 kids—took their lives. Ten to twenty times that many attempted self-destruction.

How do you come up with life pictures that illustrate what you want to communicate? Here are some ideas:

- Keep in mind what you'll be writing about and keep your eyes open to the larger picture of life. When something reminds you of something else make a note of it.
- Ask other people in your ministry or church what reminds them of salvation or grace or any other topic you wonder about.
- Be prepared to do research. When I got the idea for the suicide illustration above, I called high schools and colleges all over the area asking about the seating capacity of their gyms.
- Keep a file of ideas for future writing and illustrations.

Tell the tiny tale

A tiny tale is also known as an anecdote, "a short entertaining account of some event." These are the stories, the life of any communication piece that make it come alive. These are the images we remember.

Anecdotes are especially useful in DTP writing because we can tell the tale, and then follow it with the lesson we want to teach. If we've shared a vivid word picture, not only will our audience understand our teaching but the picture will remain in people's minds and our lesson will be tied to it.

In the same issue of the youth newsletter on the previous page the youth minister had a message to share. The story on the next page shows how he did it.

In this story the author uses the story of his lost daughter to communicate a message about God's unconditional love.

We see God's love fleshed out in Robert's concern for his daughter.

This is an effective and powerful way to teach a lesson about God's love.

Look for events in your life that remind you of biblical truth and record them for resources in your writing.

My daughter was lost in the woods

Linn and Judy Van Norman and I were talking on their front deck when my six-year-old daughter Amanda asked if she could take a hike out around their house. The Van Normans live on a high ridge that is surrounded by woods filled with short, safe hiking trails. Off Amanda went.

When she didn't return after 15 minutes I began to worry. I realized it would be very easy for a little girl to become disoriented in the woods and end up lost. Linn and I searched the area around his house for another 10 minutes but could not find Amanda.

I was scared. I decided to make one more sweep through the woods before I called the Search and Rescue Unit. But as I set off into the woods, Amanda emerged and came running into my arms. She was crying but relieved that she was found.

Lost from God

As I reflected on what happened to us, I began to think about what it is like for God when we are lost from Him. When we become disoriented in the woods of life, we often make decisions that take us away from God.

God doesn't hate us for being lost. He just wants to help us find our way home.

When we are lost, does God hate us for it? Does God get angry with us? I don't think so. When Amanda was lost, my only concern was her welfare. I would have done anything to help her get back home.

I think that must be the way God thinks of us when we are away from Him. Like me, as our Father God will do anything to help get us out of the woods. Jesus demonstrated that to us by laying down His own life to rescue us from our lostness. As the Bible puts it, "While we were still sinners [lost], Christ died for us" (Romans 5:8).

Yet it is so easy to think Christ hates us when we stumble away from Him. But the reality is, like a parent with a lost child, Jesus searches earnestly for us in the woods. What a relief when we are found by Him.

adapted from FUMC

It's interesting how the mind works when we read stories. We can take a specific example and generalize it to our lives—from Amanda's story we feel what it is like to be searched for and found by a loving father. But it's difficult to do the reverse. If we hear a general statement like "God is waiting for you in a non-judgmental way to come to Him" —we aren't touched as deeply.

Some tips on finding tiny tales:

- Journal about how you see God working in your life and the life of others. Record when your life is similar to a lesson in the Bible. Look at your journal for stories to share.
- Read about the lives of others. It's OK to tell a story about another's life.
- Ask people to tell you stories. Ask kids, ask teens, ask seniors, "Tell me about a time in your life when God taught you a lesson."
- Don't make them up and pass them off as true. If you can't come up with a real life story be sure to say something like, "Imagine this event happening. . . ."

Practical writing how-tos

"If a writer is so cautious that he never writes anything that cannot be criticized, he will never write anything that can be read. If you want to help other people you have got to make up your minds to write things that some men will condemn. . . . If you write for God, you will reach many men and bring them joy. If you write for men, you may make some money and you may give someone a little joy and you may make a noise in the world for a little while. If you write for yourself, you can read what you yourself have written and after ten minutes you will be so disgusted that you will wish that you were dead."

C.S. Lewis

Know the length needed before you start

Make a mock-up and count words or lines on the computer or by hand—whatever you need to do to have a realistic estimate of the length you can write. Then write with that guideline in mind. If someone else is writing, give them the guidelines also.

This seems obvious, but somehow people tend to think that DTP can take a piece of writing of any length and compress it into whatever space is available just by passing it through the computer— it doesn't work that way.

Write a terrible first draft

Give yourself permission to be awful and just begin writing. Start anywhere, start in the middle, start at the end and work backwards, it doesn't matter, just get something on paper and then go back and clean it up later.

You'll always be surprised—your first draft may need work, but it's usually much better than you first thought.

After you've gotten it down, first revise for structure and then revise for readability and grammar.

Ignore the voice within

You'll always hear messages like this one writer recorded in his journal, "I'm no good. . . I'm desperately upset about it. I have no discipline anymore."

Remember Satan is the accuser, and you can bet he won't leave you alone when you are working on writing that can heal and bless and bring people to the Savior. Refuse to listen to that voice.

Know when to let go and go to press

You will rarely, if ever, have all the time you want to do a DTP piece of writing as perfectly as you'd like.

Part of the reason for this situation is the tremendous time acceleration of DTP production. In the past, you may have never even thought about doing a newsletter, let alone getting one out weekly or monthly.

Another potential problem with DTP is you can continue to make changes up to minutes before you run it off and you'll always see one more thing you'd like to do. Or someone else in the ministry will see it and they won't realize that "one little change" will cause you to have to rearrange four pages.

Set realistic deadlines; work until you meet them; then stop and save your improvements for your next project.

Desktop publishing, like the rest of our life, is a pilgrimage—nobody has arrived at perfection yet.

The study of typography should enable you to use type with such appropriateness that your message is clearly communicated and the type itself not noticed at all.

chapter 7

Typography

Every typeface has a distinctive voice as the examples below illustrate. Learn to use the one that best communicates your message.

In the first example below, the typefaces are in this order: Zapf Chancery and Helvetica. In the second example, the order of typefaces is Helvetica and Zapf Chancery. In the first example the typefaces are appropriate to the message. In the second they obviously aren't.

It's easy to tell when somebody is mad at you isn't it? It doesn't matter what they say—their tone of voice lets you know.

On the other hand, there is a tone of voice that says "I love you" even when it's asking for the potatoes to be passed.

The tone of voice we use when we talk is an important part of our message. An angry yell—a soft whisper—a stern command—each tone of voice communicates a totally different message regardless of the words used.

It's the same with type. Different type styles have different voices—some are loud and commanding, others soft and inviting, others simply state the facts.

Look at the two examples below. Which set of messages has the correct type for the message? Which one uses a type with a voice that is different from the message of the words?

Your presence is requested at the reception
for
Rev. Taylor Johnson

Men's work day scheduled for August 10

Your presence is requested
at the reception for Rev. Taylor Johnson

Men's retreat and work day scheduled for August 10

Pretty obvious isn't it?

You might not think you know the language of type, but from years of looking at books, advertisements, layouts in magazines

In the day of computers and electronically generated type, the world of typography is one still filled with history and terms from the days when type was cut by hand to make the individual letters.

Though this history can be fascinating to study, it can also be frustrating because some of the terms we use in describing type have great histories but make no sense at all in the computer age.

and newspapers, you know what is appropriate in type and what isn't. Even though you may not know the names of typefaces, you know when an inappropriate typeface is used, and you wonder what message they are really trying to get across.

In desktop publishing you need to become intentional in your knowledge of the voices of type and learn to use the proper voice for each of your publications. How do you accomplish that?

Again, it's very similar to our human voices. It isn't just one thing that makes a tone of voice angry but a combination of factors. In a human voice volume, tone, pitch and clarity are all important.

Type has a similar combination of factors that combine to lend a voice to its message including size, spacing, style and various other characteristics. These factors will be discussed one by one. The following examples will illustrate the concepts.

Don't worry about memorizing all the terms and vocabulary of type. Look at the examples, get a sense of what works and what doesn't, and then try similar typefaces in your publications.

Type terms

Below are some basic terms that will be useful as we discuss type:

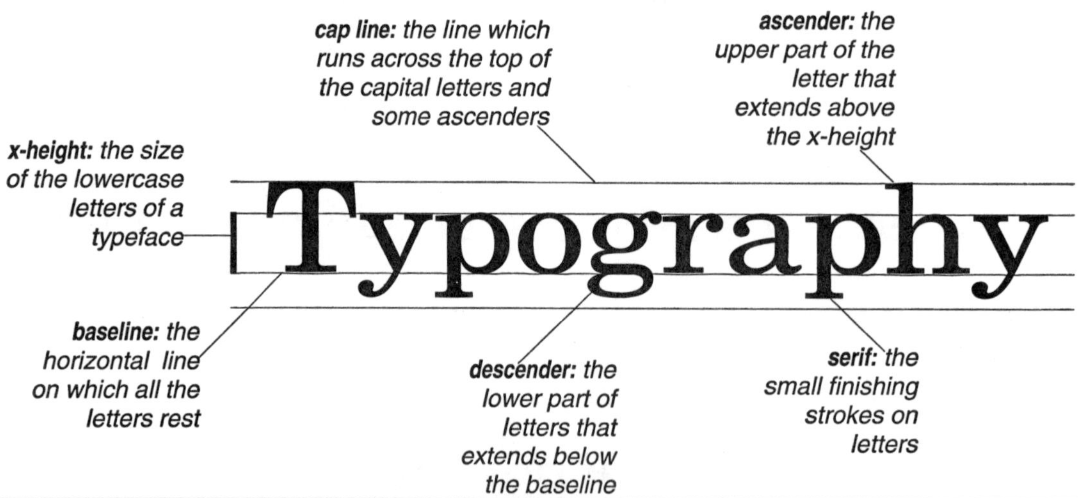

Type size

Type is measured in points which are fractions of picas. There are approximately 12 points to a pica, 6 picas to an inch.

See chapter 5 for a discussion on using points and picas to measure in desktop publishing.

This is 10 point type.

This is 18 point type.

This is 36 point type.

This seems fairly straightforward, but it causes a lot of confusion in desktop publishing because in measuring type the point size given is the measurement of the block of space around the type, not the letter itself.

You need to be aware that in desktop publishing two typefaces can be the same point size, but they can take up significantly different amounts of space in your publication. The example below illustrates how this works.

Because of its design and larger x-height, the Avant Garde typeface takes up much more space than the Times typeface even though the two typefaces are the same point size.

72 point Times

A a

72 point Avant Garde

A a

12 point Times

Different typefaces of the same size can take up different amounts of space in a publication.

12 point Avant Garde

Different typefaces of the same size can take up different amounts of space in a publication.

Type size application to DTP

- Remember different typefaces take up different amounts of space—you can't simply change the typeface of a paragraph and have it fit in the space that it did before.
- Use from 9 point to 12 point type sizes in the text of documents. Larger or smaller than that is hard to read in text.
- 10 or 11 point is an ideal text size for most typefaces.
- 12 point is good for an audience that is very young, very elderly or visually impaired.
- This book is written in 11 point type.
- Because Times is one of the most condensed yet highly readable typefaces—it is an excellent choice for text where you have space limitations.

Space between letters (kerning)

When the early typesetters set letters together to form words they found some letters just didn't look right when they were carved on individual blocks and placed next to each other. For example:

W A V E

To make the letters look like they belonged together, typesetters began to kern the letters. Kerning means to move the letters closer together so the words became easier to read, like this:

WAVE

Kerning application to DTP

Your DTP program will automatically kern for you. This autokerning works fine for body text. If larger text in headlines looks like it needs additional kerning, consult your software manual for how to tighten those letters.

Spacing between lines of type (leading)

We seldom read letters in isolation—usually they are combined into words and lines of type. How these lines are arranged has an effect on how easy or difficult they are to read.

The early typographers found that placing the lines of type one above the other, row after row, made the type hard to read.

To remedy this situation, they would insert thin strips of lead between the blocks of type. When printed with the lead inserted between the lines of type, the text now gave the eye a clean track of white space to travel from the end of one line back to the start of the next one. The lines of type were much easier to read.

Though we don't use strips of lead today, we still use the same term leading (pronounced "ledding"). This term refers to the space between lines of type. The more contemporary term "line spacing" is also used in some DTP programs. And if there is no leading between the lines of type, it is said to be "set solid."

The paragraph on the left is set with autoleading and it is easy to read because of the lines of white space between the lines of type.

The paragraph on the right is set solid and though more words can be packed into less space, it is harder to read.

"Now that I, your Lord and Teacher, have washed your feet, you also should wash one another's feet. I have set you an example that you should do as I have done for you. I tell you the truth, no servant is greater than his master, nor is a messenger greater than the one who sent him. Now that you know these things, you will be blessed if you do them" (John 13:14-17).

"Now that I, your Lord and Teacher, have washed your feet, you also should wash one another's feet. I have set you an example that you should do as I have done for you. I tell you the truth, no servant is greater than his master, nor is a messenger greater than the one who sent him. Now that you know these things, you will be blessed if you do them" (John 13:14-17).

How leading is measured

In the same way that type is measured in points by the size of the block around it, leading in your DTP program is also measured in points. When lead strips were actually used, if a 10 point type block of type had two points of lead strips inserted between the lines of type, there would be a total of 12 points (10 points for the type block plus 2 points for the strips of lead) between the top of one line of type to the one below it.

The 12 points is the leading measurement. When the leading measurement is combined with the type measurement, the combined measurement is written as a fraction, for example: 10/12 or 11/13, but pronounced "10 on 12" or "11 on 13."

Leading application to DTP

- In DTP programs the leading is determined automatically, unless manually changed. The autoleading for most programs is approximately 120% of the type size. That means that 10 point type would have 12 points of leading.

  Autoleading is fine for text but as the size of the type increases, the autoleading begins to space letters too far apart.

- For above 18 points, in headlines and subheads, etc. start the leading set solid (type and leading the same point size) and if any of the ascenders or descenders touch, increase the leading measurement until they don't touch.

When type size is above 18 points, autoleading will cause type in headers to be spaced too far apart. You need to manually tighten it up for it to look and read better.

This is a 24 point
headline that is
set with autoleading

In the second example, the leading is set 24/24. This measurement, where the leading equals the point size of the type, is refered to as set solid.

This is a 24
point headline
that is set solid

- As line length increases, increase leading to increase readability or the eye will have trouble finding the start of lines.

With a column this wide the leading was increased from the autoleading 10/12 to 10/15 to make it easier to read.

"Now that I, your Lord and Teacher, have washed your feet, you also should wash one another's feet. I have set you an example that you should do as I have done for you. I tell you the truth, no servant is greater than his master, nor is a messenger greater than the one who sent him. Now that you know these things, you will be blessed if you do them" (John 13:14-17).

Typefaces

Sizing and spacing are the same for all type, what makes it different? The same thing that makes people different—its face.

What makes up a human face? Color of eyes, shape of nose, the size of the chin—lots of individual physical characteristics that make up the whole. It's the same with type. There are individual physical characteristics that make up each individual typeface.

When we categorize people we identify them by races. Individual families belong within the various races. It is the same with type. The two most important races for desktop publishing are serif and sans serif. We'll discuss them below and then give examples of how to use each type in your desktop publishing projects.

Serifs and sans serif

Learning what typeface to use is a little bit like learning to use spices in cooking. You can cook using only salt, but your dishes will be very bland. But if you decide to use spices, you can't use any spice with any dish. One teaspoon of basil will have a very different effect on a dish than one teaspoon of cayenne pepper.

Learning what spice to use and when to use it is what distinguishes a cook from a chef.

Knowing what typeface to use in different situations is one of the skills that makes top-notch desktop publishers.

Serifs are the little feet, the strokes or projections at the end of some letter forms. Typefaces that have these are called serifed typefaces. Typefaces without them are called sans serif. (The French word for "without" is "sans.")

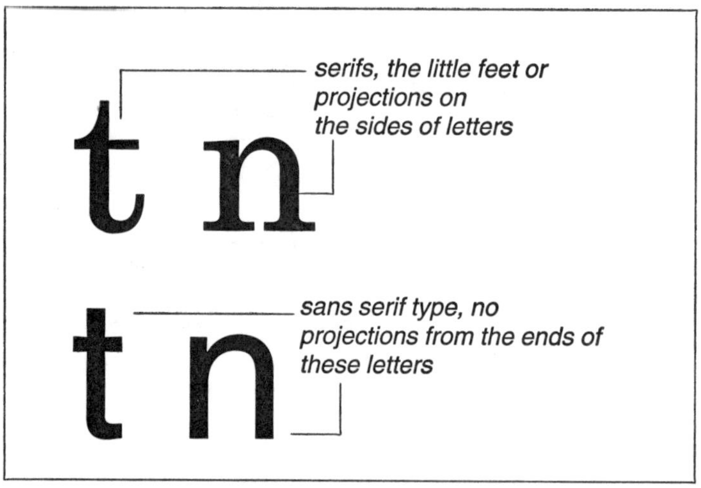

Serifed typefaces are the oldest forms of typefaces. Nobody was around making notes, but there are a couple of theories as to how serifs came to be on letter forms.

The first theory notes that the old Roman inscriptions are serif typefaces. Based on that evidence, it has been proposed that the serif developed as a stylized way of bringing the chisel out of the stone after the letter was cut.

The second theory notes that the medieval manuscripts were written with serifed letters. This theory recognizes that it is difficult to end a letter drawn with a calligraphy pen with a square edge. To try will result in a blob of ink on the paper. The scribe needed a way to bring the pen off the paper without the blob, hence the fine serif flourish to finish off the stroke and neatly remove pen from paper.

Typeface names can be different and belong to a similar typeface. Below are some of the names for Helvetica and Times.

Times, also known as:
Tymes
Dutch
Tiempo
Times New Roman
Marin

Helvetica, also known as:
Helvenica
Swiss
Geneva
Nimbus Sans
Arial

When the first type was cut for printing presses, it naturally followed the style of the handwritten manuscripts and was serifed.

Sans serif type was developed much later when it could be mechanically produced on the printing press. Though one of the first sans serif typefaces was cut in the 1800s, we tend to think of sans serif as looking modern and high tech.

With an understanding of those two major races or categories there are a multitude of typefaces to choose from.

Please note that not all DTP software uses the same names for these typefaces. The names used in the examples below are the original licensed names. Companies can create their own versions that are similar and give them their own names. For example, Times is often called Dutch; Helvetica called Swiss and Palatino called Platin. The name of the typeface isn't critical as long as the type looks similar to the examples given throughout the book.

The study of type, its history and use is fascinating. To give you a taste of what can be a lifelong study, below is a brief discussion of some of the most common typefaces that come with desktop publishing software. Each description is printed in that typeface.

The serif faces

Times

This typeface was created for the Times newspaper of London. The characteristics required of a typeface used for a newspaper make it an excellent typeface for DTP.

It is a somewhat condensed typeface, so you can fit lots of words into limited space, but it is still quite readable. It was also designed to be used in less than ideal printing conditions on the rough surface of newsprint. That makes it a good choice for the rougher printing resolution of laser printers.

Times along with Helvetica (no matter what the names given them) are the two typefaces that come with any DTP program. You can never go wrong using Times for body copy. It is great for newsletters, correspondence, brochures, books and ads. Whatever you would want to do in desktop publishing, it will work using Times.

Bookman

When I hold up a sample of Bookman in classes and ask what it reminds people of, I've literally had students call out "Dick and Jane." They're right.

Bookman is the typeface some of those early readers were printed in. It's a fat, friendly typeface and works well for children's materials.

Though it takes up lots of space limiting its use in DTP, it's great for children's or casual materials. It also can work well for ads, flyers or other material where fitting a lot of copy into a limited space is not a major concern. Don't use it in newsletters unless you don't have much to say.

Century Schoolbook

If Bookman is grade-school, Century is high school. It was created for *Century Magazine* and many high school and college textbooks are written using Century. It is not quite as condensed as Times, but is still very useful for text. The text of this book is Century.

Studies have shown that people can read Century for long periods of time without tiring. It is an excellent typeface for newsletters, training manuals, ministry reports and books.

Palatino

Publication designers love Palatino. A number of years ago typographers were asked if they were marooned on a desert island what one typeface would they take with them. "Palatino, of course" was the overwhelming answer.

It is such a lovely type without being overdone. The Y is so distinctive, as is the P. It has a touch of calligraphy about it, though it is restrained. Palatino is also a highly readable type and works well for newsletters. The result would be a bit more sophisticated than it would be with Times or Century. It is excellent for nice brochures, annual or board reports and proposals.

The sans serif faces

"Functional typography is invisible because it goes unnoticed. The aim is to create a visual medium that is so attractive, so inviting, and so appropriate to its material, that the process of reading (which most people dislike as work) becomes a pleasure."

Jan White,
Graphic Design
For The Electronic Age

Helvetica

Like Times, it is one of the most widely used typefaces in the world. It is the typeface often used as headers in newsletters.

Though often recommended for headlines, Helvetica is also frequently used as a text face and at 10 and 12 point sizes it works quite well in that role.

It is especially appropriate for scientific and contemporary publications.

Avant Garde

This is a very sophisticated type face. It is great for headlines and for advertisements.

If used in text, extra leading or space between lines is needed (9/13 works), but even then only use it for short sections of text in publications such as brochures, flyers or ads.

New Helvetica Narrow

This isn't just Helvetica condensed to get more words on a line. Be careful of this or any typeface that has the words narrow or condensed in its name. This type works well for tabular material and all sorts of charts and graphs, but the letters are too closely spaced together to work well for reading.

Specialty typefaces

Other than serif and sans serif there are other races of type used in DTP. Some do not strictly fit into the serif or sans serif category but are worth noting because they come with many DTP software programs. Examples of the most popular follow.

Of the making of typefaces there is no end

The examples in this section are of the most common typefaces that come with DTP programs, but they are by no means an exhaustive sample.

The cost of typefaces continues to drop. New technology, such as True Type, makes a large variety of typefaces easily and inexpensively available to everyone.

Write for catalogs from the type resource list in the Resource section to get an idea of some of the typefaces available.

Courier

This is the typeface that looks like it came from a typewriter. You may wonder why this is needed or included in DTP programs. The reason has to do with what we expect from type.

Back in the days when magazines had to be typeset, the majority of the publication would be typeset in a face such as Century, pasted up and laid out in the traditional method. This could take weeks to accomplish. In addition to these standard pages, perhaps the magazine had a news or update section that they would bind into the magazine at the very last minute. There wouldn't be time to get it typeset, pasted up and proofed so the editor would sit down at the typewriter and type out fast-breaking news which would be copied and inserted into the publication.

Even today, in news magazines there is often a typewritten-looking page, even though the editor most likely did not create it on the typewriter but on the computer.

Why use the computer if we make it look like a typewriter? The tone of voice of the typewriter-looking typeface says this is hot off the press, last minute news, an update. Many ministries use Courier for their donor letters. It is also good to use for correspondence.

Zapf Chancery

Use this typeface for invitations and announcements. This typeface was designed to resemble hand-calligraphied writing. Please do not use it for headlines or for text. It was never designed to be read in great quantity, just as you would never want to write an entire letter in calligraphy.

It is also a typeface that looks nice centered.

Do not use it IN ALL CAPS.

ZAPF CHANCERY CAPS ARE DESIGNED TO BE THE DECORATIVE BEGINNING LETTERS OF WORDS AND ARE HARD TO READ IF PLACED TOGETHER TO FORM WORDS.

Zapf Dingbats or Wingdings

The term dingbats comes from the printing world and was the term for a decorative symbol the older publishing houses used to identify themselves. It now means a set of symbols such as:

▲ † ❈ ✐ ✎ ✄ ❤ ❊ ❒ ✖ ✶ ➻ ✘ ❦ ✦

What is important to remember about these characters is that they can be used not only for bullets, etc. but they can be blown up into any size that your program will allow you to.

There are many other dingbat fonts available in a variety of designs. Carta, Adobe Wood Type Ornaments and Minion Ornaments are some of them.

Type styles

When we talk about "calligraphy" we are referring to letters or words that have been written with a brush or pen. Today there are DTP typefaces that have the look of being hand drawn.

The term "calligraphy" comes from the Greek word "kalligraphia," which means "beautiful writing."

Type Terminology
On the Desktop

We've talked about the races of type (serif and sans serif) and just as with people, races are divided into families or faces like Times or Helvetica. Families or faces of type all share a common likeness, but the individual members are distinctive. In human families we have father, mother, children and cousins. In type we have various styles and they can apply to each typeface.

The primary styles are roman or normal, **bold**, *italic*, condensed, expanded and combinations of each of these—depending upon the type and software available to you. Combining the type face with the style you can have for example: Times, Roman; *Times, italic*; Helvetica, Roman or *Helvetica, italic.*

There are other styles on your DTP program including outline and shadow. Use these sparingly in professional publications. They can be hard to read and were primarily designed for decorative uses.

Type style application to DTP

It's tempting to use various type styles because we like how they look or are bored. Remember when that temptation comes that each style has a different voice. Ask yourself if the message you want to get across is consistent with that voice. You don't want to use a voice that whispers when you want to shout.

Here are what the basic styles say:

As this illustration shows, each of the basic type styles—normal, bold, and italic—have a distinctive tone of voice.

Roman or normal

This is like a normal tone of voice. Sometimes this style is even called normal in DTP programs. It is the straight up and down, no slant, no boldness, ordinary style. This is the style used in writing this book. You will use this style to write the majority of your material.

Italics

This is the soft emphasis tone of voice. It is the tone used when your mother says, "Jeremy, *please*, pick up your room."

Bold

Bold speaks with a raised voice. How loud you raise it depends upon the size of type as the two examples below illustrate.

Stop doing that.

Stop doing that!

Expanded and condensed

More than a specific tone of voice, these are typographic variations that are primarily to be used in display type.

Save their use for headlines, subheads, advertisements, and similar areas. They are not meant for use in text.

*Outline and **shadow** don't have a tone of voice. They are primarily decorative styles of type and are more useful in applications such as the creation of flyers, logos and banners than they are for text.*

Tips for use of type styles

Below is the Pagemaker style sheet for this book and the type specs for body text.

Style sheets can change the specs for any level of type throughout your publication by simply changing the style sheet instead of reselecting each section.

- Use your type styles consistently. If you don't, your message won't be as clear as it should be. Keep your headlines, subheads and text the same size throughout your publication.
- If your DTP program has style sheets, where you can consistently define the styles for various parts of your publication, be sure to use them. Using style sheets will save you a tremendous amount of work because you won't have to format each paragraph individually, the style sheets do it for you.

Below are some examples of the Pagemaker style sheets.

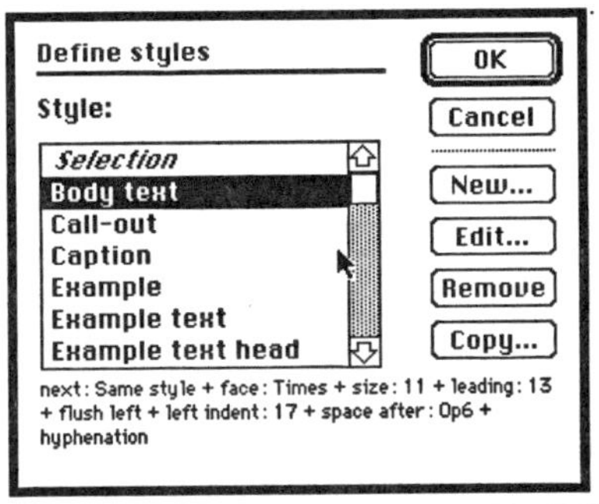

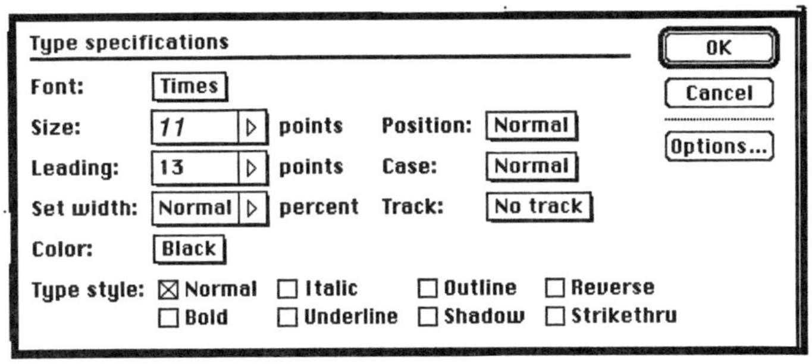

Combining typefaces and styles

It is generally accepted that a serif typeface is a good selection for body text and a sans serif typeface works well for headlines. This works well because there is enough of a difference between the two kinds of typefaces that readers can clearly see the differences in meaning. If you were to use two serif faces, the difference wouldn't be significant enough. It would be confusing to the eye. Below are some combinations that work well.

This box illustrates some combinations of headline and text type that will always work well.

They follow the classic recommendation of sans serif for headline type and serif for body copy.

Helvetica for headlines

Times works well for body copy in this example.

Helvetica for headlines

Century Schoolbook works well for body copy in this example.

Avant Garde for headlines

Palatino works well for body copy in this example.

In addition to using different typefaces to distinguish between different parts of your publication, you can also use one typeface in different styles.

Typefaces that work well when used this way include:

A variety of typefaces is not essential to provide typographic interest and variation in your publications.

Any of these listed typefaces can be used by themselves in various sizes and styles to create good-looking and effective communications.

Times

Century Schoolbook

Palatino

Helvetica

The newsletter Desktop Publishing and New Media in Ministry uses various styles of Times for typographic variation.

When people first start in DTP, they think they need many different typefaces and sizes to produce professional publications—but nothing could be farther from the truth. This publication is very professional-looking and easy to read, yet it only uses one typeface in a limited number of sizes and styles.

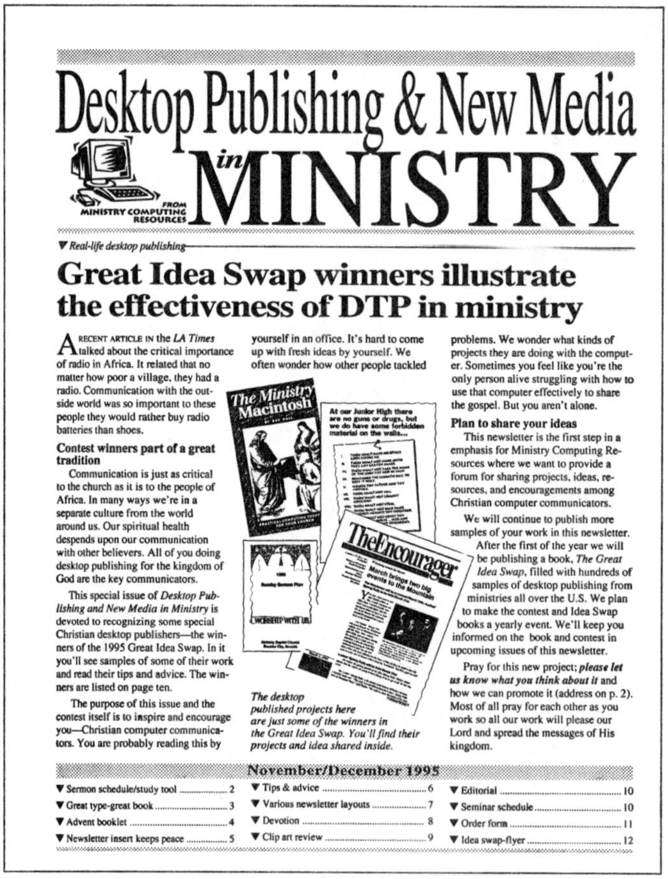

Desktop Publishing & New Media in MINISTRY

FROM MINISTRY COMPUTING RESOURCES

▼ *Real-life desktop publishing*

Great Idea Swap winners illustrate the effectiveness of DTP in ministry

A RECENT ARTICLE IN the *LA Times* talked about the critical importance of radio in Africa. It related that no matter how poor a village, they had a radio. Communication with the outside world was so important to these people they would rather buy radio batteries than shoes.

Contest winners part of a great tradition

Communication is just as critical to the church as it is to the people of Africa. In many ways we're in a separate culture from the world around us. Our spiritual health despends upon our communication with other believers. All of you doing desktop publishing for the kingdom of God are the key communicators.

This special issue of *Desktop Publishing and New Media in Ministry* is devoted to recognizing some special Christian desktop publishers—the winners of the 1995 Great Idea Swap. In it you'll see samples of some of their work and read their tips and advice. The winners are listed on page ten.

The purpose of this issue and the contest itself is to inspire and encourage you—Christian computer communicators. You are probably reading this by yourself in an office. It's hard to come up with fresh ideas by yourself. We often wonder how other people tackled problems. We wonder what kinds of projects they are doing with the computer. Sometimes you feel like you're the only person alive struggling with how to use that computer effectively to share the gospel. But you aren't alone.

Plan to share your ideas

This newsletter is the first step in a emphasis for Ministry Computing Resources where we want to provide a forum for sharing projects, ideas, resources, and encouragements among Christian computer communicators.

We will continue to publish more samples of your work in this newsletter. After the first of the year we will be publishing a book, *The Great Idea Swap*, filled with hundreds of samples of desktop publishing from ministries all over the U.S. We plan to make the contest and Idea Swap books a yearly event. We'll keep you informed on the book and contest in upcoming issues of this newsletter.

Pray for this new project; ***please let us know what you think about it*** and how we can promote it (address on p. 2). Most of all pray for each other as you work so all our work will please our Lord and spread the messages of His kingdom.

The desktop published projects here are just some of the winners in the Great Idea Swap. You'll find their projects and idea shared inside.

November/December 1995

The newsletter is 12 pages per issue and comes out six times a year. ***There is no other resource that gives information, resources and inspiration to Christian desktop publishers like this one does.*** *To order, send a check or MC/VISA info for $36 (for a year's subscription) to: Ministry Computing Resources, P.O. 202730, Arlington, TX 76006, phone 817-861-9535.*

Type manipulation programs

If you would like even more variation in your type, you can use a type manipulation program to create special effects such as rotated type, type that is twisted or formed into different shapes, type that looks like neon or chrome. These effects are useful for posters or creating nameplates for newsletters.

Some programs that can manipulate type in this way include CorelDRAW, Typestyler, Canvas and Adobe TypeAlign.

Justifying text

Numerous studies have shown that the easiest type alignment to read is ragged right or left justified or aligned.

In theological terms, justification is the process wherein sinful humanity is put right with God. When the medieval scribes were copying the Bible by hand they wanted it to be "justified" also. Their way of doing that was to copy the text with both edges perfectly lined up or "justified."

When Gutenberg printed the Bible, he followed that form and arranged his pages in perfectly justified columns also. This remained the preferred style in printing for many hundreds of years even though it was very difficult to do.

Today theology and printing are no longer mixed and a number of additional options for setting text desktop publishing projects are illustrated below:

The other methods of justification or alignment do have their uses:

Justified
Use this in formal materials such as annual, board, or mission reports. It has the most traditional feel and look. You can also fit more words into a justified column than you can in the same amount of space in the others.

Ragged left or right justified or aligned
Use for captions or titles when you want to align them to right hand margin. This alignment is what you are reading now. Please limit your use of this alignment because in lines of text wider than one column, it can be confusing to the eye.

Ragged right or left justified or aligned
Use this whenever possible. It is easiest to read, most contemporary in look and feel, and provides more restful white space in publications. Excellent for manuals, newsletters, brochures, most publications.

Centered
Use for announcements, short sections of text in advertisements or flyers. Traditional way to set type in invitations. Please do not use it in a column of text in a newsletter or similar publication. The constant change in starting point for the eye makes it difficult to follow.

Justified text

Then Moses said to the Israelites, "See, the Lord has chosen Bezalel son of Uri, the son of Hur, of the tribe of Judah, and he has filled him with the Spirit of God, with skill, ability and knowledge in all kinds of crafts—to make artistic designs for work in gold, silver and bronze, to cut and set stones, to work in wood and to engage in all kinds of artistic craftsmanship. And he has given both him and Oholiab son of Ahisamach, of the tribe of Dan, the ability to teach others" (Exodus 35:30-34).

Ragged left or right justified/aligned text

Then Moses said to the Israelites, "See, the Lord has chosen Bezalel son of Uri, the son of Hur, of the tribe of Judah, and he has filled him with the Spirit of God, with skill, ability and knowledge in all kinds of crafts—to make artistic designs for work in gold, silver and bronze, to cut and set stones, to work in wood and to engage in all kinds of artistic craftsmanship. And he has given both him and Oholiab son of Ahisamach, of the tribe of Dan, the ability to teach others"(Exodus 35:30-34).

Ragged right or left justified/ aligned text

Then Moses said to the Israelites, "See, the Lord has chosen Bezalel son of Uri, the son of Hur, of the tribe of Judah, and he has filled him with the Spirit of God, with skill, ability and knowledge in all kinds of crafts—to make artistic designs for work in gold, silver and bronze, to cut and set stones, to work in wood and to engage in all kinds of artistic craftsmanship. And he has given both him and Oholiab son of Ahisamach, of the tribe of Dan, the ability to teach others" (Exodus 35:30-34).

Centered text

Then Moses said to the Israelites, "See, the Lord has chosen Bezalel son of Uri, the son of Hur, of the tribe of Judah, and he has filled him with the Spirit of God, with skill, ability and knowledge in all kinds of crafts—to make artistic designs for work in gold, silver and bronze, to cut and set stones, to work in wood and to engage in all kinds of artistic craftsmanship. And he has given both him and Oholiab son of Ahisamach, of the tribe of Dan, the ability to teach others" (Exodus 35:30-34).

Professional typesetting guidelines

Probably nobody told you when you began your desktop publishing adventures that you would need to learn the skills and traditions of professional typesetters, but learning typography and typesetting skills is part of the challenge of learning desktop publishing. If you want to make your publications look professional, you must spend some time learning this craft.

As with any craft, typesetting has traditional ways of doing things. The following guidelines are based on typesetting traditions. Many of them may seem difficult to get used to because they are a complete break with how you created text with a typewriter. There was nothing wrong with what you did then, but typesetting on the computer (and that is what you are doing even if you only use a word processor) is a totally different process than typewriting. What looks good with a typewriter will look unprofessional with a computer. Make your publications look their best by following these guidelines.

One space after periods and other punctuation

The spacing is very different in typesetting on the computer than on a typewriter. If you place two spaces after a period in DTP it will look like too much space.

The first example is correct. It uses only one space after a period.

The second example is incorrect for DTP typesetting. It uses two spaces after a period. This produces too much space. With other typefaces and in larger sizes, the gap becomes even greater.

"Love is patient, love is kind. It does not envy, it does not boast, it is not proud. It is not rude, it is not self-seeking, it is not easily angered, it keeps no record of wrongs. Love does not delight in evil but rejoices with the truth. It always protects, always trust, always hopes, always perseveres" (1 Corinthians 13:4-7).

"Love is patient, love is kind. It does not envy, it does not boast, it is not proud. It is not rude, it is not self-seeking, it is not easily angered, it keeps no record of wrongs. Love does not delight in evil but rejoices with the truth. It always protects, always trust, always hopes, always perseveres" (1 Corinthians 13:4-7).

Use true quote marks and apostrophes

True quote marks and apostrophes are the curly marks; the straight ones are the abbreviations for inches and feet.

Each desktop publishing program has a way to change this, so look in your manual. In some you set the change once and it does the proper ones automatically; in other programs, it may require a series of keystrokes defined in the manual.

The first example below is correct. It uses proper typographers' quote marks.

The second is incorrect. The straight up-and-down marks denote feet and inches, not quotation marks.

“For God’s gifts and his call are irrevocable” (Romans 11:29).

"For God's gifts and his call are irrevocable" (Romans 11:29).

Use proper hyphens or em dashes, not two short dashes

Again, this is a series of key strokes in most DTP programs that you must look up for your particular software. What you want is a solid hyphen or em dash, not two short dashes.

The first example is correct; it uses a proper em dash mark.

"Therefore, I urge you, brothers, in view of God's mercy, to offer your bodies as living sacrifices, holy and pleasing to God—this is your spiritual act of worship" (Romans 12:1).

The second one is incorrect. Two hyphens are not an em dash mark.

"Therefore, I urge you, brothers, in view of God's mercy, to offer your bodies as living sacrifices, holy and pleasing to God--this is your spiritual act of worship" (Romans 12:1).

Avoid using all caps

When using a typewriter, typing all caps was one of the few ways to make text stand out. Even though all caps are very hard to read it was one of the few tools of emphasis available.

Now you have a large number of options for emphasis: bold, size change, italics, a change in typeface. All of these are more readable than all caps because they preserve the shape of the word and the text remains easier to read.

You read words partly by the patterns they form, not letter by letter. When words are printed in all caps, similar words have the same shape and take you longer to read.

All caps can still be used for emphasis for very short portions of text, such as in a label over a column of text in a formal report or a section head in an order of service. When used as a one or two word label, the increased reading difficulty of all caps is minimal. Difficulties arise when they are used for headlines or subheads.

It is acceptable to use all caps for brief headings or labels in desktop publishing.

They are especially appropriate in formal reports, centered over justified margins.

MISSION RESULTS

Lorem ipsum dolor sit amet, consectetuer adipiscing elit, sed diam nonummy nibh euismod tincidunt ut laoreet dolore magna aliquam erat volutpat. Ut wisi enim ad minim veniam, quis nostrud exerci tation ullamcorper suscipit lobortis nisl ut aliquip ex ea commodo consequat. Duis autem vel eum iriure dolor in hendrerit in vulputate Velit esse

MISSION GOALS

molestie consequat, vel illum dolore eu feugiat nulla facilisis at vero eros et accumsan et iusto odio dignissim qui blandit praesent luptatum zzril delenit augue duis dolore te feugai nulladuis dolore tedehy feugait.

To add emphasis to headlines or subheads, try making them bold and increasing the size. Doing this will make your type look professionally typeset, instead of modified typewriting. Emphasize individual words the same way.

If you find yourself wanting to write it in all caps, make it bold and/ or increase the size.

The type setting variations available with DTP give you many ways to emphasize your type instead of using all caps.

The second example is preferred by some for creating headlines. It is referred to as "downstyle."

YOUR HEADLINE IS ONE OF THE MOST IMPORTANT PARTS OF YOUR MESSAGE— IN ALL CAPS IT'S HARDER TO READ

Your headline is one of the most important parts of your message—in all caps it's harder to read

Don't underline

Underlining was the only way to distinguish a type as italic or to emphasize it when you used a typewriter. Now you can set type in *true italic* when it needs to be italic, such as in book titles or you can **make it bold** when you want to emphasize a word or short phrase.

In addition, when you underline, you cut off the descenders of letters and that makes them harder to read, as in the example.

Reverse type with care

The guidelines on reversed type are similar to those on using all caps. It isn't too bad when used as a short label, but legibility and readability suffer when it is used for more than a word or two.

Regular type that is not reversed, black on white paper, reads 40 percent faster than type that is reversed from black or overprinted on gray.

For short, graphic labels, reversed type can work. In most situations stick with black type on a light background.

As a label, reversed works

But when it is used for more than a label, reversed type becomes much harder to read. It is even harder to read if you try to reverse it out of a photograph.

Be aware of the importance of line length.

When you used a typewriter, you could change the size of margins, but the width of your column didn't vary much. Now to make your columns readable, the width should be about 9-10 words or 55-60 characters wide. This is important because your eyes don't read individual words. You scan a line and pause to read groups of three or more words at a time. If a line is too long the eye tires and finds it difficult to find the beginning of the next line. If the lines are too short, the eye must stop too frequently.

"Visual communication of any kind, whether persuasive or informative, . . . should be seen as the embodiment of form and function: the integration of the beautiful and the useful." Paul Rand, Thoughts on Design

chapter 8 Graphics

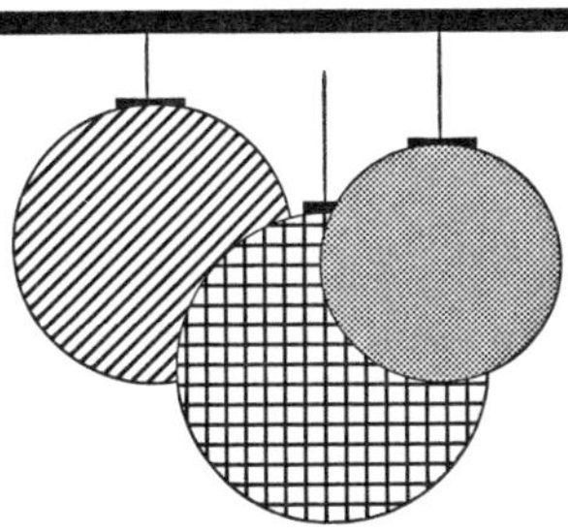

The Christmas ornaments above were created with the simple drawing tools in Pagemaker.

First a circle was drawn and filled. Then a small rectangle was added at the top and sent to a back layer. Finally, a line was drawn to hang the ornament.

Circles, lines, boxes and fills form the raw materials of many illustrations and these flexible tools come with all DTP and integrated programs.

Be adventuresome and experiment with them.

One of the great selling points of desktop publishing is its ability for the user to combine text and graphics.

Using pictures, charts and drawings in your publications is easy. You can encircle text, box it, underline it. If you haven't taken the time to play with the various drawing tools in your DTP program, do it. It's amazing what you can do with them—don't worry about creating great art, just have some fun.

This chapter discusses using rules, borders and screens, clip art, scanned art and photos. In addition to words, you'll have another visual set of tools to use in communicating your message. The tips and guidelines that follow will help you get maximum use from your graphic communication.

How do drawing and paint programs fit into DTP?

DTP programs are primarily designed to do page layout. They have limited art creation capabilities in comparison to drawing and paint programs. However, to say that the capabilities of a DTP program are limited, does not mean you need to rush out and buy another program.

Most ministries doing newsletters, brochures, flyers, and many other publications never have a need for an illustration program. Learn to use the drawing tools you have in your DTP program. If you find yourself wanting to create complex drawings and are limited by what you have, check into an illustration program.

Before getting into specific uses of graphics in DTP, remember that graphic elements in desktop publishing are not put there to look "pretty" or "interesting." Every graphic element is a medium of information. Just as each typeface has a different voice, so each graphic element conveys a message.

Lines, borders and screens—easy and available

There is no such thing as a simple line in desktop publishing—where you put a line, its thickness or complexity, all contribute to your message.

Examples on the next page illustrate various ways lines are used. Even though you can't read the words, notice the different message of the lines. When you want to add lines, or any kind of graphic, think about this illustration and ask yourself what the graphic is doing to the basic message. If it isn't making it more clear, illustrating it or at least echoing its tone, leave it out. Boring is better than confusing if you have a message to communicate.

A gallery of lines

Though the text is the same for all of the illustrations below, the style of the lines and their placement make the message of each page look very different.

From dotted to double, from thick to thin, many DTP programs have 15 or more types of lines available for your use. Experiment with them to clarify your message.

Here the line is between the title and the text. It visually cuts them apart and that can be confusing.

Here the line acts as a header or top border for the text. Also changing the line to a line of dots makes the page look more informal.

Here the line doesn't do anything. Don't put lines or any graphic on the page to just fill up an empty space.

Here the double line with a square at the corner emphasizes the importance of the title.

Here the line has some fun leading your eye from the author's name into the text.

Here the line becomes a formal border to enclose the whole page.

Borders

- Any of the line patterns available in your DTP program can also be used to make borders around text, graphics or pictures in your DTP publications.
- Borders emphasize the information contained within them. Boxed material is one of the first things people will read, so it is a good place to put in event details.
- Leave plenty of space around the text placed in a border.

The border around this text is too tight and the crowded text is hard to read.

Remember
Food Pantry Sunday is
November 21, 1992
Please bring these items:
• tuna fish
• peanut butter
• canned vegetables
Drop off donations in
church entry.

The same text is in this box, but it is much easier to read because enough space is around the text to make it stand out.

Also the text is arranged in a variety of sizes to the help the reader pick out the various parts of the message.

The stars, which are Zapf Dingbats, add a little graphic interest.

Think of your boxed material as a mini-billboard and design it for impact.

★ Remember ★

Food Pantry
Sunday is
November 21, 1992

Please bring these items:
• tuna fish
• peanut butter
• canned vegetables

Drop off donations in
church entry.
★

Screens

In DTP, the term screen has a graphic definition as well as being a term for the computer monitor. In graphic terms a screen is a dot pattern made up of a percentage of black. If you are printing in color, the screen will come out a pastel shade of a color. For example a 20 percent red screen will look pink.

Screens are often used to set off text and they can be used as a graphic to call attention to the text. At the same time they can be tricky to use in DTP because often the roughness of the dot pattern of the screen or the darkness of the screen interferes with the legibility of what is printed over them.

Here are some tips and examples for effective screen use:

- Use sans serif type such as Helvetica for your text.
- Make your text bold.
- Be sure to indent your text column .5 pica inside the border of the section you have screened.
- Use a 10-20 percent screen of black if you print text over it. Percentages can vary if you are using colors.

If you are overprinting, don't use a screen that is darker than 10-20 percent for grey/black screens. Notice how much easier this block is to read with its bold, sans serif typeface and text indent, than the example at the bottom of the page.

"But seek first his kingdom and his righteousness, and all these things will be given to you as well. Therefore do not worry about tomorrow, for tomorrow will worry about itself. Each day has enough trouble of its own" (Matthew 6:33, 34).

- Use 100 percent black if you reverse text.

If you are reversing text out of a solid color block use 100 percent coverage for the background.

"But seek first his kingdom and his righteousness, and all these things will be given to you as well. Therefore do not worry about tomorrow, for tomorrow will worry about itself. Each day has enough trouble of its own" (Matthew 6:33, 34).

- Don't use a delicate, serif typeface such as Times or Zapf Chancery. The little lines of the serifs will get lost in the dots.
- Italics make the confusion even worse.
- Be sure your screen is light if you are going to overprint on it. The exact percentage depends on the color. Ask your printer.
- Don't run your text to the edges of a column on which you are using a screen.

This example illustrates a number of common mistakes in printing on a screened block. The screen is too dark at 30 percent. The serifed, italic text gets lost in the screen. By not indenting the text .5 pica from the edge, the text looks jammed into the box.

"But seek first his kingdom and his righteousness, and all these things will be given to you as well. Therefore do not worry about tomorrow, for tomorrow will worry about itself. Each day has enough trouble of its own" (Matthew 6:33, 34).

Don't forget dingbats

From 200 points to 20 points, you can make dingbats any size you can make type in your DTP program.

If you have a dingbat font (such as Zapf Dingbats, see discussion of this font in the chapter on typography), you have a mini art gallery hiding in your computer.

Because dingbats are a typeface, whatever you can do with type in your DTP program you can do with them. Depending upon your program that means you can:

- Make them any size you want from very small to as large as your program will allow.
- Tilt and rotate them as a text block.
- Select outline, shadow, or reverse style and watch them become a different shape.
- Use them as artwork just as they are.

The telephone, the envelope, the cross, the pen, and the flower are just some of the Zapf Dingbats you can use as pieces of artwork.

You can also apply any type style to a dingbat. Here is a heart in bold, outline, shadow and reversed type style selections.

Clip art

There are numerous excellent Christian clip art companies, but they can be difficult to find because they don't have big advertising budgets. In the newsletter, Desktop Publishing and New Media in Ministry, *each issue reviews and gives examples of Christian clip art. Ordering information for the newsletter is in the back of this book. In addition, in the back of the book is an updated resource sheet with some of the companies listed.*

In the past you've probably cut out pieces of clip art to paste on your publications. You can continue to do that with your DTP publications, but you have additional options with clip art.

Scanned-in clip art

If you have a scanner, you can take your files of clip art and scan them onto a disk. The advantage of doing this is that you can then place, size, duplicate, reverse or manipulate the artwork any way you want in the computer program.

If you don't have a scanner, you can take your clip art to a print shop that has a scanner and the staff at the print shop can scan your images onto a disk for you. This is handy to do if you want to have something like the church logo on disk.

If you do a lot of scanning, you may need a program to clean up and modify your images. If you purchase a scanner, a program to modify images usually comes with the scanner.

A scanner can also be used to scan in photos on disk. Scanned-in photo quality is not as good a quality as you would get from having traditional halftones made. However, if you have a scanner, they are inexpensive to produce and work fine for many DTP applications.You can scan in either color or black and white photos for similar results.

- You can also use a scanner to scan onto disk any kind of original drawings (created by someone in your ministry and used with their permission) or signatures that you can then size and place in your publications.
- You must have permission to scan in the materials that you scan to disk. Most clip art books allow you to do this for ministry purposes.

It is illegal however to scan in copyrighted material without permission and that includes the comics from your local newspaper or magazines.

This series of images, that came from a Christian clip art book, shows how you can manipulate scanned-in clip art. The cropping on these images was all done in Pagemaker. Cropping means to cut away part of the image. Various programs will allow you to crop and manipulate scanned art in different ways.

This first image uses the entire drawing and the text that was drawn in below it. This combined scan would be a useful illustration for a flyer for a "Fellowship Nite."

Here the first image was cropped to do away with the text and some of the people and could be used to illustrate a group meeting other than "Fellowship Nite."

Here the cropping selects just the face of one person and draws a box around it. Lines are drawn to fill in the bottom of the box. An image such as this could be used perhaps to advertise a women's event.

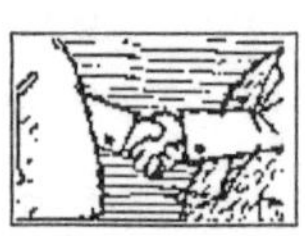

The cropping here, a severe crop down to the hands of two people, abstracts the handshake and could be used to illustrate an idea such as a Christian's word and trustworthiness.

Note that after an image has been scanned in, it can then be sized however large or small you want to make it in your program. You can also resize the image after it has been cropped.

What you do with scanned images is limited only by the capabilities of your program and your imagination.

These images are from The Church Ministry Clip Art Book, compiled by Tom Finley and published by Gospel Light. They are used by permission. For a list of other clip art sources, see the Resources section.

Clip art on disk

With a computer and desktop publishing software, you have another way to place clip art into your publications. You can purchase disks that have illustrations on them and from those disks place the clip art directly into your publications.

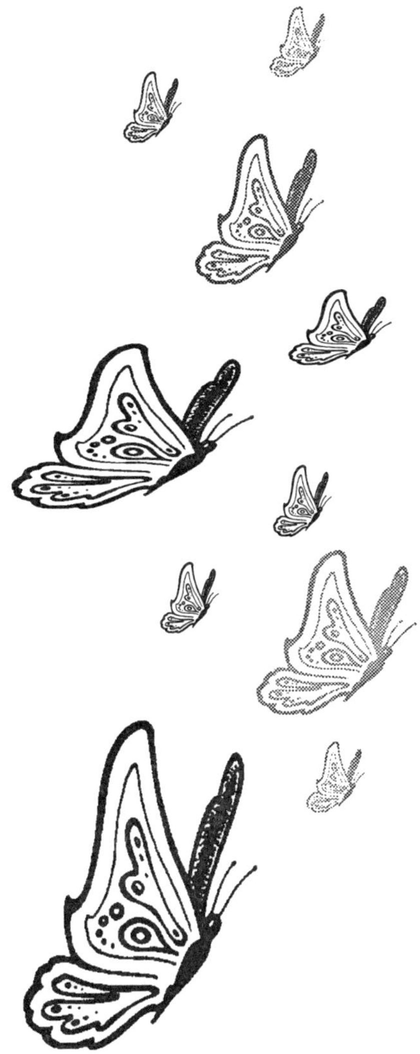

The butterflies above are variations of the same image of electronic clip art. It was copied and resized in Pagemaker. To make it the different shades of gray, various colors were selected for the clip art. On a black and white printer these come out in shades of gray.

Purchasing clip art on disk

- To find out about clip art on disks, contact the companies listed in the Resources section and they will send you brochures and sometimes samples.

  The selections are usually categorized by subject matter, such as religious, business, holidays and medical. Some are for a specific age group, such as children. Some offer a variety of subjects.

- Be sure that the electronic clip art you select is compatible with your program and system. Some clip art on disk only works on a Mac computer and others only work on PCs. Most programs however, will work on both, but you have to specify which you are using before you purchase them.

- Be sure that the clip art will work with your DTP program. Usually the clip art will state that it will work with Pagemaker, or Microsoft Publisher, or whatever programs it works with. Many DTP programs that come on CD-ROM now come with their own collections of clip art.

Instead of telling you what programs they will work with some of the clip art will give you an image format such as EPS, TIFF or PICT. It isn't important that you understand what these terms mean at this time, but just make sure that your program can use that format. All DTP software manuals will tell which graphic formats the program will accept.

Using clip art on disk

Once you have the basic images, what you can do with them is limited only by your software and your imagination.

- To edit or change the actual clip art on disk you usually need a paint or drawing program that is compatible with your system. Look in the documentation of the clip art to see which programs will work with it.

- You don't need to be able to actually edit the image itself to have lots of fun with it in your program. Most DTP programs will allow you to change the size and proportions of images in your publications. In many programs you can also crop, rotate, and reverse illustrations.

- Try cropping your image for impact. Or make it much larger.

- Repeat and change the proportions to emphasize an idea. Screen it down and overprint on it for a subtle message.

As the examples below illustrate, you can select your style of clip art and your typeface to go together to maintain a consistent look in your publications.

Heavy, bold typefaces look good with heavier graphics; the delicate typefaces could be overwhelmed by heavy, bold graphics.

- Computer clip art comes in a variety of styles. Sometimes all of the clip art from a company will have the same style, sometimes a collection will have a variety of styles represented.

In examples below are clip art images of people, flowers and money. Though they are the same basic subjects, notice the different styles of representing these ideas. Use the same style throughout your publication and pair with compatible type style to make your publication look unified.

The various artists that do clip art will have a variety of images in each collection and this makes it easy to have a consistent look.

- Times would be a good typeface choice for use with drawings with fine lines such as these.
- Palatino would also work well .
- As would Century Schoolbook.

Helvetica extended would work for headlines with heavier graphics such as these.

The bold strength of Helvetica, normal, would be a good typeface choice for text.

Bookman would also work because of its heaviness and width.

The above clip art is from the Dynamic Graphics clip art on disk collections.

A picture may be worth a thousand words, but then again it may only take up space. Take action photos and caption them to help your photos deliver their message.

chapter 9 Photography

Additional photo tips:

- *Choose your photos for placing in publications as carefully as you choose your words. Be sure the photo backs up the message of your words.*
- *A photo of a large group where you can't see anyone clearly is like a story with too many words. Just one person doing what the event is all about gets to the point of the story.*
- *Cut extra stuff from the photo as you would cut out extra words. The contemporary style for photographs, especially head shots, is very tight cropping.*

Photographs can be one of the most powerful communication tools in a desktop publication.

They are impossible to ignore. People can easily ignore page after page of what might well be very important text, but they can't flip through a newsletter or any publication without looking at the pictures and reading the captions under them.

This chapter will first briefly discuss how photos get into your desktop publication, then how to take good photos and finally some tips on using photos in your publications.

Two ways to place photographs in DTP publication

First is the traditional method. In the past if you wanted a photograph in your newsletter, you would have it made into a halftone and then either paste it into your publication before it was reproduced or have the print shop do that. This process can still be used in desktop publishing. You can create all of your text and computer graphics and then have the photographs added.

You have a second option in DTP if you have a scanner. You can scan the photograph into the computer and you can then place it into your publication in the same way you place artwork or graphics into a publication.

If you scan in photographs, and have a 300 dpi laser printer, the quality won't be as good as it would be if the print shop placed them. With some 600 dpi scanners and the right quality software, photos can look pretty good. The quality of scanned-in photos and the software used to manipulate them is improving all the time and you might want to try it for your ministry publications. The cost savings can be significant.

How to take good photos

Avoid head shots or formally posed pictures

Get people involved in action whenever possible. A head shot merely labels a person, an action shot tells a story.

Think of how much more people would learn about your leadership if instead of a mug shot of the minister each time you had his column in your newsletter, you had a picture of him in action. Instead of including the same mug shot year after year, try pictures of him with his family, interacting with a Sunday School class, or in his study. Capture him participating in a hobby, or at a church activity. A series of photos such as these would give a more rounded representation of your pastor as a person.

There is nothing wrong with the formal picture above of the pastor. As formal head shots go, it is a very good one.

But look at how much more you learn about the person when you see him interacting with children while visiting a Sunday School class.

How to get good people pictures

It is said that public speaking is people's number one fear, even above dying. I disagree. I think it's having your picture taken. I've seen countless folks in ministry who are comfortable speaking to hundreds of people turn into jelly when approached by a camera. What is even worse than the fear of getting your picture taken is the end result. A stiff, formal shot of a person clearly not enjoying the process doesn't communicate any reality about the person.

Pictures are put into publications so people can see the individuals involved in the ministry. But the strained individual standing up against a white wall with the terrified expression is not the same person who can captivate a room full of sixth graders with stories about Jesus. The severe look on the face of the man in the suit is not the same pastor who chopped wood for you when your husband was sick or counseled your niece when she lost her baby.

The pictures you take of people in ministry are of individuals God uses to inspire lives and change souls for eternity. Your challenge in taking pictures is to capture that person and share him or her in your communications.

One way to capture the real person is to photograph them doing what they do best—in the midst of ministry. If they work with kids, take a picture of them with kids; if they preach, photograph them preaching.

If you can't do that, at least take someone with you to talk to them while you are taking pictures. I've found this method works great even for people who hate to have their picture taken or don't normally photograph well. People in ministry tend to be interactive people—they come alive in relationships with others. Often when you've got them talking to someone else you can take a photograph that shows them at their best. It also takes their mind off the experience of being photographed.

Some mechanics of getting a good ministry photograph

Though you can convert any color picture from an instant camera into something you can use for your publication, your best results will come using a 35mm camera and black and white film.

Once you have a basic working knowledge of your 35mm camera, the two primary enemies of good photos are flash photography and cowardice. Here are ways to conquer them:

Flash photography

So many good opportunities for ministry photographs take place in indoor settings with low light. A camera can't see to take a good photograph in low light, so a flash is needed. The result is that though the flash may provide enough light for the photo all spontaneity of the people involved is lost and the result is often a washed-out picture.

There are a number of new ways you can get photographs into your publications. One way is have them developed on a CD-ROM and pull them off just as you would any other graphic. Most photo shops can tell you how to get this done.

A second way is to have the photographs developed on disk. The companies that do this can be found in the mail order catalogs listed in the Resource section. Seattle Film Works is one of the best known companies that put photos on disk.

The solution is to get a good high speed black and white film that will take good photos in low light without any flash such as TMAX 3200. At that speed, the objection comes up, won't the pictures come out grainy? Yes, a little bit. Does it matter? No.

You aren't shooting for *Vogue* magazine. If you place the photos in your publication using your scanner, the quality won't be the greatest anyway. And in ministry photos, what is most important is the quality of the story told, not the quality of the reproduction.

Cowardice

It isn't easy to get the good, gutsy photos by getting in the middle of ministry situations and shooting pictures. It's much easier to line people up against a wall or have them squint into the sun and smile on the count of three, but you'll never get a memorable photo doing that.

Solution: Play photo journalist; be another person. Get in the middle of the group, on a chair, on the floor, talk to your subjects, get them interacting and take lots of pictures. Forget all about yourself and catch your subjects being themselves.

Develop your own stock library of photos

If your church or ministry is doing a large number of photographs, think about getting one of the digital cameras (see budget mail order in Resource section). Though costly, $400 to $700 and up, these cameras will take photos directly on to disk. You can then put the disk into the computer and place the images directly into your publication. Once purchased they are cost-effective because using them eliminates the cost of film and photo processing.

To be able to use photos as often as would be useful and for the greatest impact, it's good to have some on hand. One way to do that would be to schedule a "Day in the Life of Your Ministry or Church." Here's how to do this:

- Plan ahead on assignments and send people out to take pictures of the ministry at different times of the day in different activities. Make sure everyone knows about it, make it a special event, and be sure several people are taking pictures.
- After it's all over and the photos are developed, publish some of the best to commemorate a day in the life of your group.
- Spend time to go through and categorize the photos. You should have enough to last you through many publications.

Photographs of sensitive situations

Sometimes photos are too real. In ministry we deal with some really tough situations: hunger, pain, disabilities, emotional and mental problems. The challenge is to illustrate these situations while retaining the dignity of the people involved.

Show the results of your ministry, not the problem that prompted it

- This means showing your youth group involved in serving meals at the senior center, not kids hanging out by graffiti-covered walls.

- This means showing children fed and at school, not starving and holding their hands out.
- This means showing women working and healed and not battered and poor.

Not only does this kind of photography emphasize the good news of the gospel, but this way a person is not forever labeled in your photograph as a victim.

Abstract the photo

I discovered this technique by accident. I was working on a brochure for a Christian counseling center. They wanted photographs, but they didn't have money for a photographer or to purchase stock photographs. In addition, it was hard to try to get somebody to pose as a couple that needed counseling.

I wasn't sure what we were going to do, so I was scanning in some photos I already had just to see how the size would work out when by accident I set the scanner to scan for line art instead of a photograph. This is what came out—

This high-contrast photo was used in a brochure describing a Christian counseling center.

It was created by scanning a photograph in as line art.

When a scanner is set to scan a photo as line art, it only picks up the light and dark areas without detail. Without the details of the faces you see the shape of the couple, you sense emotions without revealing identity. You can imagine them with heads down, perhaps discussing their situation, perhaps praying.

This technique works great with all sorts of photos—black and white, color, instant, shots with flaws in them. Run them through your scanner and see what comes out. From scenery to shots of people, you can end up with great illustrations.

By the way, that photo isn't of a couple in counseling. It's of me and a friend sitting on a hay bale at a picnic out in the sun.

DTP photo tips

- Remember this is not portrait photography or studio work. You are taking pictures to use to communicate a message.
- Drama is always more important than quality. Concentrate on taking pictures that tell a story.
- Always caption your photo. People will make up a meaning in a photo if you don't tell them what you want them to see.

The primary purpose of layout design is to clarify our message. The primary goal of layout design is not to be creative, interesting or cute—it is to communicate.

chapter 10

Layout and Examples

To save time and your peace of mind, have all your materials, graphics, text and photos together and in their final form before you begin to do the actual layout in your DTP program. If you have to, be tough to enforce deadlines to do this—it will save your sanity.

The preceding chapters taught you how to create the various parts of your publication. Now is the time to put all parts together. This act of combining typography, written text, graphics and photographs—the layout process, used to take many hours by hand. Now you can do it all in the computer.

DTP layout pulls together the skills of writer, artist, editor and publication designer into the hands of one person—you—as you create your publication. Your skill and confidence in each of these areas will increase as you gain experience. This chapter contains layout examples for you to copy and adapt to your needs.

Layout examples

You'll see lots of different styles in the examples that follow. From that, realize there is no perfect DTP design or layout. Lots of things work—just make them appropriate to your message and ministry.

Following are examples of publication pieces produced using desktop publishing for churches and ministries.

There are examples for:

- Logos and business cards, stationery and envelopes.
- Church bulletins and inserts in a variety of sizes.
- Church newsletters in a variety of styles, sizes and formats.
- A variety of miscellaneous church publications.
- A great gallery section sharing samples of real DTP work done by folks around the country.

Measurements used in the layout examples

- Measurements for margins and placement of lines and other graphic objects are in picas, abbreviated *p*. For more information on using picas as a measurement see the chapter on grids and templates.
- Typographic sizes, leading measurements and styles are in standard graphic arts terms, e.g. in point sizes. An example is Times, 12/auto, bold. This method of measuring is discussed in the chapter on typography.
- Line thickness is measured in point size.
- Any additional notes on sizes of columns, layout placement or similar measurements are given when appropriate. These sizes are suggestions only. You may vary them in any way that suits your purposes or publication procedures.
- Always check with your print shop if you will be reproducing a piece that will allow more than one item to be printed per page. Computer examples of how this can be done are included on

some of the examples such as the postcards and the attendance cards. For example you can get four postcards on one sheet of 8 1/2 x 11 inch paper. You can also combine items such as postcards and book marks. Various print shops have different ways they prefer this to be done. Ask for their suggestions and you'll save printing costs.

"Success in graphic design is measured by how quickly and effectively you communicate your ideas to your reader."

Roger C. Parker,
The Aldus Guide to Basic Design

Though most examples are reduced in size for illustration purposes, each piece prior to the gallery section has the measurements and type specs used to produce it. Many also contain an illustration of the computer layout used in the production of the piece.

Guidelines for using the examples

As you use these examples to create your own publications, remember that in the DTP process, though you may use creative, artistic or interesting techniques, always make sure the communication of your message is primary. Following are some tips illustrated in the examples to help you do that:

- Various sizes and styles of text are used to differentiate different levels of a communication piece. For example, in the church bulletins, the headings are all one size and placed one way, the people doing the activity are all another size and placed in another way.
- All of the publications for each organization use the same logo and type. Doing this assures a consistent look for the publications coming from the same organization. As much as is possible, they should also be printed on paper that is similar in color and finish. The same colors of ink should also be used.
- All of the parts of the design are coordinated to contribute a communication of the personality and message of the ministry. This means for example that Helvetica type and a clean, graphic logo is used for a more contemporary message.

Please note: none of the churches, ministries, addresses, phone numbers or people used in the illustrations are real. The only logo that is from an actual church is the tower from First United Methodist Church in Colorado Springs. Some of the text is dummy text and begins "Loren ipsum," but even the text that seems authentic is not from an actual church or ministry.

Make the examples your own

You may follow these examples and measurements exactly or modify them in any way you wish.

Remember it is your church and your ministry—communicate your message in the way that is best for you.

Logos, business cards

1 p margin around the outside of the card and the other cards on this page

Times, 14/15, bold, 120% width

Line under church name is 2 points

Logo was created from modified, scanned-in clip art

All other type is Times, 9/10 normal

Call anytime
(719) 377-9887

New Hope Church

Alan Jones
Pastor

560 North Evans
Leadville, CO 80907

Church name is Avant Garde bold and the spacing between the letters was modified in a drawing program to achieve this blocked look

Other type is Palatino, 9/10, bold, small caps

Logo is a scanned in drawing of the tower of the church

Dr. Roland Pierce
Senior Minister

FIRST UNITED METHODIST CHURCH

695 Ralston Street
Golden, CO 80917
(719) 643-7766

Helvetica, 8/10, normal

Logo was created by scanning in the two figures into a drawing program, drawing the cross and then encircling them with a round-cornered box

Helvetica, 12/13, bold, 130% width, very tight track

Helvetica, 9/10, normal

A ministry
to the homeless
in our community

All-City Social Concerns

453 Dover Ave.
Denver, CO 89765
(303) 267-7746

Stationery

The layout of the stationery should reflect the personality of the church or ministry and its logo. The style on this page would work well for many midsize churches. It would also work for more informal, perhaps newer congregations.

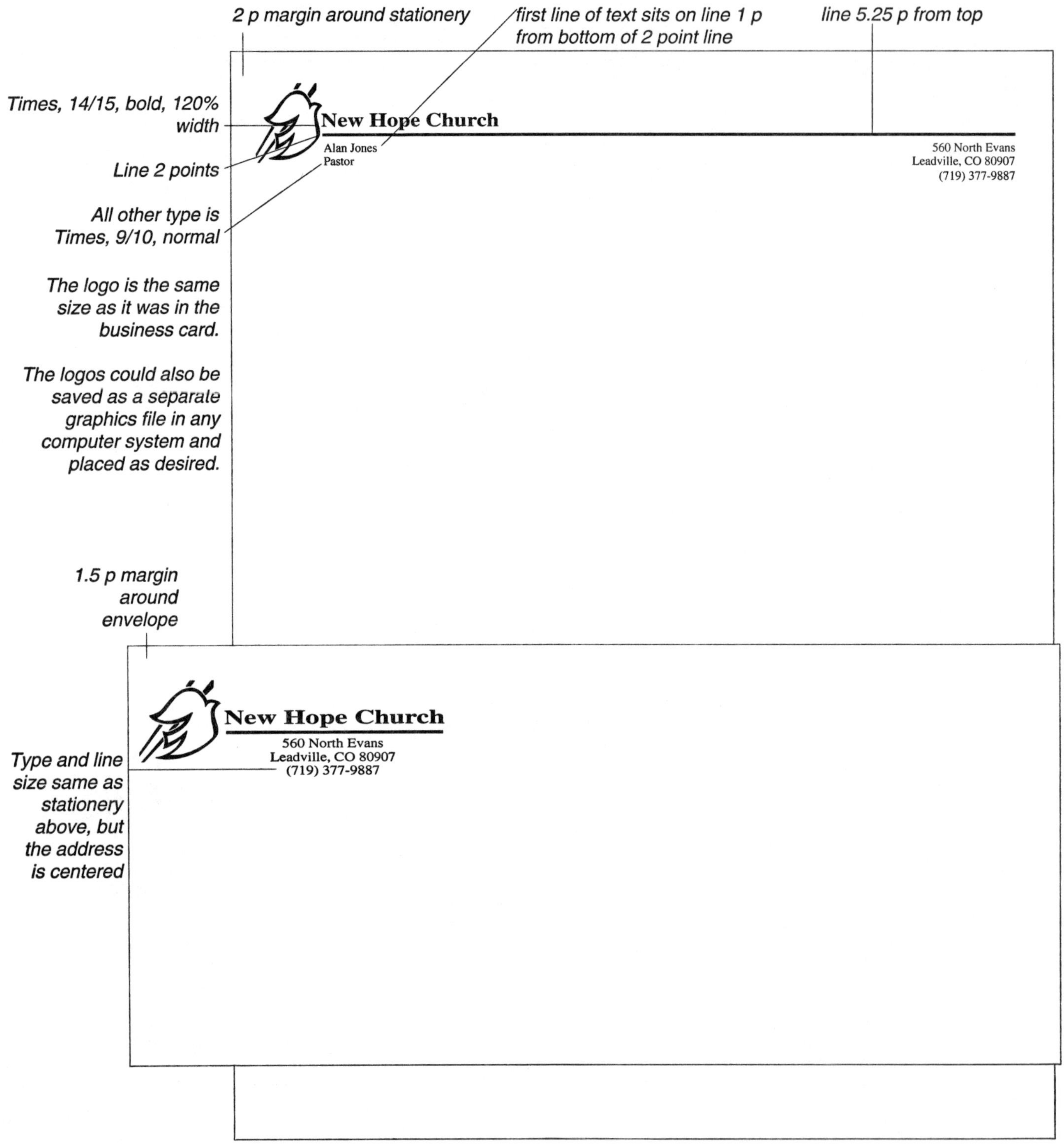

A centered design always implies formality. This layout would work well for a traditional, more established church. Many churches such as this use their building as part or all of their logo. This works well if it is a prominent landmark. In addition the building logo can be modified graphically to emphasize one part of the structure as was done with the tower of the church in this example.

There is a 2 p margin around the stationery.

The lines under the pastor's name and at the bottom are .5 point

The line at the bottom is 2 p from the bottom of the page, the line at the top is 12.5 p from the top of the page

Church name is in Avant Garde bold and the spacing between the letters was modified in a drawing program to achieve this blocked look.

The name block and the logo of the church tower were both reduced in size for the stationery. A double line square was added to unify the elements.

All other type is Palatino, 9/10, bold, small caps

FIRST UNITED
METHODIST
CHURCH

DR. ROLAND PIERCE, SENIOR MINISTER

There is a 1.5 p margin around the envelope.

The type specs are the same for the envelope as they are for the stationery.

FIRST UNITED
METHODIST
CHURCH
695 RALSTON STREET
GOLDEN, CO 80917
(719) 643-7766

695 RALSTON STREET • GOLDEN, CO 80917 • (719) 643-7766

This stationery for a ministry illustrates another style that is slightly more contemporary and not as traditional as the centered-design church stationery on the previous page.

This design would also work well with narrow, or strong graphic logos.

When typing your message on the stationery be sure to leave enough space between the logo and the body of the letter. You could also place a hairline down the length of the page to keep the areas separate.

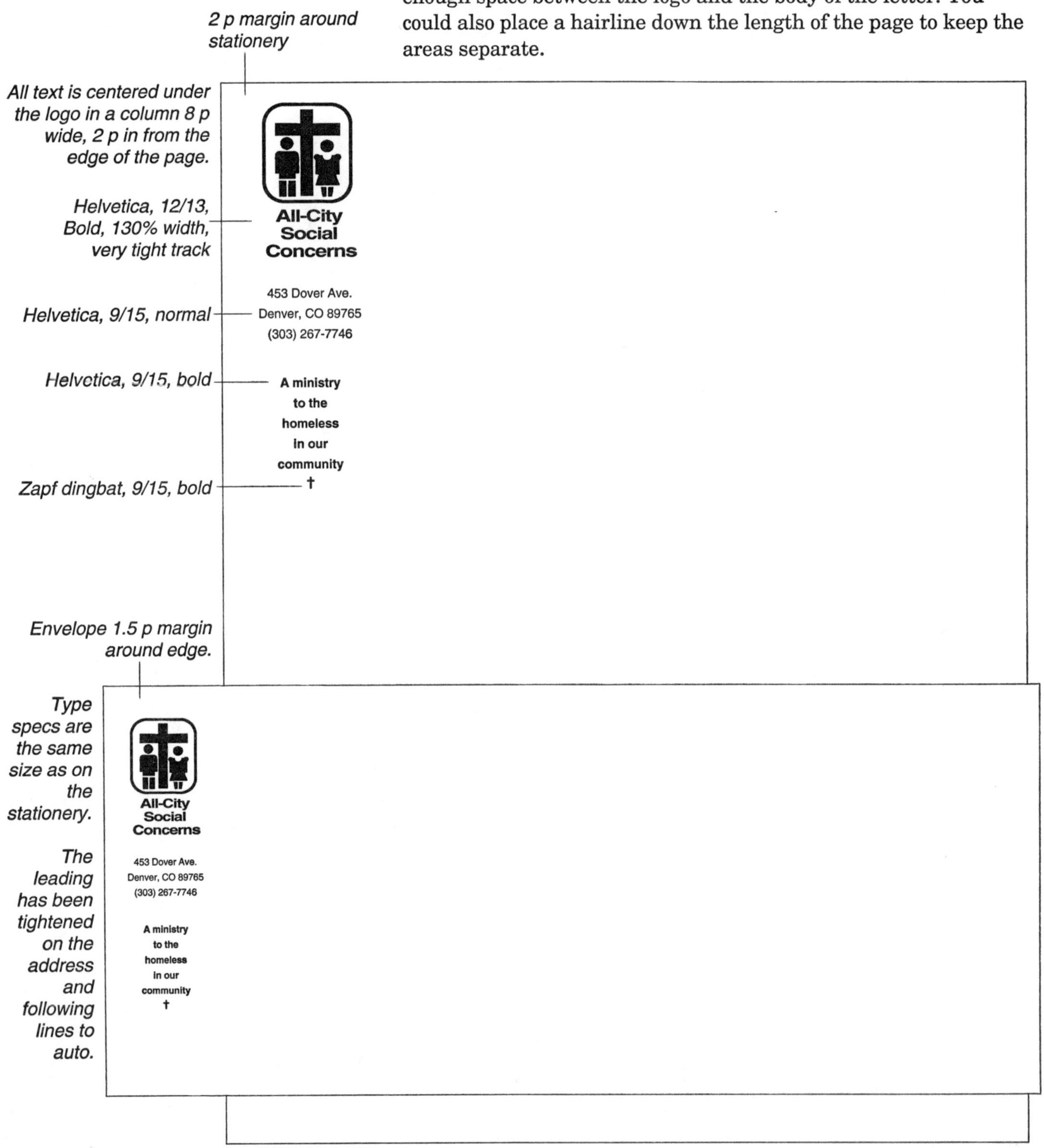

Postcards

Postcards work well to send out short messages, notices or invitations. You can get four postcards from one 8 1/2 x 11-inch piece of paper or card stock.

As illustrated below, lay out postcards four on a page in your DTP program. The following page shows a more detailed layout of two separate cards.

The cards are then reproduced on card stock. Card stock comes in a variety of colors, but it is heavier paper like that used for business cards.

Some laser printers and photocopy machines can print on card stock, but usually the master must be taken to a quick printer who will reproduce them and cut them apart.

You may also purchase envelopes this size that match the color of your paper or card stock.

Below is an illustration of how you can lay out four postcards on one 8 1/2 x 11-inch master in your DTP program.

First draw in the guidelines. Then create one card, copy it and move it into each of the remaining spaces.

These guidelines illustrate where the cards will be cut apart, but do not print them on your master.

Each of the four cards is separated horizontally and vertically by a 4 p column. That results in a 2 p margin around the edge of each individual card.

There is a 2 p margin around the entire page.

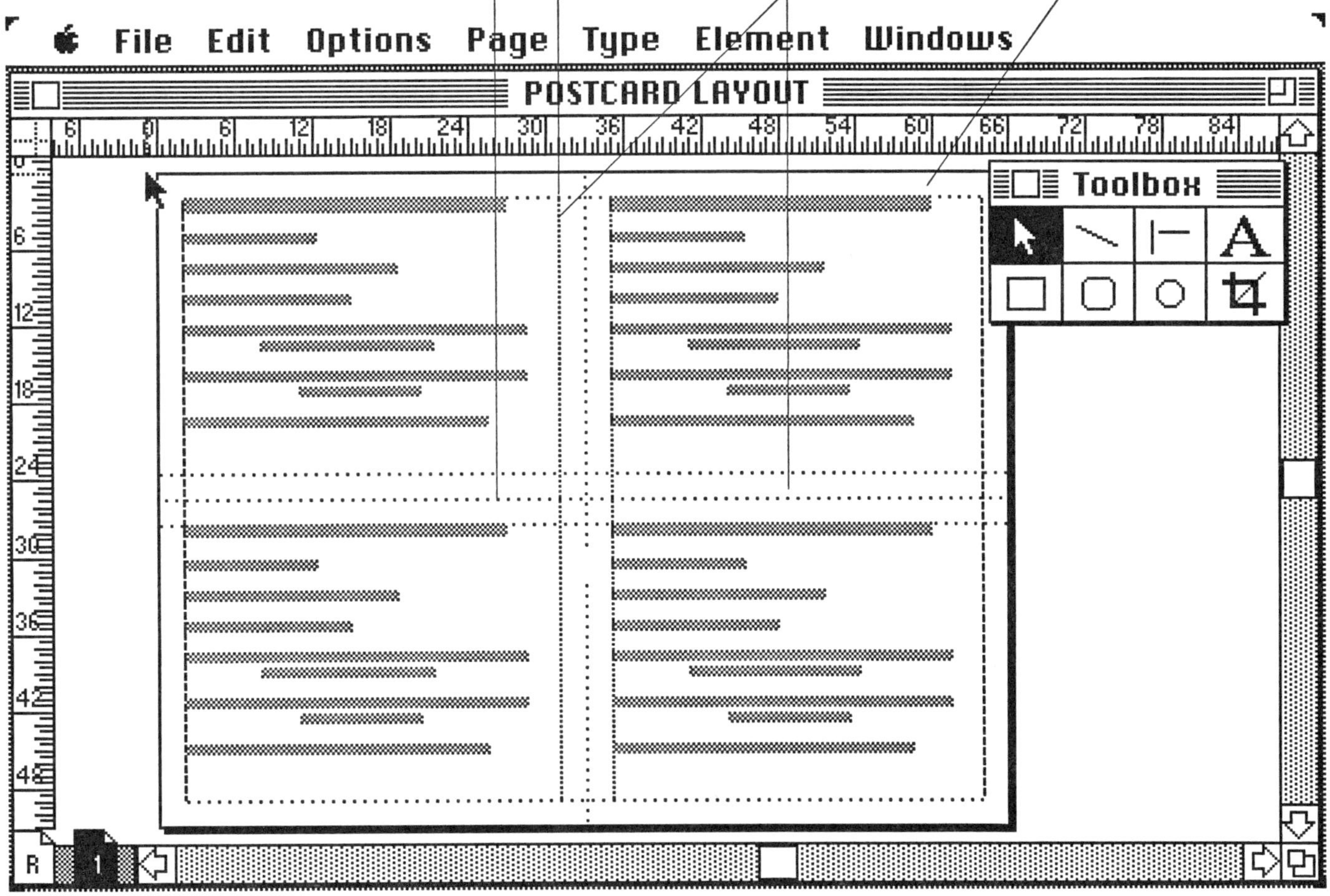

All text is centered.

Zapf Chancery 24/auto, normal

Zapf Chancery 12/auto, normal

Zapf Chancery, 18/auto, normal

Zapf Chancery, 15/auto, normal

Zapf Chancery, 24/auto, normal

Zapf Chancery, 12/auto, normal

The Chancel Choir

of

First Christian Church

Union at Cooper Street

invites you to a concert

Sunday, December 8

7:00 p.m.

featuring

A Ceremony of Carols	Benjamin Britten
The Many Moods of Christmas	R. Shaw/R. Bennett

with

The Chancel Choir and Orchestra

Free Admission   Nursery Provided

2 p margin around edge of card

Helvetica, 16/auto, bold

2 p line

Helvetica 12/auto, bold for labels, extra space between entries

Senior High Volunteer Planning Meeting

When: Monday, July 6

Time and duration: 7:00 - 9:00 p.m.

Where: Youth pastor's office

What we'll do: Plan the topics and teaching responsibilities for August and September.

Bring to the meeting: Your ideas for topics and which ones you want to lead.

Questions: Call Jenny at the youth office, 555-5555.

Church bulletins—cover

A handshake, a hug, a welcome, an invitation, a challenge and guide—a bulletin needs to be all these things for visitors. It's a very important task.

Your challenge is to communicate the best of your church and the Gospel on paper—remember it is a message folks will take home with them.

Church bulletins are one of the primary communication pieces of churches. It is the first thing a visitor sees. It is an important means of communicating with the congregation during the week.

In the past many churches purchased pre-printed bulletin covers with religious art on the front and added their order of service inside. You can still use this method with DTP.

Today with the graphic abilities of DTP, many churches are now creating the inside and the outside of their bulletin. Sometimes a church wants an illustration of the church on the front, sometimes the church wants to reproduce their logo on the cover. Either graphic treatment can work well. In addition to the logo or illustration of the church, the cover can be used to give a message of welcome and to encourage people to think about the upcoming message. The bulletin cover illustrated on this page shows how this can be done.

This bulletin is 8 1/2 -by-11-inch folded in half. There are 2 p margins around the edge of the sheet.

Helvetica, 30/auto, bold, 130% width, tight track

Welcome to Trinity

Helvetica, 12/auto, bold, paragraph indent 2 p

We're so glad you've chosen to be with us today!

Helvetica, 12/auto, normal, paragraph indent 2 p

Please relax and enjoy the music before the service starts. Quiet your heart before God. Ask Him to meet with you and teach you today.

Inside you'll find our order of service and the activities of the church for the week. On the back cover is a listing of our staff and church hours and phone numbers.

Our sermon today is on "Setting Priorities." As you wait for the service to begin, think about this verse:

Helvetica, 12/auto, bold, centered

"But seek first his kingdom and his righteousness, and all these things will be given to you as well."
Matthew 6:33

Logo created from a Zapf Dingbat triangle with a Zapf Dingbat reversed cross placed on top

Helvetica, 24, auto, bold, 130% width, tight track

Trinity Church

Church bulletin sizes

If you are producing your bulletin using DTP there are two primary sizes that are easiest and most cost-effective to use. One uses standard letter-size paper and is folded in half. The other uses standard legal-size paper and is folded in thirds.

Both work well and what you choose to work with is a matter of personal preference. The illustrations in this chapter use the 8 1/2 x 11-inch size. You can adapt them to the 8 1/2 x 14-inch size by making your columns narrower.

The basic computer layout for each size is illustrated below.

This bulletin layout is an 8 1/2 x 11-inch sheet of paper, lengthwise. It will be folded in half.

This is also the size of many preprinted bulletins. This layout can be used for your personalized information inside the bulletin.

3 p margins on each side

The page is then divided into 2 columns with a 6 p space between them.

4 p margins top and bottom

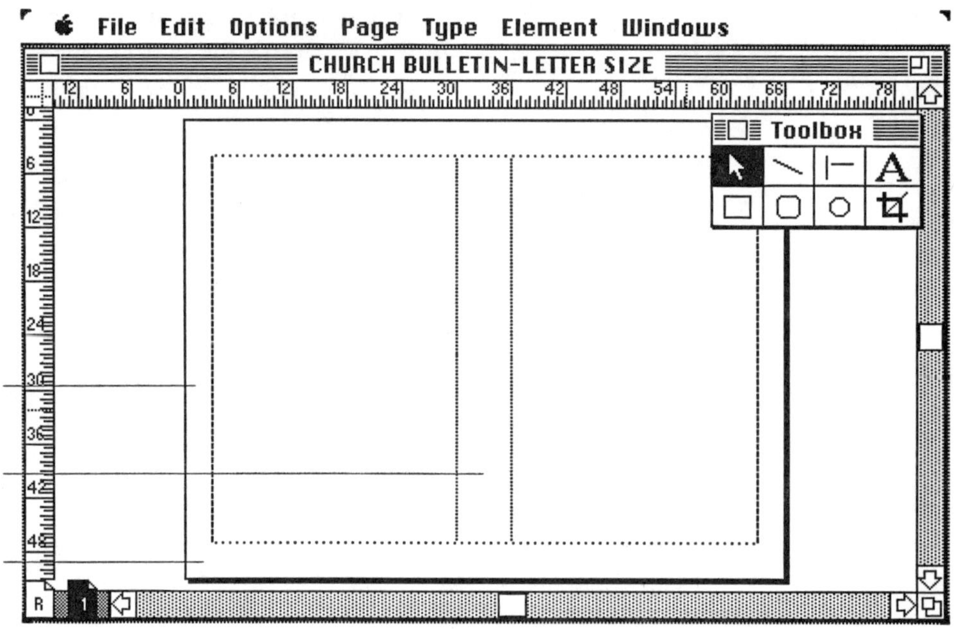

This bulletin is made from a sheet of 8 1/2 x 14-inch or legal size paper, lengthwise. It can be folded in thirds.

3 p margins on the sides

The page is then divided into 3 columns with a 6 p space between them.

4 p margin on the top and bottom

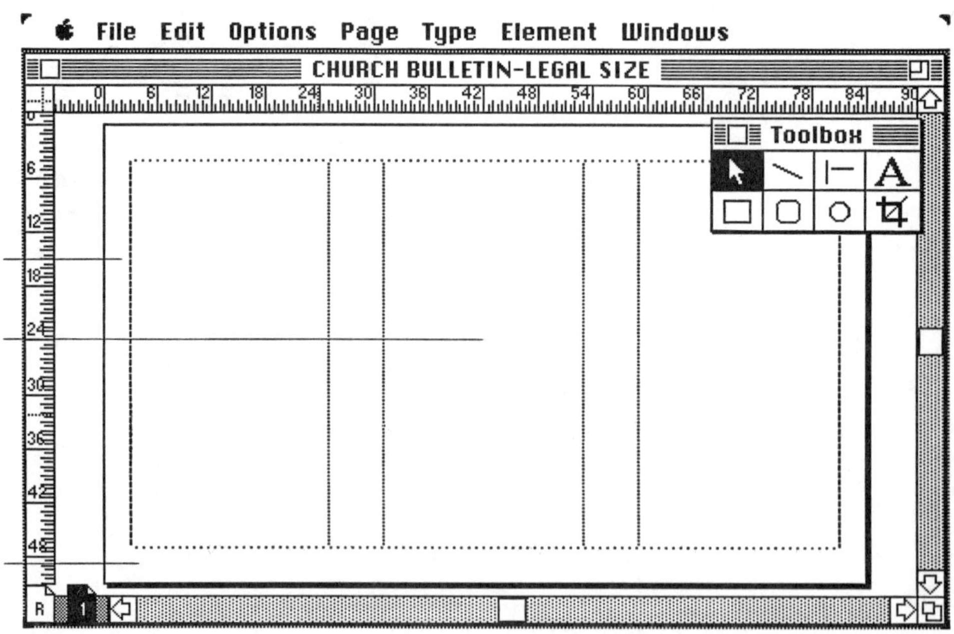

Church bulletins—order of service

Listing the main events down the left-hand margin as in the example below makes it easier to keep your place than if they were centered on the text.

The primary layout concern for the order of service of church bulletins is that they must be easy to follow. One way to do this is through consistency in type size and placement. In the example below, the order of service events are one size type and placement, the people another, the hymns and reading page numbers another.

The design should also reflect the communication style of the church. For example, the bulletin on this page has a formal, structured layout, as do the other publications from this church. On the next page is a much more informal bulletin layout, reflecting a different church personality.

There is a 2 p margin around the edge of the bulletin on all sides.

All lines are 2 points.

This bulletin is an 8 1/2 x 11-inch page folded in half. It could either be the inside of a preprinted bulletin or it could be the front and back of one sheet inserted in a preprinted piece that had announcements printed on the inside.

Logo the same as on card and stationery.

Avant Garde, 18/20, bold, all caps

Palatino, 12/14, normal

All type flush left is Avant Garde, 10/12, bold, all caps.

Remaining type is Palatino, 10/12, either normal, italic or bold depending upon function.

FIRST UNITED METHODIST CHURCH

MORNING WORSHIP SERVICE

11:00 a.m., November 8, 1992
Eleventh Sunday in Kingdomtide

PRELUDE — Darrel Nystedt, Organist
Adagio from 1st Sonata, Felix Mendelssohn

CALL TO WORSHIP — Rev. April Smith, Christian Education Director

Leader: It is good to give thanks to the Lord, to sing praises to the Most High;
People: To declare the Lord's steadfast love in the morning, and his faithfulness by night,
Leader: To the music of the lute and the harp, to the melody of the lyre.
People: For you, O Lord, have made us glad by your work; at the works of your hands we sing for joy.

PROCESSIONAL HYMN
Joyful, Joyful, We Adore Thee
Hymnal, page 89

MORNING PRAYERS — Rev. Harold James, Singles Minister

Pastor: The Lord be with you.
People: And also with you.
Pastor: Let us pray.

PASTORAL PRAYER, THE LORD'S PRAYER, AND CHORAL RESPONSES

WORDS OF WELCOME — Dr. Roland Pierce, Senior Minister

GIVING OF GOD'S TITHES AND OUR OFFERINGS

OFFERTORY ANTHEM — Mona Roger, Director of Music
How Lovely Is Thy Dwelling Place, Johannes Brahms

DOXOLOGY
Hymnal, page 95

SCRIPTURE READING — Jan Costley, Assistant for Pastoral Care
Matthew 18:21-35, pew Bible page 457

SERMON — Dr. Roland Pierce, Senior Minister
"What is Forgiveness Worth?"

HYMN OF DEDICATION
How Great Thou Art
Hymnal p. 32

BENEDICTION — Rev. Harold James, Singles Minister

POSTLUDE — Darrel Nysted, Organist
Finale from 1st Sonata, Felix Mendelssohn

GO IN PEACE THIS WEEK AND SERVE THE LORD WITH JOY

Avant Garde, 10/15, bold italic, all caps

fold line

An informal bulletin

This bulletin is very friendly. It answers visitor's questions right on the front cover without having to make them hunt for information.

Ask visitors what they want to know and then publish it on the front of the bulletin—and don't forget to tell people how welcome they are to your church.

This bulletin is half of an 8 1/2 x 11-inch piece of paper. It could either be the outside panel of a bulletin with announcements inside or one page inside an 8 1/2 x 11-inch sheet.

This bulletin reflects the more informal structure and personality of this church. Because there is less complexity to the order of service the bulletin can also contain important information for guests in an easy-to-read location.

If you put overall church information in your bulletin, be sure to be complete and clear in what you write. For example, this bulletin doesn't just say that child care is available, it tells how to get directions to it. It doesn't stop by telling you to attend an adult Sunday School class, it tells you who can attend and where to find out more information about them.

A good way to find out if your bulletin information would make sense to an outsider is to have someone who is not familiar with your church read it and tell you what it says to them.

Times, 14/16, bold, 120% width

Times, 18/20, bold, 130% width

Times, 9/10, normal

Times, 10/12, bold

Times, 14/16, bold, underneath, 2 point line

Times, 12/14, bold

Times, 10/12, normal

Zapf Dingbat, 10/12, normal

2 p margin around page, each text column is 14 p wide.

hairline to divide columns

double line at bottom and around top information

560 North Evans
Leadville, CO 80907
(719) 377-9887

New Hope Church

Sunday Service

October 27, 1992
9:00 a.m. & 11:00 a.m.

Our Order of Service

Opening Songs
-on overhead
The Lord Thy God
Cornerstone
We Bring the Sacrifice of Praise

Welcome
Tom Hanson

♦ **Singing Together**
-page 122 in hymnal
Great is Thy Faithfulness

Scripture Reading
-page 314 in pew Bible
John 14
Karen Jenson

Giving Back to God

Sermon
"God's Faithfulness is Forever"
Pastor Alan Jones

♦ **Singing Together**
-words on overhead
I Worship You
In the Name of The Lord

♦ **Closing Prayer**
Pastor Alan Jones

♦ Would all who are able please stand.

Guests

Welcome to New Hope Church.
We're glad you came!

Following is information for your first time at New Hope Church:

1. You may take your children to the Nursery or Children's classes.
Our Children's Ministry has care and classes for all ages during both services and during the Sunday School hour. The folks at the Welcome Center in the church entry will direct you to the classrooms.

2. Feel free to visit our adult Sunday School classes.
We have classes for all adults. Some study a book of the Bible and some a topic in the Christian life. If you are single, married, attending by yourself, or with your family, we'd love to welcome you to a class. The Welcome Center in the church entry has directions to and descriptions of each class.

3. Please do not feel obligated to participate in the offering.
The offering is intended for the regular attenders who consider New Hope their church home.

4. If you have any questions about our church, feel free to call us anytime.

Church bulletin inserts—sermon notes

The next four pages of inserts were all prepared on half of an 8 1/2 x 11-inch piece of paper. They can be modified for a bulletin that is either wider or narrower just by adjusting the length of the column. The sizes and placement of type will work with a large variety of sizes.

When you prepare inserts for your bulletin, printing them in different colors will make them easy to keep separate. Light colored paper is easier to read than dark colors, so stick with printing on shades of beige, gray, white and light pastels.

The church logo or a line stating that it comes from the church is helpful on the insert if people need to call for more information. Be sure to also include the phone number if a reply call is required.

When printing a sheet to take sermon notes on, a minimum amount of text works best. Some churches simply enclose a sheet with only the title and appropriate Scripture passage included.

Helvetica, 18/auto, bold, italic

Logo treatment same as bulletin cover

Helvetica, 18/auto, bold, normal

Helvetica 12/auto, bold, normal

Sermon notes

Trinity Church

Help in Temptation

Matthew 4:1-11
Rev. John Smith

There is victory over temptation.

I. Temptation is a spiritual battle, vv. 1,2.

II. Victory over physical temptations, vv. 3,4.

III. Victory over spiritual temptations, vv. 5-7.

IV. Victory over temptations to abuse power, vv. 8-10.

V. Conclusion and application, v. 11.

Though they are work to create, it's OK to have lots of inserts in your bulletin. Think of them as mini-billboards, ads or advertisements. Make it easy for diffferent members of the family to take out and post what is important to them.

Church bulletin inserts—schedule

Putting together a schedule of events for a church or ministry is far more difficult than it first appears. Not only is there usually a large amount of information to include, but to be effective more needs to be included than date and time.

You need a contact person and phone number for people who are not familiar with the program. You may need to include length of time for some programs that target working people. Words of encouragement and welcome may help get new people into the program.

Times, 10/11, bold, italic

Helvetica, 18/auto, bold, italic

Logo treatment same as previous bulletin cover on p. 93.

Helvetica, 12/auto, bold

Times, 10/11, bold for time, normal for text

Note how each level of information—date, day, time, and event is treated in a different way typographically. This makes each area easy to pick out.

You are welcome to any of the following activities at Trinity. Please call the contact person if you need more information.

This week at

Trinity Church

Sunday, Jan. 31	**8:30 a.m.**	Prayer service in chapel. All are welcome!
	9:30 a.m.	Sunday School hour
	11:00 a.m.	Worship service in sanctuary
	5:00 p.m.	Youth Bible study in senior high meeting room. Contact Jim Edwards, 655-5555. All senior high welcome.
	6:30 p.m.	Evening service
Monday, Feb. 1	**12:30 p.m.**	Ladies Brown Bag Bible Study in Church conference room. Contact Amy Wells, 654-5555.
	1:30 p.m.	Finance Committee, in Pastor's study.
	6:00 p.m.	Outreach Team meeting at Jeff and Jean Davis's home. (123 Terry Street, 765-5555)
Tuesday, Feb. 2	**6:30 a.m.**	Professional Women's Breakfast at Denny's on Union. New women very welcome. Lasts one hour. Contact Jenny Jones, 543-5555.
	7:00 p.m.	Single's Bible Study at Wayne Johnson's. (346 N. Hurlburt, 654-5555)
Wednesday, Feb. 3	**6:30 a.m.**	Men's Prayer Breakfast, Denny's on Union. Pastor Smith leading study on James. Contact John Hart, 543-5555.

Church bulletin insert—special event

If you want to do a poster for an event, use a similar layout to this bulletin insert. Make individual items and type larger in size and print on 8 1/2 x 11 inch or 14-inch paper.

Think of these inserts as mini-posters. They should be eye-catching and easy to read. You can use bright colors for the paper on these. The hot pink paper that wouldn't be appropriate for sermon notes might be just right for a youth event.

Don't put too much on them—just include the facts that are important. Always be sure to include a phone number for more information.

A map is useful to include for special events held away from the church. You can either draw one with your computer program or paste one on after you have created the rest of the insert on the computer.

Bookman, 12/auto, bold, italic

Attention senior high students!
Come celebrate an undefeated season at the

Bookman, 30/auto, bold

Church Basketball Team Victory Party!

Helvetica, 14/auto, bold, centered

at the
Berry's House
444 Pine Ave.
555-5555

Friday, 7:30 p.m. to 9:30 p.m.

Bring a munchie.
Beverages provided.

Clip art. A photo of the team could also have been used.

Helvetica, 10/auto, bold

How to get there:

Times, 10/auto, normal

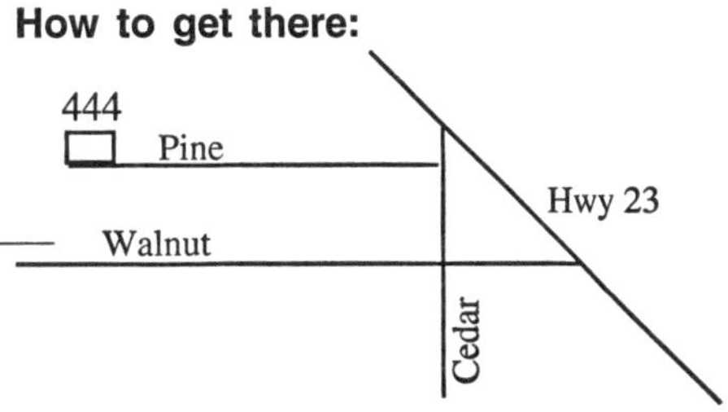

Map was drawn in Pagemaker, directly on insert.

Church bulletin inserts—back page or staff page

Every church bulletin needs a place to list the staff and the services the church provides. Some churches keep this a constant on the back page of the bulletin. Others, who may list it each week in a newsletter, include an insert in the bulletin once a month.

In addition to listing staff, you can also use this section to answer regular questions that are asked about your church.

How detailed you make your list is more a matter of the procedures at your church than of graphic design. In some churches the same people handle every ministry task. In others the lines of responsibility are more clearly structured. Just be sure your communication reflects your style of ministry.

Helvetica, 18/auto, bold, italic

Staff and service at

Logo treatment same as previous bulletin cover on p. 93.

Trinity Church
1222 Oak Road
Evans, OH 88888

Helvetica, 14/auto, bold, normal

Staff

Any of the individuals listed below can be reached at the main church office phone, 555-5555.

Times, 10/11, bold, normal

Andy Wilson
Senior Pastor
Robert Smith
Worship and Administration
Joe Sheffer
Youth Pastor

Times, 10/11, normal

Becky Johnson
Sunday School Coordinator
Lisa Smith
Church Secretary

Services

Times, 12/12, bold

At Trinity we seek to serve you in any way we can. Below are some people to contact when you have these questions or needs.

A prayer request?
Call Jean Adams, 555-5576 or the church any time to leave a request.

Information about Sunday School classes?
Call Mary Lou Seasons, 555-9876 for information about children's classes and John Lee, 576-5555 for information about adult classes.

Information to go in the bulletin or newsletter?
Contact Lisa Smith at the church office before Tuesday of each week.

A need for financial aid?
Call Kenn Otta at 765-5555 or leave a message at the church office any time.

An illness, hospitalization, birth, wedding or death in the family?
Call the church office any time.

A question about baptism, membership or any church doctrine?
Call the church office and make an appointment with any pastor.

For any question or concern not on the list—please call us anytime. If we can't talk to you immediately or help right away, we will as soon as possible.

Church newsletters

Tips for newsletters:

• Remember the two parts of the term: news and letter.

• It's news—no lengthy, flowery writing. Always include the who, what, when, where and why of events.

Be complete in the details, make them easy to find and you'll find attendance at your events increase.

• It's a letter. The newsletter from your church should reflect your church. It doesn't have to look like anybody else's.

• If you are part of a very large church, consider multiple newsletters for the various ministries in the church. Children's, youth, singles, men's ministry, women's etc. will all probably want and need their own newsletter.

These can be shorter and less complex than the overall church newsletter. Try to delegate out the production of them to someone in the group.

In the business world, newsletters are recognized as the most successful publication piece for promoting a business, marketing products and creating good consumer relations. They can also be an excellent communication tool for your church or ministry.

In putting together a church newsletter, there are two primary design decisions to make. The first is the size of the newsletter. The most popular sizes include:

- One or two pages, 8 1/2 x 11 inches, printed on both sides.
- Four or eight pages, using one or two 11 x 17-inch sheets, printed on both sides and folded in half. Each page measures 8 1/2 x 11-inches.
- One or two pages, 8 1/2 x14-inches, printed on both sides.
- Four or eight pages using 8 1/2 x 14-inch, folded in half lengthwise. Each page measures 7 x 8 1/2 inches.

Each of these sizes works well for a newsletter. What will work best for you depends upon the amount of content you have for the newsletter and how you reproduce it.

Each size will be illustrated in the pages that follow. One option, the 8 1/2 x 14-inch folded lengthwise, is particularly useful for churches or ministries with limited budgets and reproduction facilities. It uses a standard legal size piece of paper, but with DTP the design and layout possibilities are great. Below is how to set the margins for this newsletter. The following two pages will illustrate layout ideas for this size newsletter.

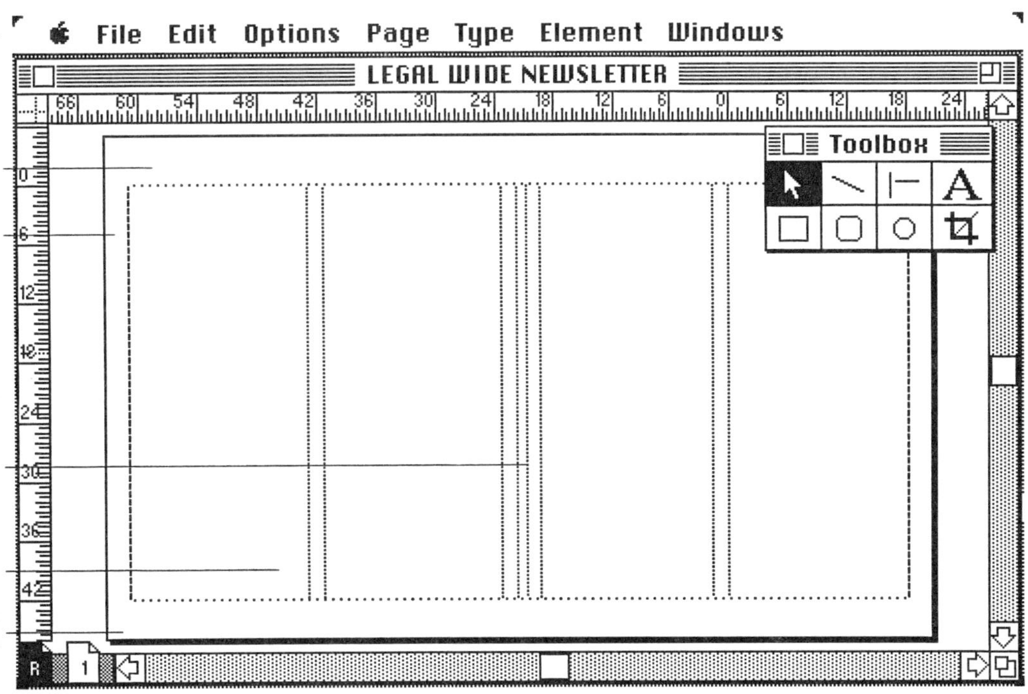

5 p margin at top of newsletter

2.5 p margin on both sides of the newsletter

The newsletter is set up with 5 columns with a 1.5 p gutter between them. To make the layout come out like this, move the two center gutters together to make a total space of 4 p. Then move the remaining gutters so each column is 18 p wide

3 p margin at bottom of newsletter

The one thing to never print in a newsletter: "Call the church office for more information." Print the "more information" in the newsletter. Much more efficient and kinder to church staff.

This size and layout is one of the most cost-effective for any size church to produce because it is simply a legal-size piece of paper folded in half. This size is easy to reproduce on in-house photocopy machines. At the same time, depending upon the amount of sheets used, this size of newsletter can contain quite a bit of information.

Clip art and photographs may be used, but you do not need them to make an effective newsletter.

Even though the size is small, the newsletter will be more readable if the text is set up in two columns rather than having the text extend across the entire page. To make the newsletter easy to read, decide upon continuing sections or columns for the newsletter and place them in the same location for each issue.

Grid measurements for this newsletter are given and illustrated on the previous page.

Name plate, Helvetica 32/auto, bold, 130% width, tight track

1 p line

Times, 11/auto, bold

2 p line around nameplate

Helvetica, 10/auto, bold, italic

Main headine, Helvetica, 16/16, bold

Body text, Times, 10/auto, normal

2 p line between stories

Other headlines, Helvetica, 14/ auto, bold

2 p box

Times, 10/auto, bold

Trinity Church Tidings

News, notes, and updates about our church family at Trinity

Pastor's column

Congregation challenged to renew commitments

Lorem ipsum dolor sit amet, consectetuer adipiscing elit, sed diam nonummy nibh euismod tincidunt ut laoreet dolore magna aliquam erat volutpat. Ut wisi enim ad minim veniam, quis nostrud exerci tation ullamcorper suscipit lobortis nisl ut aliquip ex ea commodo consequat.

Duis autem vel eum iriure dolor in hendrerit in vulputate velit esse molestie consequat, vel illum dolore eu feugiat nulla facilisis at vero eros et accumsan et iusto odio dignissim qui blandit praesent luptatum zzril delenit augue duis dolore te feugait nulla facilisi.

Lorem ipsum dolor sit amet, consectetuer adipiscing elit, sed diam nonummy nibh euismod tincidunt ut laoreet dolore magna aliquam erat volutpat. Ut wisi enim ad minim veniam, quis nostrud exerci tation ullamcorper suscipit lobortis nisl ut aliquip ex ea commodo consequat.

Duis autem vel eum iriure dolor in hendrerit in vulputate velit esse molestie consequat, vel illum dolore eu feugiat nulla facilisis at vero eros et accumsan et iusto odio dignissim qui blandit praesent luptatum zzril delenit augue duis dolore te feugait nulla facilisi. Nam liber tempor cum soluta nobis eleifend option congue nihil imperdiet doming id quod mazim placerat facer possim assum.

Lorem ipsum dolor sit amet, consectetuer adipiscing elit, sed diam nonummy nibh euismod tincidunt ut.

New Bible Study Groups forming—see Pastor Johnson to sign up!

Llaoreet dolore magna aliquam erat volutpat. Ut wisi enim ad minim veniam, quis nostrud exerci tation ullamcorper

suscipit lobortis nisl ut aliquip ex ea commodo consequat. Duis autem vel eum iriure dolor in hendrerit in vulputate velit esse molestie consequat, vel illum dolore eu feugiat nulla facilisis at vero eros et accumsan et iusto odio dignissim qui blandit praesent luptatum zzril delenit augue duis dolore te feugait nulla facilisi. Lorem ipsum dolor sit amet, consectetuer adipiscing elit, sed diam nonummy nibh euismod tincidunt ut laoreet dolore magna aliquam erat volutpat.

Ut wisi enim ad minim veniam, quis nostrud exerci tation ullamcorper suscipit lobortis nisl ut aliquip ex ea commodo consequat. Duis autem vel

Mission giving increased for second year in a row

Eum iriure dolor in hendrerit in vulputate velit esse molestie consequat, vel illum dolore eu feugiat nulla facilisis at vero eros et accumsan et iusto odio dignissim qui blandit praesent luptatum zzril delenit augue duis dolore te feugait nulla facilisi. Lorem ipsum dolor sit amet, consectetuer adipiscing elit, sed diam nonummy nibh euismod tincidunt ut laoreet

1222 Oak Road, Evans, OH 88888 • Church office phone: (555) 555-5576
Sunday School Hour 9:30 a.m. • Sunday Worship Service 11:00 a.m. • Wednesday Service 7:00 p.m.

This is an illustration of the center page of the newsletter illustrated on the previous two pages. Since it is a piece of 8 1/2 x 14-inch or one legal size sheet, you can do a center page spread like this because you can lay out the entire page as one in your DTP program.

A full-page layout like this works well if you have a topic that warrants several small articles and an overall graphic emphasis, such as the children's program illustrated here.

For information that consists of a variety of topics, pages can also be laid out in two columns per page without a centered headline.

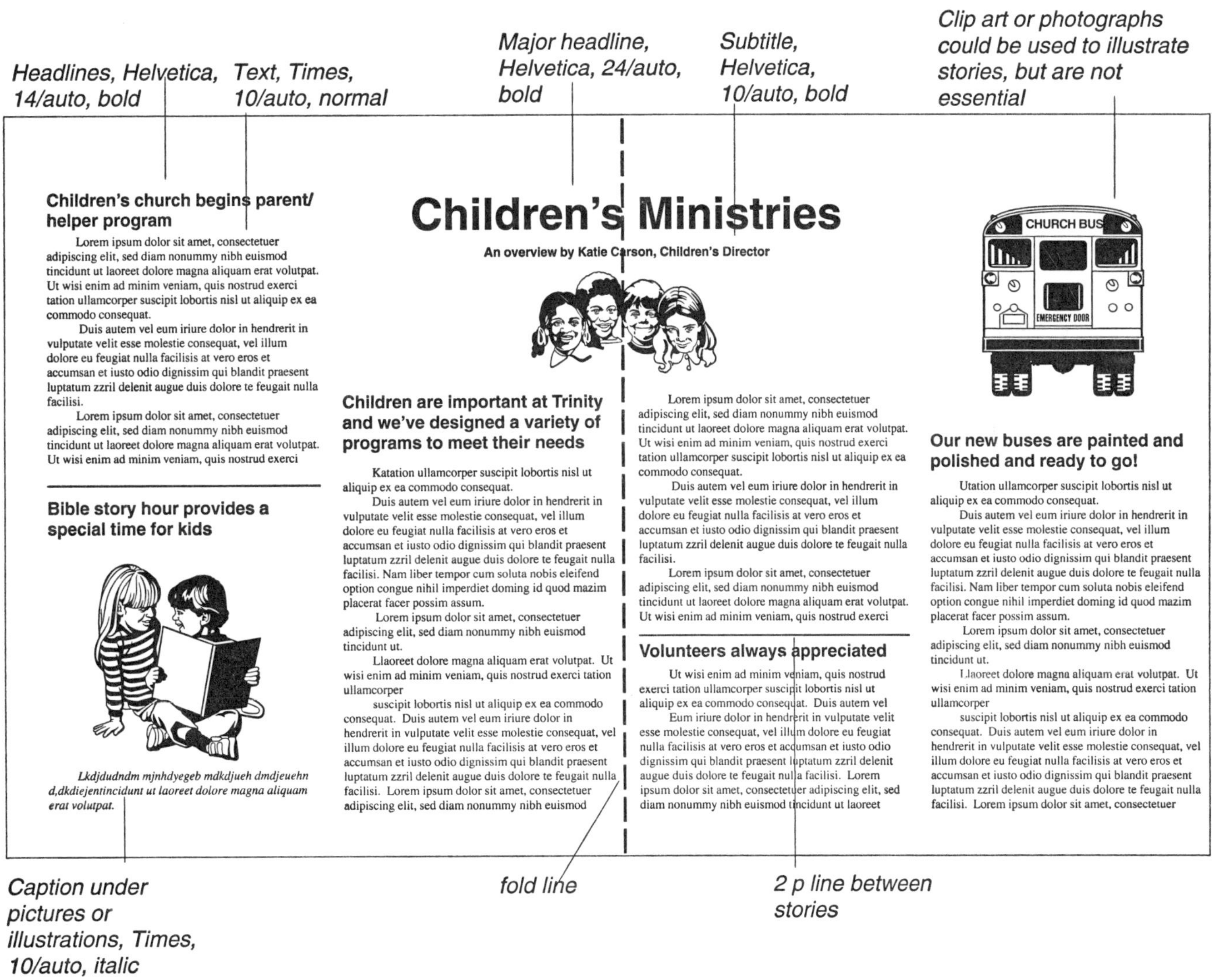

Children's Ministries

An overview by Katie Carson, Children's Director

Children's church begins parent/helper program

Lorem ipsum dolor sit amet, consectetuer adipiscing elit, sed diam nonummy nibh euismod tincidunt ut laoreet dolore magna aliquam erat volutpat. Ut wisi enim ad minim veniam, quis nostrud exerci tation ullamcorper suscipit lobortis nisl ut aliquip ex ea commodo consequat.

Duis autem vel eum iriure dolor in hendrerit in vulputate velit esse molestie consequat, vel illum dolore eu feugiat nulla facilisis at vero eros et accumsan et iusto odio dignissim qui blandit praesent luptatum zzril delenit augue duis dolore te feugait nulla facilisi.

Lorem ipsum dolor sit amet, consectetuer adipiscing elit, sed diam nonummy nibh euismod tincidunt ut laoreet dolore magna aliquam erat volutpat. Ut wisi enim ad minim veniam, quis nostrud exerci

Bible story hour provides a special time for kids

Lkdjdudndm mjnhdyegeb mdkdjueh dmdjeuehn d,dkdiejentincidunt ut laoreet dolore magna aliquam erat volutpat.

Children are important at Trinity and we've designed a variety of programs to meet their needs

Katation ullamcorper suscipit lobortis nisl ut aliquip ex ea commodo consequat.

Duis autem vel eum iriure dolor in hendrerit in vulputate velit esse molestie consequat, vel illum dolore eu feugiat nulla facilisis at vero eros et accumsan et iusto odio dignissim qui blandit praesent luptatum zzril delenit augue duis dolore te feugait nulla facilisi. Nam liber tempor cum soluta nobis eleifend option congue nihil imperdiet doming id quod mazim placerat facer possim assum.

Lorem ipsum dolor sit amet, consectetuer adipiscing elit, sed diam nonummy nibh euismod tincidunt ut.

Llaoreet dolore magna aliquam erat volutpat. Ut wisi enim ad minim veniam, quis nostrud exerci tation ullamcorper

suscipit lobortis nisl ut aliquip ex ea commodo consequat. Duis autem vel eum iriure dolor in hendrerit in vulputate velit esse molestie consequat, vel illum dolore eu feugiat nulla facilisis at vero eros et accumsan et iusto odio dignissim qui blandit praesent luptatum zzril delenit augue duis dolore te feugait nulla facilisi. Lorem ipsum dolor sit amet, consectetuer adipiscing elit, sed diam nonummy nibh euismod

Lorem ipsum dolor sit amet, consectetuer adipiscing elit, sed diam nonummy nibh euismod tincidunt ut laoreet dolore magna aliquam erat volutpat. Ut wisi enim ad minim veniam, quis nostrud exerci tation ullamcorper suscipit lobortis nisl ut aliquip ex ea commodo consequat.

Duis autem vel eum iriure dolor in hendrerit in vulputate velit esse molestie consequat, vel illum dolore eu feugiat nulla facilisis at vero eros et accumsan et iusto odio dignissim qui blandit praesent luptatum zzril delenit augue duis dolore te feugait nulla facilisi.

Lorem ipsum dolor sit amet, consectetuer adipiscing elit, sed diam nonummy nibh euismod tincidunt ut laoreet dolore magna aliquam erat volutpat. Ut wisi enim ad minim veniam, quis nostrud exerci

Volunteers always appreciated

Ut wisi enim ad minim veniam, quis nostrud exerci tation ullamcorper suscipit lobortis nisl ut aliquip ex ea commodo consequat. Duis autem vel

Eum iriure dolor in hendrerit in vulputate velit esse molestie consequat, vel illum dolore eu feugiat nulla facilisis at vero eros et accumsan et iusto odio dignissim qui blandit praesent luptatum zzril delenit augue duis dolore te feugait nulla facilisi. Lorem ipsum dolor sit amet, consectetuer adipiscing elit, sed diam nonummy nibh euismod tincidunt ut laoreet

Our new buses are painted and polished and ready to go!

Utation ullamcorper suscipit lobortis nisl ut aliquip ex ea commodo consequat.

Duis autem vel eum iriure dolor in hendrerit in vulputate velit esse molestie consequat, vel illum dolore eu feugiat nulla facilisis at vero eros et accumsan et iusto odio dignissim qui blandit praesent luptatum zzril delenit augue duis dolore te feugait nulla facilisi. Nam liber tempor cum soluta nobis eleifend option congue nihil imperdiet doming id quod mazim placerat facer possim assum.

Lorem ipsum dolor sit amet, consectetuer adipiscing elit, sed diam nonummy nibh euismod tincidunt ut.

Llaoreet dolore magna aliquam erat volutpat. Ut wisi enim ad minim veniam, quis nostrud exerci tation ullamcorper

suscipit lobortis nisl ut aliquip ex ea commodo consequat. Duis autem vel eum iriure dolor in hendrerit in vulputate velit esse molestie consequat, vel illum dolore eu feugiat nulla facilisis at vero eros et accumsan et iusto odio dignissim qui blandit praesent luptatum zzril delenit augue duis dolore te feugait nulla facilisi. Lorem ipsum dolor sit amet, consectetuer

This page illustrates a newsletter printed on one 8 1/2 x 14-inch sheet of paper. This brief newsletter format is useful for either a small church or for a ministry that is part of a larger church such as the singles' ministry illustrated here. The grid measurements for this page include a 3 p margin around all edges, center divided into 3 columns, one for headlines, two for text.

Nameplate, Palatino 48/auto, 130% width, tight track, bold, italic

2 p line

Palatino, 12/auto, 130% width, tight track, bold, italic

Headlines, Palatino, 18/35, bold, with a 1 p line above them,

Text, Palatino, 10/auto, normal

Subtitle information Palatino, 12/auto, bold.

Quotes or comments on stories, Palatino, 12/auto, bold

Dotted line from line menu in DTP program.

Singles Update

What's new and what's news for singles at First Church
675 Old Stage Road, Beacon, CO 88888 • 555-9876

Relationships to be topic of April classes

Lorem ipsum dolor sit amet, consectetuer adipiscing elit, sed diam nonummy nibh euismod tincidunt ut laoreet dolore magna aliquam erat volutpat.

Ut wisi enim ad minim veniam, quis nostrud exerci tation ullamcorper suscipit lobortis nisl ut aliquip ex ea commodo consequat. Duis autem vel eum iriure dolor in hendrerit i.

Mulputate velit esse molestie consequat, vel illum dolore eu feugiat nulla facilisis at vero eros et accumsan et iusto odio dignissim qui blandit praesent luptatum zzril delenit augue duis dolore te feugait nulla facilisi. Lorem ipsum dolor sit amet, consectetuer adipiscing elit, sed diam nonummy nibh euismod tincidunt ut laoreet dolore magna aliquam erat volutpat.

Pot-luck dinner to follow church choir concert

Date
Time
Place

Lorem ipsum dolor sit amet, consectetuer adipiscing elit, sed diam nonummy nibh euismod tincidunt ut laoreet dolore magna aliquam erat volutpat.

Ut wisi enim ad minim veniam, quis nostrud exerci tation ullamcorper suscipit lobortis nisl ut aliquip ex ea commodo consequat. Duis autem vel eum iriure dolor in hendrerit i.

Mulputate velit esse molestie consequat, vel illum dolore eu feugiat nulla facilisis at vero eros et accumsan et iusto odio dignissim qui blandit praesent luptatum zzril delenit augue duis dolore te feugait nulla facilisi. Lorem ipsum dolor sit amet, consectetuer adipiscing elit, sed diam nonummy nibh euismod tincidunt ut laoreet dolore magna aliquam erat volutpat. UtMulputate velit esse molestie consequat, vel illum dolore eu feugiat nulla facilisis at vero eros et accumsan et iusto odio dignissim qui blandit praesent luptatum zzril delenit augue duis dolore te feugait nulla facilisi. Lorem ipsum dolor sit amet, consectetuer adipiscing elit, sed diam nonummy nibh euismod tincidunt ut laoreet dolore magna aliquam erat volutpat.

Mission team forming for summer projects

Contact person
Phone number

Lorem ipsum dolor sit amet, consectetuer adipiscing elit, sed diam nonummy nibh euismod tincidunt ut laoreet dolore magna aliquam erat volutpat.

Ut wisi enim ad minim veniam, quis nostrud exerci tation ullamcorper suscipit lobortis nisl ut aliquip ex ea commodo consequat. Duis autem vel eum iriure dolor in hendrerit i.

Mulputate velit esse molestie consequat, vel illum dolore eu feugiat nulla facilisis at vero eros et accumsan et iusto odio dignissim qui blandit praesent

Prayer partner program being planned

"Lorem ipsum dolor sit amet, consectetuer adipiscing elit, sed diam nonummy nibh."

Lorem ipsum dolor sit amet, consectetuer adipiscing elit, sed diam nonummy nibh euismod tincidunt ut laoreet dolore magna aliquam erat volutpat.

Ut wisi enim ad minim veniam, quis nostrud exerci tation ullamcorper suscipit lobortis nisl ut aliquip ex ea commodo consequat. Duis autem vel eum iriure dolor in hendrerit i.

Mulputate velit esse molestie consequat, vel illum dolore eu feugiat nulla facilisis at vero eros et accumsan et iusto odio dignissim qui blandit praesent luptatum zzril delenit augue duis dolore te feugait nulla facilisi. Lorem ipsum dolor sit amet, consectetuer adipiscing elit, sed diam nonummy nibh euismod tincidunt ut laoreet dolore magna aliquam erat volutpatipsum dolor sit amet, consectetuer adipiscing elit, sed diam nonummy nibh euismod tincidunt ut laoreet dolore magna aliquam erat

Newsletters can take a variety of forms depending upon your communication goals. Below, the newsletter is in the form of features, photos and profiles of church activities. On the next page is a newsletter that uses the form of short news pieces and notes

Overall grid measurements for the newsletter are: 3.5 p margin on all sides, 3 columns of 13.5 p with 1.5 p space between columns.

Logo is the same as on business card and stationery. Double lines are the same as those used on bulletin.

Times, 36/36, bold, 120% width, tight track
2 point line
Times, 11/13, italic
1 point line
Times 11/13, bold
Times, 24/24, bold
Times, 11/13, italic
Times, 10/12, normal
Times, 14/16, bold
2 point line

New Hope Church News

News, updates and encouragements for the church family at New Hope Church.

560 North Evans, Leadville, CO 80907 **(719) 377-9887**

Adults and children grow in giving during Becomer's class project day

While adults painted a house for Habitat for Humanity, the kids made Christmas cards for the senior center

Lorem ipsum dolor sit amet, consectetuer adipiscing elit, sed diam nonummy nibh euismod tincidunt ut laoreet dolore magna aliquam erat volutpat.

Ut wisi enim ad minim veniam, quis nostrud exerci tation ullamcorper suscipit lobortis nisl ut aliquip ex ea commodo consequat. Duis autem vel eum iriure dolor in hendrerit in vulputate velit esse molestie consequat, vel illum dolore eu feugiat nulla.

Macilisis at vero eros et accumsan et iusto odio dignissim qui blandit praesent

Luptatum zzril delenit augue duis

Lorem ipsum dolor sit amet,

Adults and kids shared in a delicious chili supper at the church after their projects.

Lorem ipsum dolor sit amet, consectetuer adipiscing elit, sed diam nonummy nibh euismod tincidunt ut laoreet dolore magna aliquam erat volutpat.

Ut wisi enim ad minim veniam, quis nostrud exerci tation ullamcorper suscipit lobortis nisl ut aliquip ex ea commodo consequat. Duis autem vel eum iriure dolor in hendrerit in vulputate velit esse molestie consequat, vel illum dolore eu feugiat nulla.

Macilisis at vero eros et accumsan et iusto odio dignissim qui blandit praesent luptatum zzril delenit augue duis dolore te feugait nulla facilisi.

Lorem ipsum dolor sit amet,

The adult members of the Becomer's class were able to get the outside of the Johnsons's house painted for Habitat for Humanity during the class project day last Saturday.

While their parents were busy painting, the children made 50 Christmas cards for the Senior Center. They also heard lessons about giving and sharing from the high school volunteers.

Join one of these Sunday School classes and become involved in fun and service

consectetuer adipiscing elit, sed diam nonummy nibh euismod tincidunt ut laoreet dolore mkiuj ggfvc deesw kmjmn ggvfd ccxse bgtfmagna aliquam erat volutpat.

Ut wisi enim ad minim veniam, quis nostrud exerci tation ullamcorper suscipit lobortis nisl ut aliquip ex ea commodo consequat.

Luptatum zzril delenit augue duis dolore te feugait nulla facilisi.

Lorem ipsum dolor sit amet, consectetuer adipiscing elit.

Sorm nnmui ed diam nonummy nibh euismod tincidunt ut laoreet dolore magna aliquam erat volutpat. Ut wisi enim ad minim veniam, quis nostrud exerci tation ullamcorper suscipit lobortis nisl ut.

November 1992

Ministry update or newsletter

The basic grid for this publication is an 8 1/2 x 11-inch sheet. The text margins are 3.5 p side margins, 11.5 p top margin and a 6 p bottom margin. There are three columns of 13.5 p with a 1.5 space between each column.

A 1 point box encloses two columns and is set out 1 p from the text on the left side.

Below is a layout that can be used for either an update sheet or a newsletter for a church or ministry. This format would not have any photographs. The text in it would consist of short news and information pieces. A schedule or other list of information can be placed on the side.

This design takes into account the busy schedule of volunteers and the little time they have for reading. It is designed to provide maximum input of information in a brief amount of space.

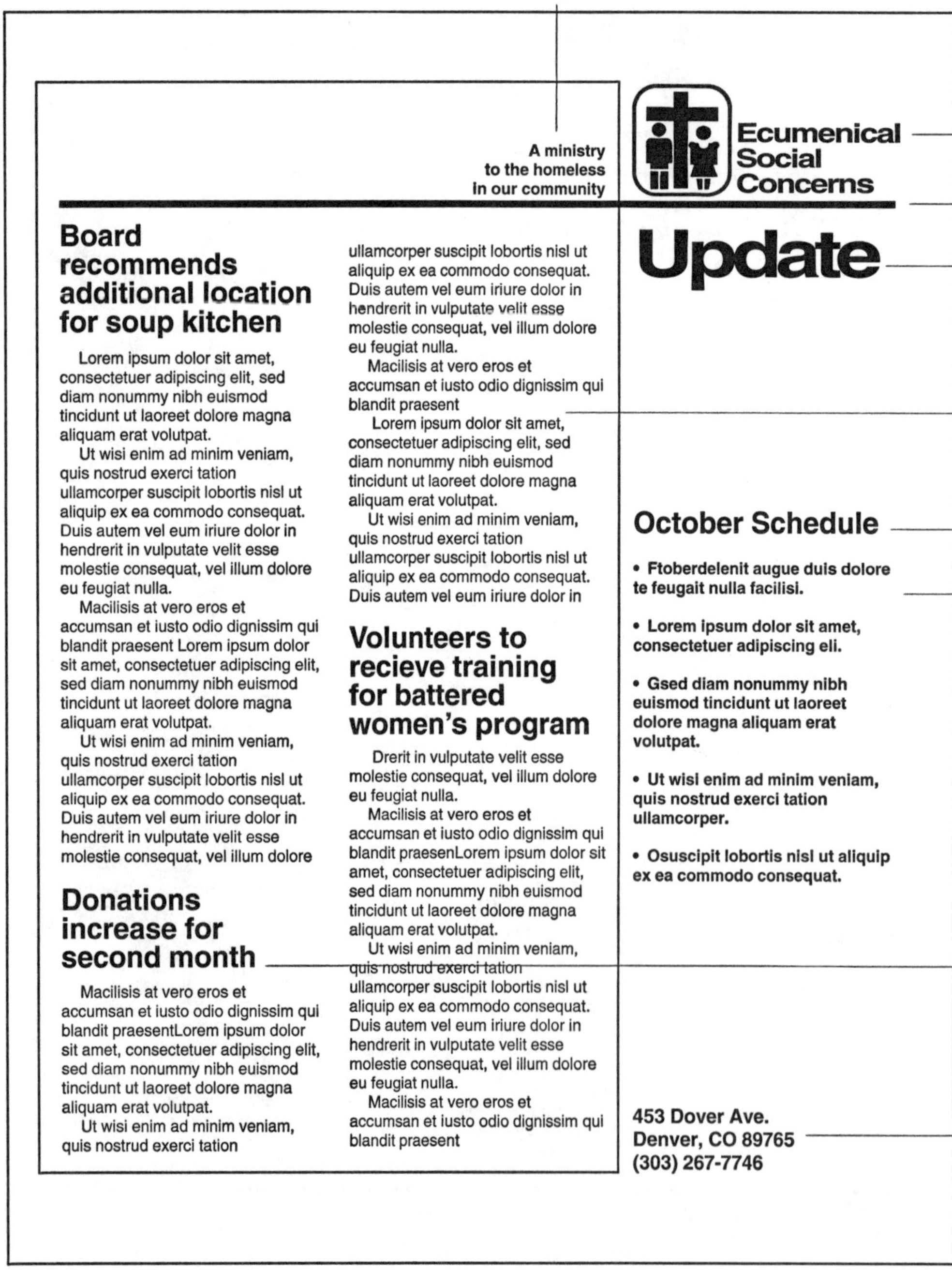

A ministry to the homeless in our community

Ecumenical Social Concerns

Update

Board recommends additional location for soup kitchen

Lorem ipsum dolor sit amet, consectetuer adipiscing elit, sed diam nonummy nibh euismod tincidunt ut laoreet dolore magna aliquam erat volutpat.

Ut wisi enim ad minim veniam, quis nostrud exerci tation ullamcorper suscipit lobortis nisl ut aliquip ex ea commodo consequat. Duis autem vel eum iriure dolor in hendrerit in vulputate velit esse molestie consequat, vel illum dolore eu feugiat nulla.

Macilisis at vero eros et accumsan et iusto odio dignissim qui blandit praesent Lorem ipsum dolor sit amet, consectetuer adipiscing elit, sed diam nonummy nibh euismod tincidunt ut laoreet dolore magna aliquam erat volutpat.

Ut wisi enim ad minim veniam, quis nostrud exerci tation ullamcorper suscipit lobortis nisl ut aliquip ex ea commodo consequat. Duis autem vel eum iriure dolor in hendrerit in vulputate velit esse molestie consequat, vel illum dolore ullamcorper suscipit lobortis nisl ut aliquip ex ea commodo consequat. Duis autem vel eum iriure dolor in hendrerit in vulputate velit esse molestie consequat, vel illum dolore eu feugiat nulla.

Macilisis at vero eros et accumsan et iusto odio dignissim qui blandit praesent

Lorem ipsum dolor sit amet, consectetuer adipiscing elit, sed diam nonummy nibh euismod tincidunt ut laoreet dolore magna aliquam erat volutpat.

Ut wisi enim ad minim veniam, quis nostrud exerci tation ullamcorper suscipit lobortis nisl ut aliquip ex ea commodo consequat. Duis autem vel eum iriure dolor in

Donations increase for second month

Macilisis at vero eros et accumsan et iusto odio dignissim qui blandit praesentLorem ipsum dolor sit amet, consectetuer adipiscing elit, sed diam nonummy nibh euismod tincidunt ut laoreet dolore magna aliquam erat volutpat.

Ut wisi enim ad minim veniam, quis nostrud exerci tation

Volunteers to recieve training for battered women's program

Drerit in vulputate velit esse molestie consequat, vel illum dolore eu feugiat nulla.

Macilisis at vero eros et accumsan et iusto odio dignissim qui blandit praesenLorem ipsum dolor sit amet, consectetuer adipiscing elit, sed diam nonummy nibh euismod tincidunt ut laoreet dolore magna aliquam erat volutpat.

Ut wisi enim ad minim veniam, quis nostrud exerci tation ullamcorper suscipit lobortis nisl ut aliquip ex ea commodo consequat. Duis autem vel eum iriure dolor in hendrerit in vulputate velit esse molestie consequat, vel illum dolore eu feugiat nulla.

Macilisis at vero eros et accumsan et iusto odio dignissim qui blandit praesent

October Schedule

- **Ftoberdelenit augue duis dolore te feugait nulla facilisi.**
- **Lorem ipsum dolor sit amet, consectetuer adipiscing eli.**
- **Gsed diam nonummy nibh euismod tincidunt ut laoreet dolore magna aliquam erat volutpat.**
- **Ut wisi enim ad minim veniam, quis nostrud exerci tation ullamcorper.**
- **Osuscipit lobortis nisl ut aliquip ex ea commodo consequat.**

453 Dover Ave.
Denver, CO 89765
(303) 267-7746

Ministry brochures

Brochures such as the one below can serve a multitude of ministry purposes. They can describe special programs or departments within a church. They can promote and raise funds for ministries.

Above is the basic grid for the brochure on this page and the next.

It is based on an 8 1/2 x 11-inch piece of paper lengthwise.

The margins are 2 p top margins, 3 p side margins. The space inside the margins is divided into 3 columns, 16 p wide, 6 p space between them. This forms the three panels of the brochure.

It is very important that you place the 6 p of space between the columns. It will look like too much space when you are putting together your brochure on the flat computer screen, but the fold takes up more space than it seems it should. If you don't leave that much space, when the brochure is folded the text will be too crowded.

Board or mission report

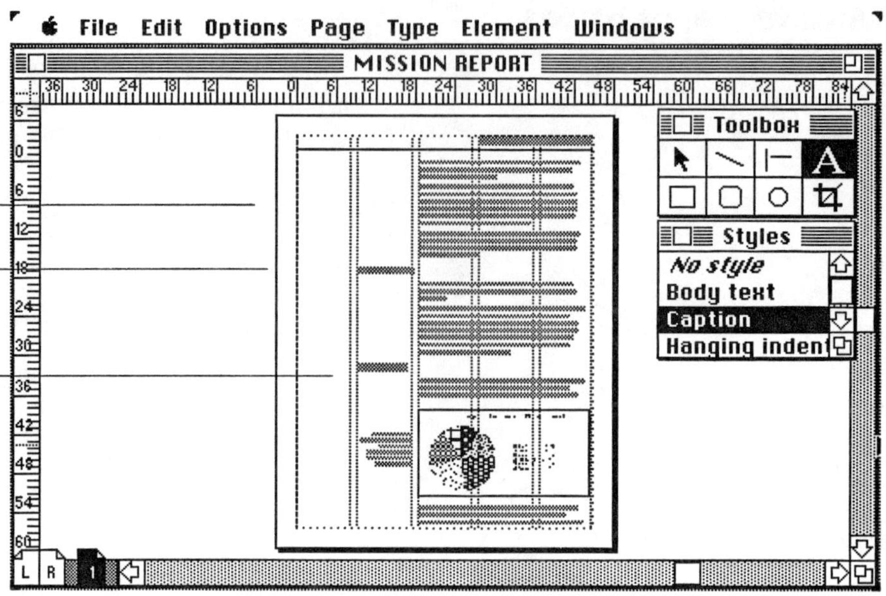

Layout—
The report layout is based on a 5-column grid

The page has a 3 p margin on all sides.

There are 1 p spaces between each column.

Helvetica, 24/auto, bold, flush right, 2 p line underneath

Palatino, 10/auto, normal, left indent 18.5 p

Helvetica, 14/22, bold, 1 p line .5 before, hairline .5 after, left indent 9.25 p

Helvetica, 12/auto, bold, italic

Chart imported from Microsoft Works

MISSION REPORT

Lorem ipsum dolor sit amet, consectetuer adipiscing elit, sed diam nonummy nibh euismod tincidunt ut laoreet dolore magna aliquam erat volutpat.

Ut wisi enim ad minim veniam, quis nostrud exerci tation ullamcorper suscipit lobortis nisl ut aliquip ex ea commodo consequat. Duis autem vel eum iriure dolor in hendrerit in vulputate velit esse molestie consequat, vel illum dolore eu feugiat nulla facilisis at vero eros et accumsan et iusto odio dignissim qui blandit praesent luptatum z

zril delenit augue duis dolore te feugait nulla facilisi. Lorem ipsum dolor sit amet, consectetuer adipiscing elit, sed diam nonummy nibh euismod tincidunt ut laoreet dolore magna aliquam erat volutpat.

OUR PURPOSE

Ut wisi enim ad minim veniam, quis nostrud exerci tation ullamcorper suscipit lobortis nisl ut aliquip ex ea commodo consequat.

Duis autem vel eum iriure dolor in hendrerit in vulputate velit esse molestie consequat, vel illum dolore eu feugiat nulla facilisis at vero eros et accumsan et iusto odio dignissim qui blandit praesent luptatum zzril delenit augue duis dolore te feugait nulla facilisi. Ut wisi enim ad minim veniam, quis nostrud exerci tation ullamcorper suscipit lobortis nisl ut aliquip ex ea commodo consequat.

OUR PEOPLE

Duis autem vel eum iriure dolor in hendrerit in vulputate velit esse molestie consequat, vel illum dolore eu feugiat nulla facilisis at vero eros et accumsan et iusto odio dignissim qui

This is a caption describing the graph. It emphasizes whatever point the writer of the report wants to make.

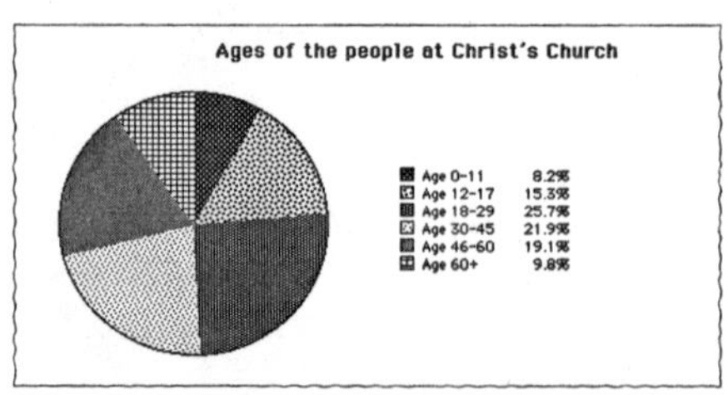

blandit praesent luptatum zzril delenit augue duis dolore te nulla facilisi. Lorem ipsum dolor sit amet, consectetuer adipiscing elit, sed diam nonummy nibh euismod tincidunt ut

Gallery of examples

It's exciting to see how folks take the basic DTP principles and apply them to their specific ministries. The following pages are some great examples of applied DTP in real-life ministry settings.

There are just as many ways to accomplish the goal of good communication in DTP as there are churches and ministries with a message. In the following pages are some examples of DTP projects accomplished by folks just like you working on the computer in the church office.

These are part of the Great Idea Swap conducted by Ministry Computing Resources. Folks from all over America shared their samples and their names are listed below.

For information on how to receive a complete copy of the results, call Ministry Computing Resources at 1-817-9535 and ask for the Great Idea Swap book.

The examples that follow came from these people and churches:

Anthony L. Jones
First United Methodist Church
Downers Grove, IL

Steve Waterman
Olive Branch Church of God
Rockford, OH

If you'd like to be part of the next Great Idea Swap, contact Ministry Computing Resources, P.O. Box 202630, Arlington, TX 76006 or call 817-861-9535 for entry guidelines.

It's a great way to see your work nationally published, to get prizes and recognition for what you do!

Keith Shimfessel
Church of Christ at Mountain View
Winchester, VA

Edith Nedrud
Fellowship Church
Greeley, CO

Jackie Meyer
Bethany Lutheran Church
Burlington, IA

Phil Jones
Prince Avenue Baptist
Athens, GA

Brian Carmack
Pendleton Faith Center
Pendleton, OR

Rob Geraltowski
St. John's Evangelical Lutheran Church
Bloomington, IL

Their examples will encourage and inspire you.

Also, as you consider how much you can learn from other folks doing DTP in ministry, consider getting together a group of people in your area to share samples, ideas and encouragements.

Church stationery

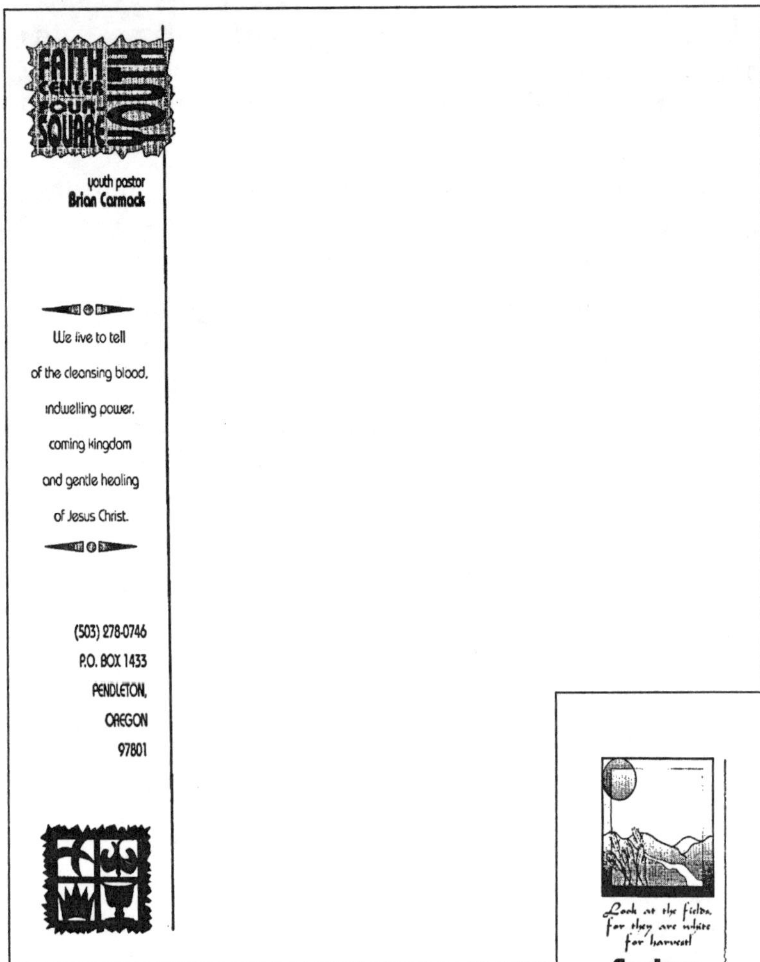

Very attractive design for youth stationery, lively and yet legible enough for correspondence sent to adults.

Here stationery has been specifically designed for an event. This adds importance, impact and identity to an event more than if the regular church stationery was used for it.

Both of these examples show that church stationery doesn't have to always be "professional" and serious looking.

You know you've gotten a message from a real person when you get something on Pastor Steve's notepaper.

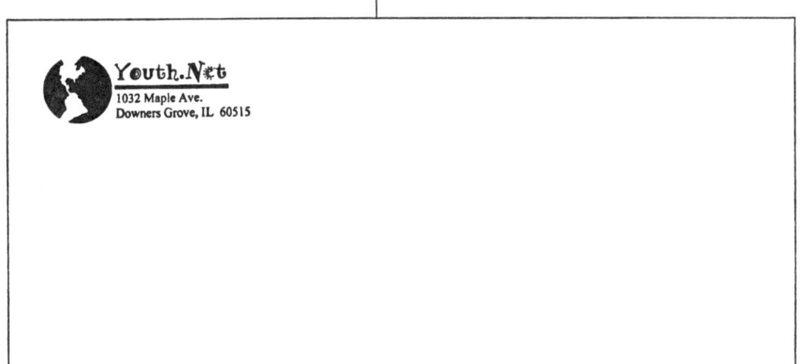

Church bulletins

Great example of a bulletin that is welcoming and yet traditional. The clear clean format makes it easy to follow the order of service and to know what's going on in the church.

You will always find a warm fellowship here on the mountain

We have classes and programs for everyone of all ages. Our worship services are filled with dynamic preaching, uplifting praise and worshipful singing.

Are you looking for a church home?

If so, then we are here for you. We would be thrilled to have you come join our ever growing church family. Our ministers and leaders will be more than happy to explain how you can become a part of our church. **Call the office at 703-869-2244 (24 hour answering service).** The friendly office staff will put you in contact with someone to answer all your questions.

We have a wonderful nursery

We would like for your worship experience to be pleasant and uplifting. For that reason, we have a nursery program for children under the age of two, and a Kinder Church for ages two to five years old. **The nursery is located halfway down the north corridor (to the left from the vestibule).** Our caring and loving staff will make sure that your little ones have a pleasant time during the worship service.

Times of Worship

Sunday	Bible School	9:30 AM
	Morning Worship	10:30 AM
	Youth Meetings	6:00 PM
	Seekers Service (Evening Worship)	7:00 PM
Wednesday	Adult Bible Class	
	Young Peoples Classes	
	Choir Practice	7:00 PM

Church of Christ at Mountain View
Rt 11 South (Next to DMV) • P.O. Box 2702 • Winchester, VA 22604
(703) 869-2244 (24 hour answering service)
Charles W. Doughty/Evangelist • Doug Hardman/Youth Evangelist
Keith Shimfessel/Music/Worship Minister

Come *Alive* in '95

We would like to extend a cordial welcome to you from the Church of Christ at Mountain View. We are pleased to have you worship with us. If you are visiting with us today, please know that we are honored to have you and invite you to come worship with us again. You are always welcome here on the mountain

Church of Christ at Mountain View
Order of Worship

Welcome to our morning worship hour. Members please fill out the membership cards located in the pew in front of you. Visitors can fill out the special visitor cards also located in the pews. All cards can be placed in the offering plates as they are passed later during the service. Thank you.

Prelude .... The Mountain View Praise Band

Opening Song
(Words on the screen)

Opening Prayer .... Chris Straley
Welcome and Fellowship

Worship In Singing .... Keith Shimfessel
Music/Worship Minister

Morning Prayer .... Charles Doughty
Evangelist

Special Music

Worship in the Word
Charles W. Doughty
"We Have An Altar"

Invitation .... "Just As I Am"
#306

Worship in Communion .... "Near the Cross"
#403

The Lord's Supper is served to all Christians. You may partake of the loaf and the cup as they are passed.

Worship in Giving

Announcements

Closing Prayer .... Calvin Gant

Closing Chorus .... "Faith Is The Victory"

Announcements for the week of May 21,1995

Communion for the Sick And Shut -In
May 21 - Robert Pifer, Wayne Keiter, Allen Kibler
May 28 - Alfred Armel, Garland Whitlock, Don Pridham

Let's Talk About Your Child's Education
We are currently enrolling students for our 1995-1996 school session at Mountain View Christian Academy. Please call the office at 869-2941 for more information or pick up an interest inventory form from the Welcome Center, fill it out and drop it in the offering plate.

Congratulations Graduates!
It's that time of year again. We want to honor and recognize all of our high school and college graduates. If you are graduating this year, please call Maxine at the church office(869-2244). We want to make sure we have your name and school you are graduating from.

June 25-30 "Summer In The Son" - This high energy week for youth (Grades 9 through 12) and sponsors is held on the campus of Kentucky Christian College. There is information on the bulletin board. See Minta or Doug for more information.

Attention Ladies- Don't forget our next meeting on Monday, May 22nd at 7:00 in the fellowship hall. Bring a finger food and come join in the great fellowship! Hope to see you there. - Barb Fauver

You are invited to attend the graduation ceremonies at Hampshire High School for Kathy Alkire and Steve Hyson on Sunday May 28th at 2:00. Following graduation on Sunday, the Raums will host an Open House to honor Steve.
On Monday, May 29th at 2:00 the Alkires would like to invite you to their 3rd annual Memorial Day picnic and will also honor Kathy at that time.
You are requested to bring a covered dish to both the Open House and the Picnic.

For a seeker-friendly church, this is a great bulletin cover. Clean, clear, almost business-like in appearance, it doesn't put visitors off with images they may not be familiar with.

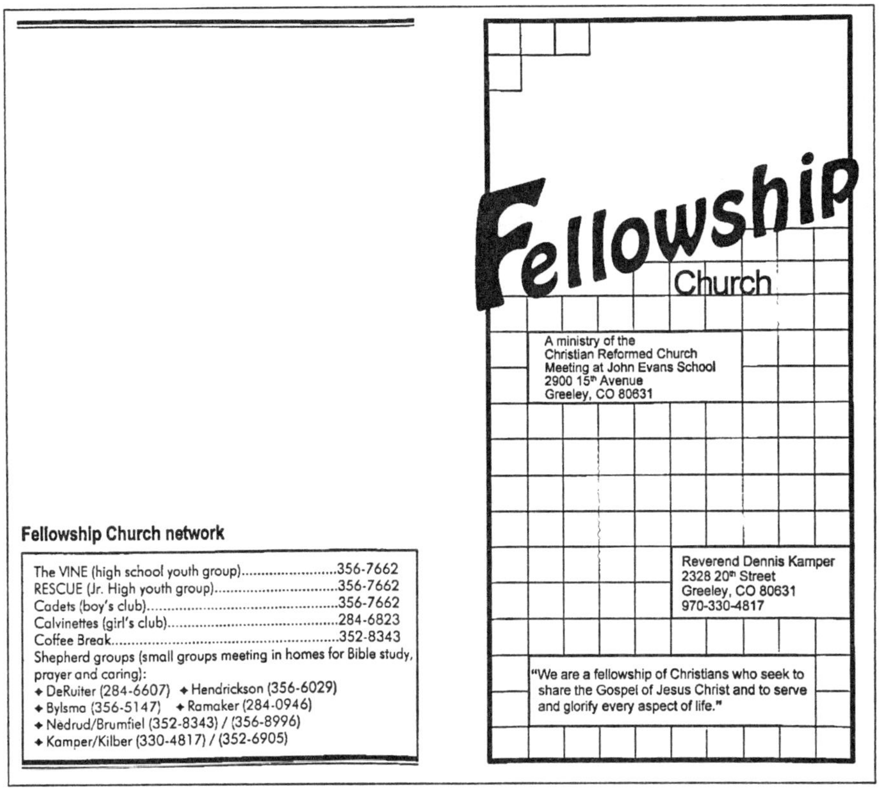

Fellowship Church

A ministry of the
Christian Reformed Church
Meeting at John Evans School
2900 15th Avenue
Greeley, CO 80631

Reverend Dennis Kamper
2328 20th Street
Greeley, CO 80631
970-330-4817

"We are a fellowship of Christians who seek to share the Gospel of Jesus Christ and to serve and glorify every aspect of life."

Fellowship Church network

The VINE (high school youth group)........................356-7662
RESCUE (Jr. High youth group)..............................356-7662
Cadets (boy's club)..356-7662
Calvinettes (girl's club)...284-6823
Coffee Break..352-8343
Shepherd groups (small groups meeting in homes for Bible study, prayer and caring):
✦ DeRuiter (284-6607) ✦ Hendrickson (356-6029)
✦ Bylsma (356-5147) ✦ Ramaker (284-0946)
✦ Nedrud/Brumfiel (352-8343) / (356-8996)
✦ Kamper/Kilber (330-4817) / (352-6905)

Fellowship Church
47th Avenue, 24th Street • Greeley, CO • 80631

A ministry of the Christian Reformed Church Reverend Dennis Kamper • 303/330-4817

Here is a copy of the church stationery from the same church. It has the same professional, clear, clean look that would be very appealing to a non-churched person.

Church newsletters

The Chimes

Newsletter of Bethany Lutheran Church

Volume 35 Number 8 August, 1995

"Awesome Adventures"

All kids three years old through sixth grade are invited to come along for some "Awesome Adventures" and learn about God's amazing deeds at this summer's Vacation Bible School.

The Awesome Adventures begin August 7 - 11. Each night the adventures begin at 5:30 p.m. with a light supper (there will be a free-will offering to help pay for the supper) and ends at 8:00 p.m.

The lessons will teach us about God's Amazing Deeds, and there will be games, great arts and crafts, and music. We will also have a nursery for younger children.

There is still time to register! Just call the office or Dean McDanel at 753-0883.

Praise at the Port!

An evening of music and praise to the honor and glory of God is being planned for Friday, August 25, from 7 to 10 p.m. at the Port of Burlington. (Bring your lawn chairs)

All area churches are invited to attend and/or participate in the service. A mass choir and band is being organized. If you are interested in taking an active part in the program (musical group, solo, quartet, mass choir or band, etc) contact First Church of the Nazarene at (319) 752-4245.

Preschool Open House and Registration
August 16, 1995
10 a.m. to noon

Meet Pastor from Tanzania

On Sunday, August 13, you are invited to participate in a special mission opportunity. You can meet Rev. Esther Ngomuo of the Pare Diocese, in Tanzania, East Africa, at a potluck luncheon beginning at 12:30 p.m., at Immanuel Lutheran Church, located at 607 North Orchard Street in Mediapolis.

The Pare Diocese of Tanzania, East Africa, is a companion synod to our own Southeastern Iowa Synod. That means we have a reciprocal "sister synod" relationship in which we share

An attractive, traditional church newsletter, but look at all the information they managed to put on the outside sheet.

Staff, schedules, mission statement, all sorts of important information is in an easy-to-read and very accessible form.

Our Mission Statement

Bethany Lutheran Church is dedicated to serving God by gathering to worship, to share in the sacraments, to proclaim the Gospel of Jesus Christ, to express the love of God through our service to others in order that all people may grow in faith to fulfill the teachings of our Lord.

Adopted by Congregational Council 7-9-92

1995 Congregation Council

Richard Bock - President & Social Ministry
Robert Sogard - Vice-President, Scholarship & Evangelism
Bonnie Rosenberg - Secretary & Christian Ed.
Mel Kopping - Treasurer & Finance
Mark Borchardt - Remembrance Treasurer
Dan Cox - Property
Carol Dodge - Worship & Music
Art Felgum - Evangelism
Annie McCabe - Youth
Greg Shottenkirk - Stewardship
Bob Volgt - Fellowship
Ebert Wischmeler - Remembrance

Bethany Lutheran Church
A Church For All People
2515 Madison Avenue
Burlington, Iowa 52601

Come ...Share The Spirit!

Services Every Sunday
7:30 a.m Worship
9 a.m Worship
10 a.m. Fellowship

Pastors
Rev. Carl J. Engstrom
Richard A. Bailey, Visitation

Staff
Organist Jean Zink
Custodian Bill Piper
Choir Director Romanne Mehaffy
Preschool Teacher/Director Tamara Levins
Preschool Assistant Cathy Frankforther
Executive Secretary Jackie Meyer
Our Missionaries - Tom & Keiko Dillon

Telephone (319) 752-3621 or 752-3622
Office hours 8:30 a.m. to 4:30 p.m. weekdays

A monthly newsletter published by Bethany Lutheran Church
Jackie Meyer, editor

Bethany Lutheran Church
2515 Madison Avenue
Burlington, Iowa 52601-6697

Address Correction Requested

Non-Profit Org
U.S. Postage
PAID
Permit No. 557
Burlington, IA 52601

Inside: Sneak Preview page 7

CHOIR NOTES

VOLUME 9 ISSUE 26
JULY 5, 1995
PRINCE AVENUE BAPTIST CHURCH

PRAYER REQUESTS

THOSE ON VACATIONS
BRENDA SPRATLIN
BYRON DAVID
DIANNE BAHNSEN
DONALD MITCHELL
GLENDA AND JERRY LEMONS
LINDA GORE
DARLA RICKETTS
STEVE HEMKEN
KELLIE DICKERSON
RALPH AND SUZANNE
ROGER BEVELS

PATTI WARREN
QUICK RECOVERY FROM
EMERGENCY APPENDECTOMY

BETTY MARTIN
CONTINUED RECOVERY

CONTINUED GROWTH
IN OUR ADULT CHOIR

PRAY THAT THE SPIRIT OF THE LORD WILL HAVE FREEDOM TO WORK IN OUR HEARTS SUNDAY!

PRAY FOR HOWARD AS HE PREACHED THIS SUNDAY MORNING AND EVENING!

HAPPY BIRTHDAY!

GLENDA LEMONS	JULY 6
SARAH WASHINGTON	JULY 6

THIS SUNDAY MORNING!!

ADULT CHOIR
"THE MUSIC OF YOUR PRAISE"
"HALLELUJAH! I LOVE HIM!"

SOLO
MARDIE SMITH

THIS SUNDAY NIGHT!!

ADULT CHOIR
"HOW MAJESTIC IS YOUR NAME"
"SINNER SAVED BY GRACE"

SOLO
ROSE ANN CARSON

WEDNESDAY NIGHT!!

ONE AWESOME REHEARSAL!!

THE SYSTEM SOUNDS GREAT

THE PARTY LAST FRIDAY NIGHT WAS ONE OF THE BIGGEST AND BEST SURPRISES OF MY LIFE!! ALTHOUGH WE DID SEE THE UNKIND AND NASTY SIDE OF A LOT OF PEOPLE I'M GRATEFUL THAT I WAS ABLE TO EXHIBIT A CONTROLLED AND ENCOURAGING SPIRIT IN THE FACE OF SO MANY ORNERY AND UNTRUE COMMENTS. SERIOUSLY, I LOVED IT ALL!! YOU ALL ARE SPECIAL PEOPLE AND I'M GRATEFUL FOR YOUR SUPPORT AND ~~ENCOURAGEMENT~~ - WELL, YOU UNDERSTAND! LET ME SAY A SPECIAL WORD OF THANKS TO TIP AND HIS CREW FOR THE GREAT JOB THAT THEY DID ON THE MEAL!! FANTASTICO!! FOR THOSE WHO PLANNED AND "EXECUTED" (SO TO SPEAK) THE PROGRAM I HAVE A SPECIAL "THANKS" THAT WILL COME WHEN YOU LEAST EXPECT IT!! FOR THE SOUND SYSTEM - I DON'T KNOW HOW TO SAY THANKS - IT'S GREAT!!

This is a great newsletter! There are many reasons why:

- *It's great to look at, has a fun, upbeat design.*
- *It is targeted to a clearly defined audience—the choir.*
- *An attitude of caring comes through in listing birthdays in a prominent place.*
- *Wonderful ministry attitude in its listing of "one awesome rehearsal!" The whole newsletter just makes a person want to sign up for this group—I bet they sound great also!*

October, 1994 Vol II Issue 5

The Parent Gazette

The monthly newsletter for parents of teens

The Power of Prayer

See You at the Pole!

What is "See You at the Pole" you ask? Well, it is a student-organized, student led and student-run gathering all across America. It began in Texas and has now spread to ever state in the union. The idea is that youth who truly care about the cause of Christ will stand up for their faith and for their school and spend a day in prayer for their school and the students in their school.

This year "See You at the Pole" was held on **Wednesday, Sept. 21st.** Downers South High School had more than 80 youth present at 7:00 a.m. to pray for their school. At Downers North, there were over 35 youth. Other schools in our area where youth gathered include Hinsdale South, Hinsdale Central and Westmont. Our church alone was represented at these school by over 20 youth! If you happen to see some of the youth, ask them about "See You at the Pole." You'll be glad you did!

Inside This Issue

Are You Successful?

There is more to success than merely external rewards. Have you considered that you might be more successful than you think? Consider the following suggestions:

1) Emphasize how what you do contributes to the greater good. Think about how you contribute to your family and friends.
2) Take pride in how well you do your job. Lean back occasionally to enjoy what you have accomplished.
3) Find rewards in the process of doing your job. Do not be overly concerned about results. Focus on the process and relish the quality of the experience.
4) Avoid depending on others to tell you how well you are doing. Develop an internal set of standards to guide you. But, keep your mind open to others' suggestions.
5) Do not be afraid to fail! Consider: "What one great thing would you do if you knew you could not fail?"

News for You . . .

Family Facts

The Barna Research Group is an organization that specializes in research for church leadership. It is the Christian equivalent of the Gallup Poll. George Barna has some new information out on the family that might surprise you. Here is a sampling:

- People who live together before marriage actually have a substantially higher divorce rate than those who live separately before marriage.
- Parents do not credit themselves with having the greatest influence on their children. Nor do they charge the media with that, either. They cite their children's friends as the biggest influencers.
- Before they reach the age of eighteen, two out of three children born this year will live in a single-parent household.
- Contrary to the popular belief most homemakers more satisfied with of their lives than who have children outside of the home.

If you would like to about the family, look Barna's book, *The Fut American Family*. You very interesting and info

It is often difficult for ministries who work with youth or children to know who to write the publication for—the kids or the parents.

This newsletter solves the problem by creating a newsletter specifically for parents. Doing this makes the editorial process and focus so much easier. You can have material that is directed precisely to parents without boring kids.

THE PARENT GAZETTE 3

"The times they are a changing" as the old saying goes. It is the time of year when we "fall" back into short days and early darkness. At the end of this month, **October 30th** to be exact, it is time to set our clocks ***BACK*** one hour. Actually, it would be better for you to set your clock back before you venture into deep REM sleep on the 29th (that way you do not forget and show up to church an hour early).

Don't forget to set your clocks back at the end of this month!!

Some news you can use

Why Teenagers Leave

The "Pastoral Ministry Newsletter" conducted a study recently on people who drop out of churches. Their results show that the greatest percentage of people leaving are teenagers, those usually in their upper teenage years. The reasons that teenagers gave for leaving the church are:

1. They get involved in other things.
2. They are put off by hypocrites. (of which they perceive as many in the church).
3. Church is dull and boring.
4. They do not like organized religion.
5. They move and do not get connected with a new church.
6. They have questions the church cannot answer.
7. They do not like the minister.
8. Their spiritual beliefs change.
9. Self-righteous people turn them off.
10. They resent the appeal for money.
11. Church people are unfriendly.
12. Their parents stop attending.

It is important for youth to remain connected at this critical stage in their lives. If you notice your youth's attendance slipping, ask why and see if there is a way to help them. Remember: a little encouragement can go a long way!

The Stress Factor

The term stress comes from the Latin word *stringere* meaning to bind tight or constrict. It is the result of unrelieved tension. Below are some questions that can help you assess your level of stress. Answer them as honestly as possible.

- Do you live under a constant sense of urgency and hurry?
- Do you find little time to unwind and relax?
- Does tension affect your relationships and cause sharp words?
- Do you feel time is passing too quickly?
- Do you seem to have little time just for you?
- Are you concerned about losing your job?
- Do you suffer from feelings of guilt for not doing everything you want?
- Are you always racing against the clock?
- Do you become irritable over things that are not important?
- Do you blame yourself for things over which you have no control?

If you answered yes to more than two of these questions, you may be experiencing stress. Perhaps, some stress management could improve your situation.

When Junior Highers Have Crushes

Many parents have a hard time admitting that their sweet, innocent children have now entered that stage of life where the opposite sex appears attractive. However, sooner or later, every parent must face the fact that the opposite sex has some portion of your youth's attention. Junior highers' crushes are common and good for them, according to child psychiatrist Dr. James Comer. "A crush is the junior highers' first step in attracting and being attracted to non-family members," says Comer. "It's the first step toward social and sexual intimacy."

Crushes generate new and powerful feelings that junior highers can experiment with safely. A crush lets youth learn more about romance without the risk of involvement. So, how can you as a parent help make this transition smoother?

- Tell your junior higher that it is normal for emotions to come and go, so he or she should enjoy the moment without expecting deeper involvement.
- Avoid making too much or too little of your youth's feelings. Be willing to talk about your own past experiences and acknowledge that you understand your youth's feelings.
- Keep the lines of communication open so that your youth will feel comfortable coming to talk to you about these often confusing emotions.

Youth.Net Journal

A Network of News and Notes Just for Youth Workers

Scripture Search

" My people come to you, as they usually do, and sit before you to listen to your words, but they do not put them into practice. With their mouths they express devotion, but their hearts are greedy for unjust gain."

— Ezekial 33:31

Attendees at the
May 2, 1995 Meeting:

Dan Amato
Tony Jones
Bruce McEvoy
Mike Peres
Mike Phillips
Kurt Richards
David Winkowitsch

Next Meeting: Mon., May 15 at Westmont Alliance Church
117 N. Cass Ave.

Upcoming Events

May 12 **SEDIT Meeting**
Admin. Building
at 63rd & Springside

June 12 "Volleyball Extravaganza" (Youth.Net)

Prayer Concerns

• A joy for Bruce McEvoy's graduation on May 6

• A joy for Bill Terry's installation on May 7

Vision for Ministry

We were fortunate to have David join us all the way from Wheaton. David first approached us with a devotional which was inspiring and motivating. He quoted Ezekiel 33:31 and shared how that verse had really impacted his own life recently. He shared that when we consider our ministries, it is not enough to just get them in the door. It is not enough to simply count the numbers present. Rather, we need to work on giving youth the drive and motivation to put their faith into action.

David went on to speak about his foundation and the purpose of it. This could possibly be a source of income for *Youth.Net* down the road. He also worked with us on helping us to think about how we define success in our ministry. He shared a diagram that speaks of the key elements to a strong ministry. Here it is:

He mentioned that many people do not really have a philosophy of ministry, nor have they defined what a successful ministry would be. He encouraged us to do so. The fact that we have our ministry statement finalized was a good step. Let's keep thinking about this as we go along.

Volleyball Extravaganza

We need to step up our planning for our Summer kick-off volleyball tournament. The date is **Monday, June 12.** At our next meeting we need to really begin to finalize this. Bruce said that his one sand court should be ready by then. Mike offered the YMCA acreage out back if we need. Also, Tom is still checking on the Illinois Tollway courts. All of this activity is due to the fact that McCullom is booked for leagues which begin on that day.

We talked about having a big banner and letting people see *Youth.Net* for some great exposure. This could be a fun day.

The details still need to be worked on, so come to the next meeting ready to plan for this. Here are some of the responsibilities that we have assigned:

• **Bruce:** will check on getting refs, through his own sources and others.

• **Tony:** He will also make registration forms for teams, flyers to advertise, etc.

• **Tom:** will check with the Illinois Tollway to see if their facilities on Finley Road are available on weekends.

Other Random Thoughts

- Dan says that he r getting us a treas definitely on our build *Youth.Net* while remaining

- Dan was the off "Hoops Hysteri great pictures, p own teens. If yo to show your yo Dan wouldn't mi

Here the newsletter has a more teen oriented look, but it is still clear and clean and could be enjoyed by parents also.

National Day of Prayer

On Thursday, May 4 the annual **National Day of Prayer** was observed by many churches. Did you take time out to pray, or were you too busy? Well, none of us should be too busy to pray. It is a vital part of that which goes into our ministry, and something that, without it, would make it impossible to truly do ministry. Here is what author John Biersdorf had to say in his book, *How Prayer Shapes Ministry*:

"When we pray, we essentially meet the silence of God. Not hearing an audible answer or seeing a picture before our eyes does not mean that God is absent or that prayer is futile. It means that God's answer is to create us anew, according to our freedom, our vocation, and God's self disclosing love. The essential insight here is that in an encounter with diving reality, we do not hear a voice, but rather acquire a voice."

Interesting thoughts on why prayer is so important to our ministries. As Matthew Fox puts it in his book, *How to Be a Musical, Mystical Dancing Bear*, "Prayer does not change God, but rather it changes us." Why not take some time now and pray . . . it will do both of you (God and you) some good.

Summer Ministry

Most of you probably have your summer all planned out. But, just in case you need a few more ideas, here are some events that you might find helpful in ministering to your youth. Possibly, we might be able to get a few groups together to head off for a fun event that would strengthen our groups. Watch the next few issues to see many ideas for the summer.

The first place to start is where most of your kids are . . . in the music realm. There are several summer music festivals each year that offer great contemporary Christian music, workshops, Bible studies, and great fellowship. Here is a list of some of the major ones:

- **Cornerstone '95:** June 29 - July 2 at the Cornerstone Farm in Bushnell, IL (near Peoria). 60 different artists will perform. The crowd is usually around 15,000. Call (312) 989-2087.

- **Atlanta Fest '95:** June 14-17 at Six Flags over Georgia. This fest averages around 30,000. DC Talk, Steven Curtis Chapman, Tony Campolo, Andy Stanley and Josh McDowell are already on the docket. Call (404) 424-8839.

- **Joy Jam '95:** June 24 at Cardinal Stadium in Louisville, Kentucky. They attract more than 20,000 each year. Over 10 artists will preform, including DC Talk and Susan Ashton. Call (502) 244-9614.

- **Son Shine '95:** July 6-8 at Wilmar, Minnesota. Son SHine brings in about 12,000 youth per year. Over 25 artists, including DC Talk, White Heart, Newsboys, Audio Adrenaline and more. Call (612) 235-0119.

- **Spirit Song II '95:** July 7 at King's Island in Cincinnati, Ohio. Approximatelt 10,000 youth are there. Amy Grant and Gary Chapman are on tap. Call (800) 898-1092.

News and Notes

★ Several things are on the horizon for the next month. Here is one way that we can help get involved with the community and begin to make inroads in order to help communicate the Gospel down the road: The first is **Downers North Graduation With Pride.** This is an all-night party that is completely alcohol and drug free. The school is always looking for more chaperones. Possibly we could help out with the early morning shifts, since they seem to be the most difficult to get volunteers for. The date for GWP is **Friday, June 9, 1995.**

★ **Mike Phillips mentioned that on his "Teen Nights" he would like to have us help and possibly give a devotional.** They are almost the same program as the Youth Group nights, except with the Christian emphasis. I think we are open to helping reach youth in whatever ways we can. If you would like to help, let Mike know.

★ The National Youth Workers Seminar is coming this fall. The dates are **October 4-8** in San Francisco, or **November 16-20** in Nashville. Perhaps we could car pool (or fly) and room together if more than one of us is going. Check your calendars.

page 2

YOUTH QUAKE

SR. HIGH SUMMER 1995 JUL-SEPTEMBER SPECIAL ACTIVITIES

Mega Worship and Bible Study

God's Gym

Sunday's at 6pm
HDC - room 13

don't miss out on this great time of being together with lots of other students for a "spiritual workout"! Tim Hartman and the Praise Band will lead worship and Craig and other leaders will be teaching from God's Word. *DON'T MISS OUT!!!!*

☞ **no God's Gym on August 27th (gone to Hume)**

Beach Days

July 13 to Huntington Beach
August 4 to Newport Beach
August 18 to Corona Beach

meet the bus at HDC each morning at 9am to head down to catch some gnarley beach action. Bring $5.00 to help pay for gas and parking. Bring a sack lunch or $ for the snack bar. Make sure to have a **MEDICAL RELEASE FORM** on file with Craig.

Tsunami!

July 17,18
details in God's Gym

this ALL NEW TSUNAMI features a day at **MAGIC MOUNTAIN** (amusement park) and **HURRICANE HARBOR** (water park). We'll be staying overnight at Master's College. **Sign up soon!**

Definitely designed for youth.

Fun, upbeat, something that a teenager wouldn't be embarrassed to leave around at school.

SPECIAL ACTIVITIES

T.R.A.S.H. NIGHTS

one Sunday night each month we get together as a group and head out on the bus to one of our "bud's" house for a great time of munchin' and funnin'. Don't miss these dates:

July 2nd
August 6th
September 10th

FUND RAISER

need money for camp, or other Sr. High Activities? Here are some more opportunities to make some of the much needed bucks:

JULY 27 BOWL-A-THON
AUGUST 5 CARWASH-A-THON

check with Craig to get details and sponsor sheets!

MAV'S GAME
Aug. 11th
7pm Cost:$5.00
SIGN UP IN GOD'S GYM
(it's 50cent hotdog/Pespsi night!)

HIKING AT BIG BEAR

Sat. July 29
9am
Cost: $3.00
sign up in GOD'S GYM

ALL-CHURCH PICNIC AT MAVERICK'S STADIUM

Sunday, Sept. 3rd
stay tuned for all the hot details!

PICNIC

NEWPORT DAY

September 23rd
Cost: $5.00
1 - 10pm

grab your ROLLERBLADES, BIKE, or just your swimsuit for a great day down at the Balboa Pier at Newport Beach. The evening will end with a bonfire and smores. Invite your friends and get signed up in God's Gym.

HUME LAKE SUMMER CAMP

August 27 - September 2
Cost: $250.00

spots are going very fast for the hottest camp in the west, so don't wait any longer...get a registration form in to Craig right away and be sure to have your spot reserved! Fundraisers and partial scholarships are available. Speakers this year are: Dave Moore, and Charlie Scanlon. Oh, by the way..***KA JABI KAN KAN?!?***

SEE YOU AT THE POLE!

Wednesday, September 20th
(at your high school campus' flagpole)Before school starts
☞ don't miss the first **WEDNESDAY NIGHT LIVE!** of the school year that night!!!

Church surveys

Bethany Evangelical Lutheran Church
2515 Madison Avenue
Burlington, IA 52601

Stir us Lord

Offering Our Time and Abilities

___I/We will attend worship and receive Holy Communion faithfully.

___I/We will make daily devotions a part of our life.

___I/We will pray daily.

Please check areas where you are willing to help in 1994:

10 Christian Education
- ❑ 01 Christian Ed. Committee
- ❑ 02 Sunday School Coord.
- ❑ 03 Vac. Bible School Coord.
- ❑ 04 Church & SCS Librarian
- ❑ 05 Christmas Program
- ❑ 06 Nursery Attendant

Teachers:
- ❑ 07 Adults
- ❑ 08 High School Youth
- ❑ 09 Youth (Grades 5-8)
- ❑ 10 Children (Grades K-4)
- ❑ 11 Nursery and Toddlers
- ❑ 12 Vacation Bible School

11 Property
- ❑ 01 Property Committee
- ❑ 02 Building Maintenance (Carpenter, Painting)
- ❑ 03 Grounds Maintenance (Lawns, Snow removal)

12 Evangelism
- ❑ 01 Evangelism Committee
- ❑ 02 Member Visitations
- ❑ 03 Prospective Member Visitor
- ❑ 04 Make Phone Calls
- ❑ 05 Visit Members in Hospital

13 Finance/Remembrance
- ❑ 01 Finance Committee

14 Social Ministry
- ❑ 01 Social Min. Committee
- ❑ 02 Visitation of Shut-ins
- ❑ 03 Transportation Coord.
- ❑ 04 Transportation to and from worship

15 Stewardship
- ❑ 01 Stewardship Committee
- ❑ 02 Member Visitor

16 Worship and Music
- ❑ 01 Worship and Music
- ❑ 02 Adult Choir Member
- ❑ 03 Youth Singer Member
- ❑ 04 Nursery Attendant
- ❑ 05 Usher
- ❑ 06 Greeter
- ❑ 07 Altar Guild Member
- ❑ 08 Piano and Other Instruments
- ❑ 09 Lector
- ❑ 10 Communion Assistant
- ❑ 11 Acolyte

17 Youth
- ❑ 01 Youth Committee
- ❑ 02 Middle School Leader
- ❑ 03 High School Leader
- ❑ 04 Camping Leader
- ❑ 05 Program Participant

19 Congregational Council
- ❑ 01 Council Member

20 Women of the Church (WELCA)
- ❑ 01 Circle Membership
- ❑ 02 Circle Bible Study Leader
- ❑ 03 WELCA Participant
- ❑ 04 Help Make Quilts

21 Public Images
- ❑ 01 Banner Making
- ❑ 02 Sign an
- ❑ 03 Newsle

We offer thanksgivin the work of

Name______________________Phone______

Address______________________Zip___

Surveys like these are excellent tools for ministry.

They give the staff a way to get to know their congregation better and they give church members a way to respond and offer their gifts and services.

BETHANY LUTHERAN CHURCH
EVERY MEMBER SURVEY REPORT

Name ______________________ Home Phone ____________

Address ______________________ Birthdate ___/___/___

____

Marital Status __________ Membership Status: Baptized ________ Confirmed ________

Employer ______________________ Job/Occupation ______________________

Other Family Members: If appropriate, list school attending and current grade level.

______________ ______________________________

______________ ______________________________

______________ ______________________________

______________ ______________________________

______________ ______________________________

ACTIVITIES: (Circle all that apply)

Baseball	Cards	Ice skating	Choir	Other ____________
Softball	Hiking	Roller Skating	Band	____________
Basketball	Running	Swimming	Orchestra	____________
Bicycling	Track	Bingo	Volleyball	____________
Bowling				

HOBBIES: (Circle all that apply)

Bird watching	Needlepoint	Sewing	Reading	Other ____________
Woodworking	Crocheting	Knitting	Crafts	____________

ORGANIZATIONS: (Circle all that apply)

B.A.D.C.O.	Lions	Chamber of Commerce	Other ____________
Optimists	Coin Club	Rotary	____________
Eagles	Boy Scouts	Elks	____________
Kiwanis	Girl Scouts	YMCA/YWCA	

Have you ever served on the church council? YES NO

Have you ever served on any of the following church committees? (Circle if yes)

Christian Education	Evangelism	Social Ministry
Worship & Music	Property	Stewardship
Youth	Other ____________	

Posters

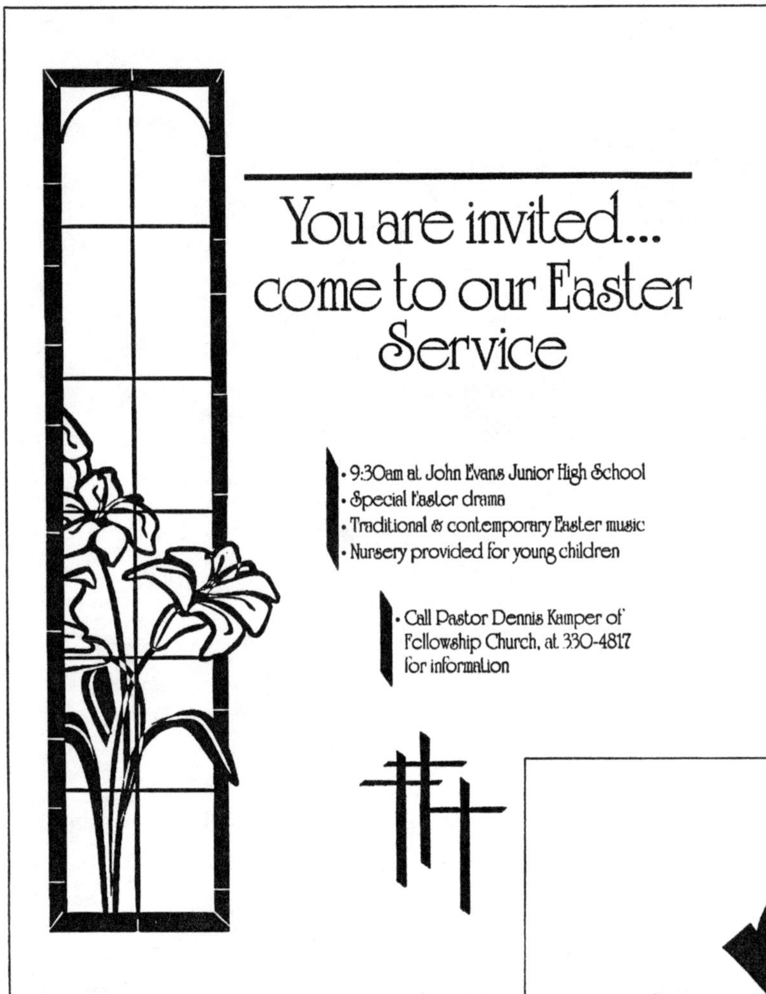

As these two pages illustrate, posters can be used for a variety of ministry reasons. You can print them for serious reasons or fun reasons.

They can be any size, from small bulletin inserts, to full-size sheets of paper. If you want them larger, Kinkos printing shops have an enlarger that can take your master 8 1/2 x 11-inch piece of paper and turn it into an 18 x 24-inch sheet.

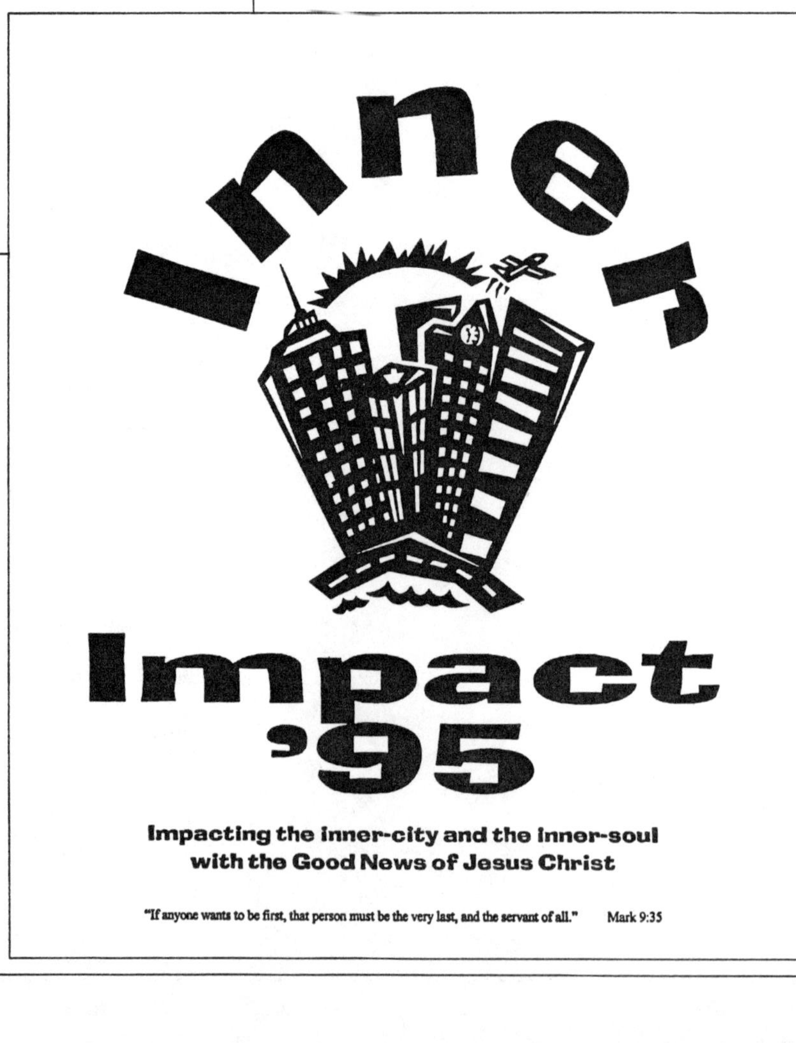

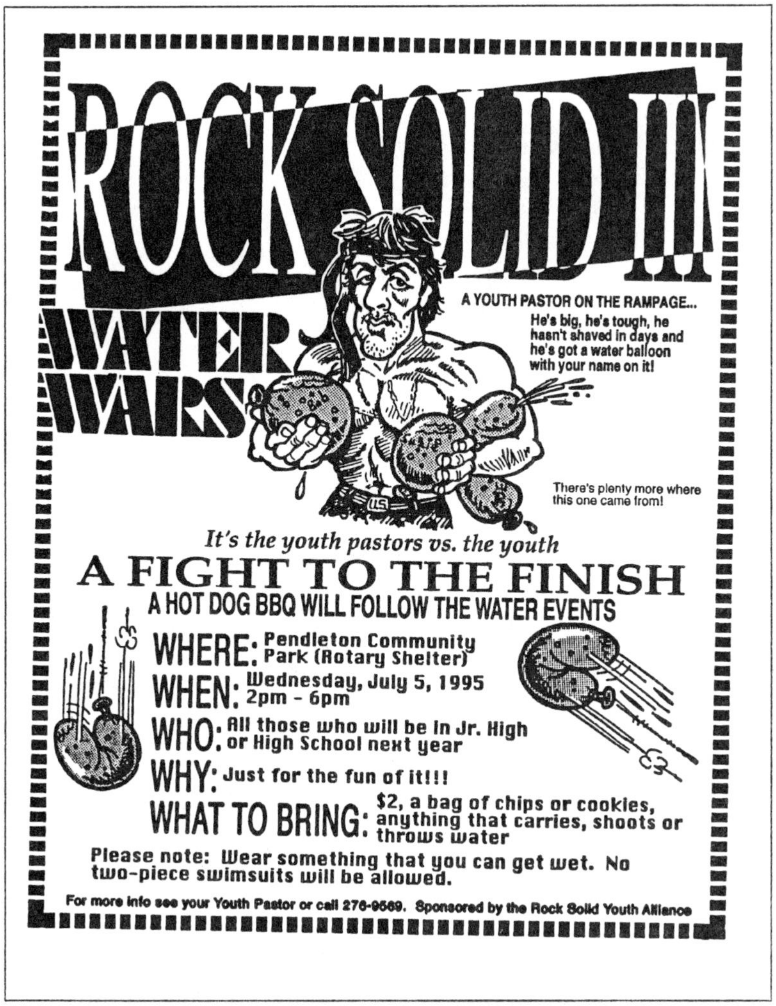

Strong graphics make both of these posters winners. They draw your eye into the page and then to the message.

Miscellaneous DTP projects

Door hangers are great invitations that you could easily pass out around your neighborhood. You can make them out of cardstock and either cut them out of regular sheets, or you can buy precut door hangers at paper stores that you can print your image on.

SOMEONE FROM

Olive Branch Church of God

Came by to wish you a wonderful Christmas and to invite you to worship with us.

SERVICES

Christmas Cantata "Jesus Is Born"
Sunday evening, Dec. 17 7:00 p.m.

Christmas Eve Candlelight & Communion
Sunday evening, Dec. 24 at 10:00 p.m.

Sunday School 9:30 a.m. Worship 10:30 a.m.

Here a bookmark does triple duty as bookmark, prayer list and reminder of the building project the church is involved in.

BUILDING *by* FAITH

REMEMBER TO PRAY

- ✦That all we do will glorify the Lord.
- ✦For wisdom and leadership for our steering committee.
- ✦For all those who serve in the "Building by Faith" campaign.
- ✦That all will seek and follow God's will.
- ✦That each individual will experience *Sacrificial Giving.*
- ✦For all to trust in God.
- ✦For the Special Event on December 4th.
- ✦For the Celebration Sunday on December 18th.

Postcards are a great way to invite, advertise and motivate. Since the recipient doesn't even have to wrestle with getting an envelope open, it's much more likely they will be read also.

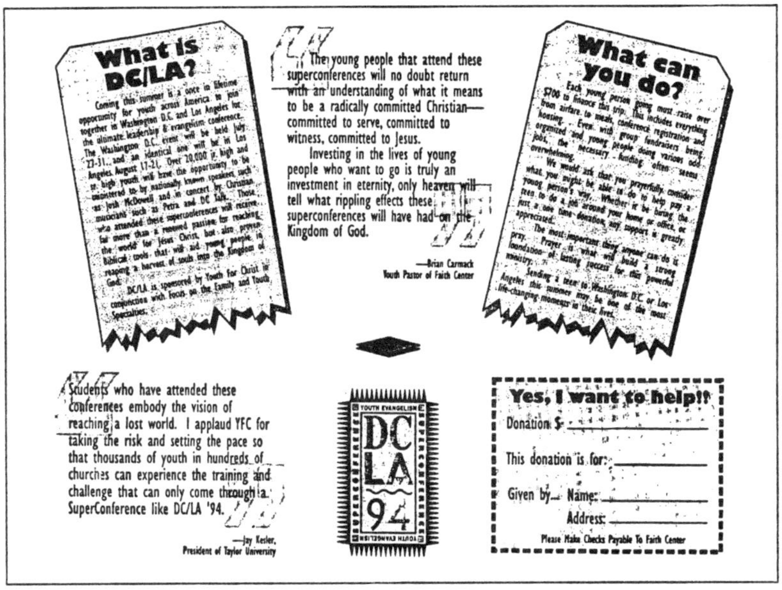

Church report

St. John's Midyear Resource Report 1995

Contents

Cover artwork by congregation member, Jim Koertge

Proverbs tell us to know the status of our ministry, and this flyer does a fantastic job—beautiful graphics, clear text. It's the quality of an annual report for a company.

St. John's Is Changing.

The congregation of St. John's church is in a time of rapid growth. Growth takes different forms. Becoming larger is only one indication of growth. Another form of growth is becoming stronger, able to deal with new forces, in better ways, with more effective impacts. This is the growth we are now enduring. The stress has been difficult for many, but the opportunities for growth have been plentiful.

During the past few months several changes have been made which hope to lay the foundation for other forms of growth in the future.

The most obvious changes is the process of selecting a senior pastor. Unfortunately we were not able to convince the first candidate to accept the call issued by the congregation, so we continue the process by looking at other candidates. The first call was not lost time. Through the process we have reexamined our expectations of the senior pastor and the associate pastors as well as the role of all lay members and staff of the congregation. We now have a refined concept of being a pastor, a lay leader, and a member of this congregation. This effort will make us a stronger congregation in the future.

The selection of a senior pastor is not the only significant growth for strength going on. Over the past few months, an increased number of congregation member have increased their level of participation in various committees and task forces established by the Council. This change has allowed members to fulfill their roles for becoming effective members of the congregation. Most of these committees include a staff member and a council member along with several other members of the congregation. Other methods for increasing communication have also been developed.

The Council has spent considerable time this spring dealing with other issues such as the financial status and changes needed in the constitution and bylaws. We have also spent time addressing the role of the council, the way meetings are conducted, and ways to respond to the congregation expressed needs.

During the difficult times, no group has felt the impact more than the staff. These individuals work with the issues on a daily basis. It is obvious to me that each wants what is best for the congregation. When you see them, tell them how much you appreciate what they do. Then contact them when you have questions or suggestions.

Proofing is the one desktop publishing skill that you cannot do on your own. It is impossible to see all of your own mistakes.

chapter 11 Proofing

"The urge in a human to love or to hate, is never as strong as the urge to amend the writings of another."

quote from a class on editing

Once you've written, illustrated and laid out your material, you need to proof it to correct mistakes and to make certain you've accomplished your communication goals. For successful proofing in desktop publishing, you need to learn to proof on each level of your work—text, type, graphics and layout.

It's very important to not try to proof on all levels at the same time. If you do, you'll skip mistakes because you're concentrating on too many things at one time.

Following are tips for proofing each level of your DTP project. Go through them one at a time to polish your work.

Proofing text

One of the most fun things about E-mail and the Internet—no proofing required!

Nobody worries about proofing messages sent through E-mail. Typos, misspellings, sloppy grammar—you see it all the time and it really doesn't matter. You know what the person is trying to say.

We do need to be more careful in our professional church publications, but it's nice to rest from the rigors of proofing somewhere in our communications life.

Proofing text can take place in two ways. First, you can proof the text in your word processing program. Often in ministry publications, the text is first created in a word processing program (for example, the pastor or leader writes an article) and then it is transferred into a DTP program.

If text is to go through major editing and revisions, do as many corrections as you can before you put it into your DTP layout.

Second, you can place the text into your layout and then proof it at that stage. If the text comes to you close to the correct length and the changes will be minor, it is sometimes easiest to go ahead and lay it out in your publication and then proof it. If major changes are made in the text after it has been laid out, it can take excessive amounts of time and effort to make the changes.

Whatever method you use to create text, follow these tips:

- Put your copy aside for at least a few hours— a day if possible.
- Print out your text on paper. It is very difficult to catch all the errors on the computer screen.
- Have someone besides the creator proof it—it is impossible for the creator to see all the errors.
- Read it out loud or have someone read it to you; you'll catch lots of awkward constructions that way.
- Use your spell checker, but don't let it be the final authority. It can't tell the difference between words that are spelled correctly but in the wrong context. For example, your and you're will pass the spell checker, but may be incorrect in context.
- For the same reasons, don't only read text backwards to proof it. If you do, you become a human spell checker because though you catch typos, you are reading out of context.

Key proofing tip #1: Make sure everyone doing proofing uses same system to mark corrections. Nothing is more frustrating than seeing something like this:

> ? The leadership group decided to promote the Promise-makers program at the meeting next week.

What does that mean? Is the term the wrong term? Spelled incorrectly? No hyphen needed? What does it mean?

For proofing to work well, be sure everyone uses the same system and are clear about what they want changed. On the next page is a handout you can give to everyone you work with to make your proofing consistent.

The only thing that would make it worse is if the person who did the proofing did it in light pencil and you couldn't see the circle. Which brings up the second key point on proofing.

Key proofing tip #2: Use a pen for proofing that can be clearly seen. Ones that work best are felt-tipped purple or dark green. Avoid using a pencil or a red pen.

It's often misplaced kindness that causes the problems in this area. People are sometimes hesitant to proof boldly, they are afraid they will hurt your feelings. So they will proof lightly in pencil. Unfortunately, despite all of these good intentions, what often happens is that its very easy to miss corrections made in pencil.

The problem can be easily solved by giving people a bright purple or green pen and telling them to proof boldly—that clear corrections will help you make the changes wanted.

- Proof your text in levels. Some of the biggest mistakes in proofing are made in the headlines. We tend to get so focused on body text, we overlook the big stuff. Proof the body text, and then go back separately and proof headlines, call-outs, subheads, and captions.
- If you have to proof on the screen, here are some ideas that can help you see mistakes. Changing the page size from 100 percent to 200 percent will help catch a lot of errors. Change italics to normal. These changes will help in the proofing process, but be sure to change the text back before it is printed.

On the next page is a form that can be shared with everyone involved in a DTP project. If everyone uses the same system, it should make the proofing and corrections process go smoothly.

Proofing instructions for____________________

Thank you for taking time to proof this material. We all want our publications to be the best they can be and the proofing process helps us accomplish that goal.

Guidelines for proofing:

- Below are the symbols to use in making your corrections. In addition to using these symbols, please make any additional notes, such as the correct spelling of an incorrectly spelled word in the margin.
- Please use a brightly colored pen, not pencil to do the corrections. If the corrections are to be faxed, used a dark-colored felt-tip pen.
- Do not make corrections in the margin if they are to be faxed.
- If you have a question about something, write it out in the margin or place a number and clearly write it out on another page, under that number. Do not just put in a question mark.
- If you want a section of text inserted, if it is more than a few words, place a letter at the insertion point and clearly write or type the text under that letter on another page.

Proofing symbols:

Symbol	Meaning
teext	delete letter
texttext	delete word
text.	delete punctuation
text proof	
twet	transpose
sp Josahua Joshua	spelling problem
prooftext #	space
te xt	close up space
text. The	delete extra space
¶	new paragraph
proof / text	no new paragraph
text]	move right
[text	move left
Text or lc	lowercase
text or cap	capitalize
text or ital	italicize
text rom	Roman or normal type
text or bf	boldface
text wf	wrong font or typeface
text stet	let it stand, no correction
txt	insert
text text	insert hyphen
text	insert comma
texts	insert apostrophe
text	insert quotation marks
text	insert period

Style guides

One of the best tools for proofing and for creating consistent publications is a style guide created specifically for your desktop publishing projects. Instead of specifying grammar and word usage rules, a DTP style guide specifies type sizes, leading and layout specifications for the publication. This type of style guide does not replace your grammatical style guide, but is needed for DTP publications in addition to it.

If you have style guides like this on file for your publications it also makes it much easier to train others to produce the publications. If an emergency comes up, it's essential.

When you create a style guide for your publications, lay out a dummy page like this using the actual sizes and leading of the type. Then specify on the sheet the type face, size, leading measurements and any other spacing notes.

Additional guidelines including how to box photos, how to layout ads, or any additional information can also be included on the sheet.

Friday, September 21,1996 **News** The Christian Messenger/page 3

Experts discuss mission plans

• Level one head: Avant Garde 36/36 B

• A 4 pt. line can be used between some stories

Grants to be awarded to top projects

• Level two head: Avant Garde 24/24 B

Money to aid mission research and fund conference attendance

•Subtitle: Palatino, ital. 14/16, indented 5

by Jenny Murphy
The Christian Messenger

• Text: Palatino 10/12 x 10.5, l pica paragraph indent

• Byline: 10/10 Palatino, extra space between byline and start of story

Lorem ipsum dolor sit amet, consectetuer adipiscing elit, sed diam nonummy nibh euismod tincidunt ut laoreet dolore magna aliquam erat volutpat. Ut wisi enim ad minim veniam, quis nostrud exerci tation ullamcorper suscipit lobortis nisl ut aliquip ex ea commodo consequat. Duis autem vel eum iriure dolor in hendrerit in vulputate velit esse molestie consequat, vel illum dolore eu feugiat nulla facilisis at vero eros et accumsan et iusto odio dignissim qui blandit praesent luptatum zzril delenit augue duis dolore te feugait nulla facilisi. Lorem ipsum dolor sit amet, consectetuer adipiscing elit, sed diam nonummy nibh euismod tincidunt ut laoreet dolore magna aliquam erat volutpat. Ut wisi enim ad minim veniam, quis nostrud exerci tation ullamcorper

The mission development center is not only for those groups suffering from financial troubles

Duis autem vel eum iriure dolor in hendrerit in vulputate velit esse molestie consequat, vel illum dolore eu feugiat nulla facilisis at

• Callout: Avant Garde 12/14 Bold, surrounding lines 2 point

Other notes:

•Indent 1 pica for text inside boxes
•Drop down l pica to hang your headlines below previous last line
•Leave l pica of space between end of story and graphic
•Be sure all graphics and ads line up with grid lines; if they aren't big enough and cannot be altered, draw a l pt. line to box them.

Kronin elected to Mission Association Executive Council

• Level three head: Avant Garde 18/18, can be used as a main head inside boxes

Photo credit, Palatino 6/6 upward and on left side, e.g. credit FUMC

Photo captions Palatino 9/11 Bold, length of picture. Photos cropped to fill box. Use a hairline rule for the box. Caption is Palatino 8 pt.

Lorem ipsum dolor sit amet, consectetuer adipiscing eli

euismod tincidunt ut laoreet dolore magna aliquam erat volutpat. Ut wisi enim ad minim veniam, quis nostrud exerci tation

• Boxed text is 12 /14 Bold Avant Garde

Type proofing

After proofing the text, go over all of your type without looking at the words and check:

- Are all of the sections, such as headlines, captions, subheads, in the same size and the same style?
- Do you have too many conflicting typefaces or sizes in your publication?
- Do the typeface selection and size help make the organization of the message clear?

Graphics proofing

After text and type, look at your graphics. Things to check:

- Are all the lines the proper length and thickness?
- Do all photos have a hairline box around them?
- Are any photos or illustrations upside down? (It happens.)
- Are the right captions with the right illustrations? Are written captions included for all your photos and graphics?

Layout proofing

Sometimes when you get to this point, it's too late to make massive changes. At this point it is more of an evaluation of what you'll do better next time. Ask yourself:

- Does the page look too crowded or too empty? You might be able to add a quote or call-out if you need to fill some space.
- Is there a good balance of photos or illustrations and text?
- Is it easy to see what sections belong together?
- Does it look readable? Inviting? Or is it something you'd put aside?
- What changes do you want to make next time?

Fax proofing tips

If you are sending a document back and forth via fax machine to be proofed here are some tips:

- Do your proofing with a fine felt-tip black pen. A pencil and most ballpoint pens do not reproduce well enough for the receiving person to see all the changes you have made.
- Do not make any corrections in the margins. Most fax machines do not read to the edges of an 8 1/2 x 11 sheet of paper and corrections made in the margins may not come through.

If there is not enough room in the body of the piece you are working on to write your corrections, take some of the opaque tape and cover a line above or below the place you want to make the correction and write on that the correction you want to make.

Know when to quit proofing

"Perfection is spelled paralysis."

Winston Churchill

Because you can make changes up to minutes before production, one of the most important things to learn in proofing DTP publications, your own or others, is knowing when to quit. You can ruin your relationships with everyone you work with and drive yourself crazy if you don't learn this. It is especially hard to do because two things seem to be constants in working on DTP publications:

DTP projects are always done on tight deadlines

*More important than any proofing rule is the bottom-line rule of newspaper work—**meet your deadline.** Everything else is icing on the cake.*

It does no good for something to be beautiful and perfect if people get it a day before the planned event.

Better a bit untidy and out in plenty of time, than perfect and late. Lots of perfectionist folks don't like to hear that, but people are always more important than perfection and in church offices we often don't have the time or energy to be perfect.

Part of this is the overall time crunch inherent in any ministry. Part is excessive expectations of the magic of DTP. You might realize rationally that the deadline you agreed to was ridiculous. At the same time, when you're starting out and don't have the experience of knowing how long certain projects will take, it's easy to cut yourself short on time.

There are always ways to do DTP projects better

If you just edited it a bit sharper . . . if you got the two pages balanced a little more, if you could get that headline to fit a bit better or crop that picture a little tighter or . . . you can drive yourself crazy with options on DTP. Sure, some of them might make a little bit "better" publication, but when you find yourself pushing in this area, always ask, "At what cost can I make it better?"

Yes, there are monetary costs involved, if you decide to do spot color at the last minute, for example. More important are the human costs.

Maybe the person doing the desktop publishing is a volunteer. Is it really worth the cost of their time if they have to stay a couple of extra hours to make changes?

Maybe the grammar isn't perfect, but is it worth the cost in hard feelings to ask the author of the piece to rewrite it?

Maybe you don't have a perfect, powerful action photo and the shot of the youth pastor you are going to use is five years old. But do you have the money or the time to get the film, find a camera, take the pictures, and get them developed without working an extra evening and Saturday?

It's OK if you say no to all of these questions. You'll always have a chance for improvement on the next project.

Have an ice-cream cone and remind yourself that only one perfect publication was ever produced—the Bible—and it was produced in part to tell us that we aren't perfect.

The paper and production method you choose can provide the perfect completing touch to your desktop project. Think about some new methods such as faxing to reach today's audiences.

chapter 12

Paper, Printing and Production

After proofing your project, two jobs remain before your message reaches your audience—selecting your paper and production of your project.

The language of paper

There is no right or wrong, no exact rules for paper choice. You just need to match your paper to your message and budget.

The chapter on typography discussed how the different typefaces have a voice. Paper also communicates in distinctive ways. What would it say about your church or ministry if you:

a. Printed your newsletter on hot pink paper with purple ink?

b. Printed your newsletter on slick, glossy white paper, with dark, steel gray ink and four-color photographs?

c. Printed your newsletter on a creamy beige paper, with black ink and second accent color, such as rust brown, on the nameplate?

You could have exactly the same newsletter, but the paper you choose would communicate a different message.

When choosing paper consider these factors:

For a fascinating catalog of papers for desktop publishing call:

Paper Direct
1-800-A-PAPERS

Audience

Hot pink paper would probably not appeal if you were targeting your newsletter to an upper-class executive neighborhood, but it might be just right if you are promoting the junior high car wash.

In the same way, the glossy, four-color printing job would be unnecessary for the high school ski camp.

For most projects, an off-white paper, in either beige or gray tones with black ink, and maybe one accent color, would work well for a large variety of projects.

Cost

If you have a choice between a second color or using a nicer paper, go with a nicer paper. The look and feel of a good quality paper can improve the look of your publication tremendously.

To save money on paper, check the Yellow Pages for paper suppliers; go to a paper outlet and buy it by the case; see if you can get a discount by buying your paper in bulk from a supplier.

There are also companies such as Paper Direct who sell papers preprinted with colors and designed to go through your laser printer without causing it problems.

Printing process

Be sure your paper choice will work with your printing process.

If you are going to print your project using your laser printer, be sure your paper was made specifically to go through your laser printer. Otherwise paper fibers or ink of a preprinted design can sometimes flake off and ruin your printer.

Design considerations

Are you going to use photos? If so do not print on blue or purple or green paper, because the color of the paper will show through and you'll have blue, purple, or green people.

Are you printing on both sides of the paper? If so, you'll need a paper that is fairly opaque. You pay more as the degree of opacity increases, especially in white paper.

If you want to figure out how opaque something is, just hold a sample of the paper over printed material. If you can see the printed material through the paper, ask for a more opaque paper.

To learn more about papers

Contact paper suppliers listed in the Yellow Pages and ask them for paper sample books. These sample books will show you the look and feel of different kinds of paper and samples of how they can be used.

Printing tips

Mock-ups —for you and the printer

Put together a dummy of your publication before you take it to the printer. Cut, paste, staple and color to make your piece fit together and look as much as possible as it will after it is printed. Use photocopies of pictures, if you will be using them, and paste them in their proper places. A detailed mock-up will help you spot any problems and will give the printer an exact picture of what you want.

After you have chosen your paper, printing is the final operation of your project.

Whether you are printing your project in-house on a laser printer or photocopy machine or having a commercial printer do it, follow these two steps:

Talk to the person doing the printing in the planning stages of your project

The more complex your job and the less you understand about the printing process, the more important it is to do this. Tell the printer what you are planning to do and ask if there are any problems with achieving your desired result. Ask them for suggestions, but remember you have to make the final design decisions.

Printers are your partners, not adversaries. So often when folks have trouble with their printers it is because they didn't take time to talk through a project. Take the time to get to know them and your projects will go much more smoothly.

Be honest with them about your schedule and don't expect miracles if you get your material in later than you planned.

Always take a mock-up of your project to whoever is doing the printing.

Assume nothing. The page order of your newsletter or brochure might make perfect sense to you, but it doesn't always make sense to the person doing the printing. A mock-up is also a great final check for you to make sure your project goes together as you planned. Finally, if something goes wrong in the printing, with a mock-up and clear written directions you can tell who is responsible for the mistake.

Distribution beyond paper—audiotapes, videos and CDs, faxes

"Multimedia is changing the nature of reading itself. Instead of . . . the linear presentation of text as printed in books, multimedia makes reading dynamic by giving words an important new dimension. In addition to conveying meaning, words in multimedia serve as triggers that readers can use to expand the text . . . by providing more text [and] by bringing it to life with sound, pictures, music and video."

Fred T. Hofstatter,
Multimedia Literacy

Though desktop publishing makes it easier than ever to reap the benefits of the miracle of printing, the medium you now use to deliver your desktop published message to your audience can go beyond paper printing to multimedia.

Audiotapes, videos and CD-ROMS and faxes are familiar technologies you can make use of. If you've got facilities and people working in your church or ministry who are skilled in some of these areas, encourage them to venture into new areas for the sake of the gospel.

These are also great areas to recruit volunteers to become involved in, especially younger folks. Many of these people have skills they have developed in high tech jobs and they don't have a way to use these skills for the sake of the kingdom of God. Many times they can also get permission to use extremely expensive equipment on their time off. Ask around, you'll probably be surprised at the expertise available to you.

Audiotapes

Businesses and corporations have long recognized the usefulness of creating audiotapes to pass along training or motivational information. If you live in an area where lots of folks in your congregation commute, why not try an audio newsletter once a quarter? Most churches have tape duplication systems for sermons already.

Have the senior pastor and various staff members talk about what they are doing, what is on their hearts, what they are praying for. Edit it by putting in opening and closing comments.

Or try an audio newsletter to the parents of your youth department. As a youth director, share the burdens of your heart, ask them to pray for specific kids and projects, pray together for the kids on tape. In today's frantic world, it may be tough to schedule a prayer meeting, but Jesus promises to be with us when we pray even if it's during a busy freeway commute.

Video and CD-ROM

Machines that master CDs have dropped under $2,000 for a quality machine, making this technology a possibility for many ministries.

High end DTP software, such as Pagemaker can be used to create much of the content for CDs.

There are numerous video editing programs for computers and many churches are getting them. Some of the programs can integrate the results of your DTP projects in with action video. Why not create a newcomer's video of your church? Have the youth of the church make it their project.

Much of the same equipment and software that is used to make videos can also be used to master CD-ROMS. Though out of the price range of many ministries now, the cost is dropping rapidly. A church produced CD could have photos, voice messages and videos of the staff and programs. It could have schedules, bios or maps of a facility. A huge amount of information could be stored that could be given to members and visitors.

Faxes

Many of the business people in your congregation have fax machines. You can broadcast fax from most PCs today. After you've created your DTP masterpiece, sending it out via fax will save you printing and postage costs.

Consider these uses:

• Send out encouragements, minutes and prayer requests to members of various ministry committees. Church and mission boards could benefit especially from this.

• Find out who would like to be on a prayer chain via the fax machine. Not only folks who work, but lots of people have fax machines in their homes.

• This is a lot more complex, but if you attend a larger, seeker oriented church, consider setting up a fax-on-demand system for your church. You need specialized software to do that and a dedicated fax machine.

Once it is operational you can have various DTP created publications stored in your system, and by dialing a number folks can have info faxed to their fax machine immediately.

Novelty items from baseball caps to billboards

For how to make decals, bumper stickers, message pads, magnets and much more get a copy of The Desktop Publishers Idea Book *by Chuck Green, Bantam Publishing.*

You can create masters from your DTP system to make any sort of imaginable gift or novelty item. I've literally created everything from coffee cups to billboards using mine, with a number of T-shirt creations thrown in. These can be used for youth groups, outreach and as awards. For ideas look in the novelty or gift item section of the Yellow Pages in your local phone directory.

What comes off your computer is just the master for DTP communication. Use your imagination for the final form it can take to communicate your message.

As disciples of Jesus Christ, we are commanded to go into all the world to preach the gospel—today cyberspace is part of that world and this book has taught you the skills to communicate in it.

chapter 13

The Internet

A digit originally meant a finger, our original counting tool. Today, digital is the basic concept for defining all computer communication.

This book is about using your computer to help you communicate better. Building on these familiar technologies is cyberspace, the Internet and new ways for us to share the gospel message.

All of the skills this book teaches you are directly applicable to communicating online and creating your own Web sites for your church and ministry. Your church bulletins, newsletters and all the other publications of your ministry can go on-line and have an outreach far beyond what you can currently imagine.

As you explore this new arena, some background definitions and explanations might be helpful. The following section is adapted from the newsletter *Cyberchurch Update.*

Digital: the building blocks of the information age

CYBERCHURCH UPDATE

News, stories, and commentary to inform and challenge the church to be an informed and effective witness for Jesus Christ in the information age.

Cyberchurch Update gets its name and inspiration from cyberspace—a term used to describe the world inside computers that has moved from the realm of science fiction to become a new frontier for the church of Jesus Christ.

Cyberspace winds through our world in the form of computers, television, the Internet and online services, CDs, video games, and virtual reality. As disciples of Jesus Christ we are commanded to go into all the world to preach the gospel—today cyberspace is part of that world.

Cyberchurch Update will help you get to know that world. It will introduce you to people ministering in it; it will challenge, inspire, and sometimes disturb you. You'll get condensed news from variety of specialized secular publications and commentary on the implications of that news.

Cyberspace—it's your space now—help make it part of the Kingdom of God.

"One of the most remarkable aspects of this new communications technology is that it will eliminate distance. It won't matter if someone you're contacting is in the next room or on another continent, because this highly mediated network will be unconstrained by miles and kilometers."

Computers used in ministry

The printing press was invented to print Bibles. The Roman roads, the technological wonders of their time, were used by the Apostle Paul to spread the gospel. In the past, technology was seen as the servant of ministry. This section features stories of computers in the service of the gospel today. Names are changed and events modified to provide privacy.

Computer baptism follows computer conversion.

Jeff assured me that it wasn't an ordinary baptism when he began telling me about it.

"We had one guy in the back of the church hooked up online with his computer," he told me. "While the baptism was going on, he was typing in everything step-by-step and there was a group of us all over the U.S. who were online receiving the message. It was a way for us to join in the baptism even though we were hundreds of miles apart.

Why did all these folks want to participate, I wondered. Was it the baptism of someone they were all related to? Jeff went on to explain. "We had this Christian discussion group online and Chris wandered into it while cruising the net one night. We started conversing with him. He asked questions, we answered them. He debated with us, we answered and prayed. Finally, one night online, surrounded by his virtual buddies, Chris accepted Jesus as his savior. So, it only seemed right that we be with him when he got baptized.

Commentary: There are no closed doors to sharing the gospel online.

Online witnessing sets the stage for salvation.

Jenny remembered she was nervous. She was meeting someone in person she'd met online, but unlike so many she'd read about this wasn't a romantic meeting. She was meeting Steve, who she had been witnessing to for the past several months online.

They'd met in a chat room entitled 40plus. What started out as a conversation about the heartache of the divorce Steve was going through prompted Jenny to ask if Steve was a Christian. As she shared, "The standard line of going to church as a child came out and from that I knew he did not know the Lord.

"Our friendship continued to grow with our discussion moving more and more into the area of a relationship with God. I suggested he find a church. . . and he did just that."

Now Jenny was attending a conference in the city Steve lived. She recalled their meeting, in spite of her nerves: "Our conversation about God continued face to face. . . after answering all his questions, Gary invited Jesus into his heart. . . . So often we are called to plant seeds but not to harvest them. It was wonderful to do both with my online friend.

MARCH 1996 PAGE ONE

CYBERCHURCH UPDATE, a newsletter of news, stories and commentary to inform and challenge the Church to be an effective witness for Jesus Christ in the information age. 4 pages, 10 times a year, $24.

To subscribe, contact: Ministry Computing Resources, P.O. Box 202730, Arlington, TX, 76006; ph: 817-861-9535.

All of the monumental changes going on in the world of technology and the reason why so much emphasis is on the Internet is based on a very simple premise that all information is digital, meaning it can be represented by a combination of two conditions—either the presence or the absence of an electrical signal. This presence or absence is represented as either a 0 or a 1 called a *bit* or a *digit.* Eight of these bits is termed a *byte* and each byte can represent either a letter or number.

In the same way that the basic dots and dashes of Morse code formed a language that could communicate messages across the globe, bits and bytes form *digital communication.* Unlike Morse code which moved very slowly, digital communication travels at the rate of billions of bits of information per second. Digitization means taking information, whether it is a word-processed document, CD recording or a color picture of Jupiter from space and converting it to digital components.

Words, music and static images are only the beginning. Full-body scans have been done of some movie stars. More than one B-grade science fiction movie has had the "soul" of a character digitized and enter the computer upon death of the body.

Once reduced to these digital components, the elements can be edited, altered, manipulated and sent or projected anywhere.

Implications of digitization

A photograph can be altered just like a word-processed document. A face, a person, an entire world can be created out of stored pieces of information. Because of this ease of creation and editing, it is often difficult to tell what the original was. We can no longer believe or trust what we see.

For believers, the 2 Corinthians 5:7 admonition that "we walk by faith and not by sight," will become more and more true as digital communication increases in sophistication. We believe in a person, Jesus Christ, and the truth of His Word no matter what our eyes and senses tell us.

Bandwidth: the pipeline for the digital river

"All this may seem more like science fiction than reality. Indeed, in the history of the world, it has been only a few hundred years since gunpowder transformed human warfare and less than a century since television connected the world. But just as those inventions brought us to the twentieth century, so will digital information transmit us into the next, transforming everything from how we learn to how we work."

Vice President Al Gore,
PC World

Understanding bandwidth is important to distinguish between reality and dreams in the information revolution. With the digitization of information, many things are *possible* today—virtual reality, interactive movies and games, 500 channel TV—but the key to translating the theory into reality is bandwidth.

Bandwidth is a measure of the carrying capacity of the communications link. It's a physical, limiting reality and you can't cram a big dream of digitized material down a little pipe no matter how innovative it is.

Bandwidth consists of a variety of communication pipelines today including the phone lines, satellite, coaxial cable and fiber optic cable. Most of them can't carry much digital data at a time and the ones that can aren't in widespread use at present.

According to one estimate, existing copper lines can handle from 4-240 phone calls at a time, coaxial cable about 5,000, satellite transmission 8,000 to 15,000 and fiber optic cable 100,000.

The problem is that we've mostly got copper wire linking everybody, while folks prototype, dream and advertise as if everyone had a direct fiber optic hookup to their homes. In practical terms this means don't count on the reality of hyped promises of interactive TV and many of the exotic applications of the Internet until more bandwidth is in place—it's coming, but it isn't here yet.

"The . .Internet is not going to disappear. The Net is becoming the next major communications medium. Your children will have to learn not only how to navigate the Net, but how to use the net wisely, with discernment and strong Biblical convictions."

Quentin J. Schultze,
Internet for Christians

Ministry limitations imposed by bandwidth

Be practical in the use of the bandwidth you've got today in ministry and communication, but dream and plan for increased bandwidth in the future.

Always check out whether or not people can actually receive what you create. Even simple desktop systems can create far more powerful images than it is realistic to communicate. By using off-the-shelf software available today you could create an interactive, virtual reality simulation of a missionary compound, but probably none of your donors have the bandwidth as yet to receive that creation.

On-line: the primary digital highway of today

This word can be used as a destination in terms such as *going on-line* or as an adjective as in *on-line communication, on-line service providers*. On-line is simply the overall term for the communications from one computer to another via telephone lines. The commercial service providers and the Internet are all *on-line.*

To go on-line usually requires the use of a modem, which connects your computer to the phone lines. A modem translates the analog or sound wave language of your telephone into the digital communication language of the computer.

Internet: the highway of on-line communication

"Newspapers are limited by space; TV broadcasts are limited by time. But the net has no time or space constraints. You can find as much information as you want, whenever you want."

Michelle Staialla,
Netguide

This on-line global connection of computers was established in 1969 by the U.S. government as a virtually indestructible military communications system that would remain intact regardless of nuclear war or other disaster. Soon large universities joined in to share research data over this system.

The Internet can be accessed directly using your computer and a modem or connecting through the commercial on-line service providers such as CompuServe or America OnLine. They provide software that makes it easier to connect to the Internet. In addition they have a variety of services from E-mail to encyclopedias on-line. They charge a monthly fee that starts at around $10 a month. They are a good way to start on the Internet. Once you learn your way around, if you find you are spending lots of time on the Internet, check into a local specialized provider.

E-mail: electronic mail—the on-line way to reach out and touch

"Since the technology behind the Internet has not 'settled into its own' yet, there is still time for the Church to establish an influence . . . . the Church must realize that there is a new mission field forming on the phone lines, modems and computer screens of the world."

Jerry Woods,
Religion Magazine

One of the most popular parts of on-line activity. It's a sort of combined letter and phone call. You type a message on your computer and then via your modem you can send it anywhere in the world online. In addition to the advantages of being almost instantaneous, there are no additional charges, beyond your basic fee, no matter where the destination.

Ministry uses of E-mail

Unlike any other form of communication, from postage to phones which can cost lots of money depending upon the ultimate destination, communication on-line costs the same no matter where the destination (very little, starting at about $10 per month) and is almost instantaneous all over the world. It's also very quick and easy. Few people worry about spelling, proper grammar or format in most on-line communication. Personal ministry and evangelism can expand tremendously.

In practical terms this means you could encourage a missionary in Canada, firm up several conference speaking engagements in Colorado and Texas, counsel a friend having trouble with their kids in Georgia, encourage teaching staff in several states and write several personal letters to friends all over the world in less than an hour's time and for a cost of pennies. I did just that through my E-mail last night.

World Wide Web: what made the Internet popular

Ministry Computing Resources is in the process of setting up a Web site that should be operational by the fall of 1996. Look us up through any on-line directory or find out our Web address by calling 817-861-9535.

Our Web site will keep you updated on materials and seminars to help you be an effective witness in cyberspace.

The Web transformed the Internet from the hangout of computer geeks and research nerds into the Disneyland that it is today by adding pictures. Just like Windows made computing seem like it was designed for human beings because you could click on a picture and something happened instead of typing in: C\\. ***.???. In the same way, the Web lets you click from picture to picture to find out about all sorts of things from ministry to movies instead of typing in complex UNIX commands.

In addition to the pictures, the pictures are linked (via *hyperlinks*) to other pictures and information of related topics that you can access by a click of the mouse.

The starting place for various topics on the Web are what are called home pages. Each home page has an address that is called a *URL.* URLs are those http//www.something.com things that you see popping up at the end of commercials on TV and in every imaginable advertisement you see these days. URL means "universal resource locator."

The Web's importance in ministry

Sooner than you imagine, E-mail addresses and home pages will be as common as phone numbers. Already many individuals and churches use E-mail to minister to people, to witness and to exchange prayer requests. Numerous ministry newsletters are being distributed on-line, saving time, paper, printing and distribution costs.

Home pages for ministries and churches allow folks from all over the world to access information about them at any time. There are no closed doors to sharing the gospel on-line.

You've got the basic skills to communicate on-line

"At current growth rates, estimated time at which everyone on Earth will be on the Internet: 2004."

Entrophy#16, A1 96

Though we don't have the time or space in this book to get into the details of how to construct a home page, be assured that you've already got the basic skills for communicating on-line.

All of the design principles you learned in this book work when designing home pages. Learning to write in levels as the writing section taught is how you write and organize your material to be able to hypertext it for the Web.

None of us could have imagined desktop publishing when many of us learned to type. The explosive growth and popularity of the Internet has taken even computer veterans by surprise. Should the Lord tarry, who knows what else we'll be confronted with before we meet Him, but we know in all of these technological changes our message and our Master never change. In the meantime, let's embrace with excitement new ways of sharing the messages of the kingdom of God.

The most important step in managing desktop publishing projects is to learn all you can about it because it is a radically different process than anything used to create traditional publications.

chapter 14

Managing DTP

Desktop publishing is more than a new technology, it is an entirely new way to produce communications. In addition, it creates new relationships between the people in organizations who produce communications using desktop publishing.

Understanding these relationship changes is as important as understanding the technology. DTP can either be an exciting adventure for a ministry team or it can become an area of misunderstanding and frustration. Work and pray to make it a source of joy and blessing.

Areas of misunderstanding in managing DTP

"Regardless of your experience and that of your staff, expect productivity to drop in the beginning, as everyone learns the new system . . . . It will probably take at least three production cycles before you can get all the kinks out . . . . Many organizations continue to use traditional production methods in parallel with their new desktop systems, phasing in the new methods gradually."

Janet Millenson
Publish! magazine

Here are some of the most common misunderstandings that occur in DTP management:

Training limitations

No matter what the sales person tells you or what the ad promises, you can't just open the package, give it to a person, and in one day have him or her producing publications. It isn't magic. It's a difficult new technology to learn.

People need training in the software and in publication design. This book is a good start on publication design, but you need to learn how to use your software before this book will be useful and before you can begin to produce publications.

Training in the software is essential either through a class or lots of time spent using the tutorial. You cannot pass up this essential time without putting the person expected to do desktop publishing through massive emotional trauma.

Software limitations

Though desktop publishing can do many things, it can't do some things that are easy to do in traditional publishing and some programs can't do what other programs do.

Know what to expect out of your specific DTP program and plan publications within those limitations. All the temper tantrums in the world and the demands made on the person doing the publication will not change what the software can and cannot do.

Trust limitations

The person who takes the time to learn the computer, the software and publication design now has a tremendous base of skills and knowledge. Again and again, latent creative skills greatly blossom when someone begins using DTP.

All members of groups learning to use DTP need to trust and affirm each other. A variety of ideas and designs need to be respected. Suggestions for production need to be discussed. Congratulate each other in learning an extremely complex and innovative skill.

DTP management suggestions

Finally, be strong in the Lord and in his mighty power. Put on the full armor of God so that you can take your stand against the devil's schemes. For our struggle is not against flesh and blood, but against the rulers, against the authorities, against the powers of this dark world and against the spiritual forces of evil in the heavenly realms. Therefore, put on the full armor of God . . . the belt of truth . . . the breastplate of righteousness . . . the gospel of peace . . . the shield of faith . . . the helmet of salvation and the sword of the Spirit, which is the word of God. And pray in the Spirit on all occasions with all kinds of prayers and requests.

Ephesians 6:10-18

Learn as much as you can together

Take a class, read this book, sit down and observe an actual project being put together. Learn firsthand what it means when you ask for one more little change. As one student of mine related to me, his boss got a whole new meaning of that request after three hours of watching him make that "one little change."

Don't forget the enemy

Remember Satan is the accuser of the brethren. DTP is a powerful tool to communicate the messages of the kingdom of God, and it isn't being ignored by the enemy.

Again and again, I've had clients tell me about the terrible fights and misunderstandings they have between staff members in implementing DTP publications. I remind them that beyond any seeming surface cause, it is a spiritual battle they are engaged in.

Pray

More important than any technology is the resource of prayer for the Christian.

Pray for wisdom in purchasing equipment and software; pray for knowledge and insight as you train; pray for understanding, kindness and patience with people you work with in creating your DTP publications.

Pray for the publications you create. Ask God to bless them and use them with power to touch lives and bring His healing and salvation.

Never lose sight of your ministry because of technology

This book began with the prayer that I might see your hearts. I want to close with a prayer from my heart for you as you do desktop publishing to the glory of God.

My prayer is that you remember that only people are eternal and only the message of the gospel is unchanging. Desktop publishing is the latest tool to communicate that message. One day, DTP and all of the exotic technologies that develop from it will be set aside like toys outgrown, when we see Jesus who is the reason for our communications and the heart of our message, face to face.

"So then, dear friends, since you are looking forward to this, make every effort to be found spotless, blameless and at peace with him" (2 Pet. 3:14).

chapter 15

Glossary

Access—To retrieve information stored in the computer.

Anecdote—a short entertaining account of an event. Anecdotes are essential for readers to "see" a story.

Ascender—a typography term which refers to the upper part of the letter that extends above the x-height.

ASCII—American Standard Code for Information Interchange. To transfer text from one program or computer to another, a user usually saves it as an ASCII ("askey") file.

Back-up—to copy software packages and work files from the computer's hard drive to a floppy disk for safekeeping in a separate location. This protects the files from loss due to a hard disk crash, an accident (fire, flood, etc.) or theft.

Baseline—a typography term that refers to the horizontal line on which all letters rest.

Bit—binary digit; the smallest unit of computer or digital information; represented by 0 or 1. Eight bits make a byte.

Byte—a common unit of computer storage. A byte is made up of eight binary digits (0s and 1s). A byte is a single character to the computer, such as a letter or a number. Computer hardware is measured in bytes. For example, old 20 MB (megabyte) hard drives held 20 million bytes.

CD-ROM—stands for compact disk, read-only memory. They look just like music CDs and these disks can store huge amounts of information, approximately 650 MB per disk. More and more software is being sold on them because they are such an efficient storage medium.

Call-outs—an interesting comment, phrase or quote set apart from the text, also called blurbs or pull quotes. May be pulled from the context of an article or is material that gives new related information or adds impact.

Cap line—a typography term; an imaginary line that runs across the top of the capital letters and some ascenders.

Captions—descriptive comments below photographs, graphs and illustrations that help convey the intended message of the graphic.

Church Management Software—specialized type of software that includes a variety of tasks specific to churches, such as keeping track of member records, contributions, attendance, outreach contacts, sermon notes and illustrations.

Clip art—copyright-free art that can be used in DTP publications. It can be scanned in and placed in documents or cut out and pasted in. Electronic clip art, available on disk, can be transferred from the disk directly into a DTP project.

Communications software—software that allows a computer to talk to other computers through a modem.

Computer User Groups—groups of people who get together to share information, ideas and tips about a particular computer. Highly recommended as a place to learn about a computer.

CPU—Central Processing Unit, the part of the computer that actually does the computing. Also referred to as the microprocessor chip.

Crash—a term used for a variety of severe computer problems involving either hardware or software. A crash can involve loss of data or difficulty in recovering it, which is why frequent saves and backups of data are recommended.

Crop/cropping—cutting down a photograph or illustration to eliminate distracting or unnecessary parts.

Cursor—the moving symbol on the computer screen that shows where data is entered. On text programs it is usually a blinking vertical line or underline; on graphic systems it is often an arrow.

Data—information entered into a computer, including names, addresses or numbers. The computer can then manipulate this information in some way.

Database software—software that can store, file, rearrange and sort the data that has been placed into the computer. Often used for mailing lists and usually a primary part of church managment software.

Deck—(See"Subhead")

Descender—the lower part of a letter that extends below the baseline.

Desktop publishing—the process of using a personal computer to combine text and graphics to produce publications. Abbreviated "DTP."

Dingbats—originally called "printer's marks." These decorative elements make up a type font. They can be scaled and sized as type, and used as artwork in DTP projects.

Disk—also called a floppy disk or diskette. A removable storage medium that usually inserts into a slot in the front of the computer. There are two sizes of floppy disks, 5.25 and 3.5.

Document—any short or long item (note, newsletter, sermon, letter, etc.) created and saved in a word processing program.

Documentation—the how-to manual that comes with software and hardware packages.

Downstyle—to write a headline or subhead without capitalizing the first letter of every word. Can also be thought of as writing headlines as a sentence without a period.

DPI—dots per inch, usually written in lower case—dpi. It is the measure of resolution of a printer or monitor. Resolutions on laser printers begin around 300 dpi. Monitors start at around 72 dpi.

Dragging—to reposition an object on the computer screen by selecting it with a cursor, holding down the mouse button and then moving the mouse.

Field—a unit of data. For example, separate fields for names, addresses and phone numbers in a database program.

File—means different things in different software packages. In word processing, a file is a single document of text. In a database, a file is a collection of related records. In a drawing program, a file is a single drawing or illustration.

Floppy disk—(see "Disk")

Floppy drive—the slot, usually on the front of the computer, in which the user can insert the floppy disk.

Flush left—to line up lines of text on the left margin of the page or column.

Flush right—to line up lines of text on the right margin of the page or column.

Font—traditionally, this term means a complete set of characters in a particular size and style of type, for example, Times, 10 point, bold. In DTP programs, this term is sometimes used interchangeably with the term *typeface.*

Footer—the line or information at the bottom of a page that is the same throughout a document.

Function keys—Special keys on a computer labeled F1, F2, F3, etc. These keys perform different operations depending on the software program being run. For example, in DTP, a specific F key (the exact number would depend on the program) might underline selected text or make it bold.

Grid—the underlying structure of a document created in DTP that identifies margins and columns, provides for consistent placement of graphic elements and assures a consistent, professional look in publications from issue to issue.

Halftoning—the process of converting a continuous-tone photograph into a series of dots that look like gray tones when printed. End product—a halftone. This process was necessary, prior to DTP, to place photographs into publications.

Hard drive or disk—an internal storage system for a computer, usually a metal, magnetic disk encased in metal. It can hold large amounts of storage.

Hardware—the part of the computer that can be touched.

Header—the line or information at the top of a page that is the same throughout a document.

Icon—a small, graphic representation of an object, such as an application, on the computer screen. First made popular in the Macintosh computers, now part of Windows software for IBM-compatibles.

Input—to enter data into the computer.

Integrated software—a software package that usually combines word processing, spreadsheets, graphics, database and communications software. Useful to churches or ministries for a variety of tasks, including DTP.

Internet—a global linkage of computers that allow users to communicate via E-mail, or electronic mail. Also the home of the World Wide Web, a graphic interface for information. For detailed definitions of the terms relating to it, see *The Internet,* chapter 11.

Justified—to line up lines of text so they touch both the left and right margins of a page or column.

Kerning—the process of tightening up the space between letters so they are easier to read. DTP programs do this automatically

Keyboard—similar to a typewriter keyboard, a computer keyboard is usually attached to the computer with a flexible cord. A computer keyboard usually has a numeric keypad, plus a row of function keys.

Laser printer—a printer that uses an electrophotographic method, similar to what is used in copy machines, to print pages. The laser printer is what makes DTP possible. Laser printers do this because they can produce type at 300 dpi and higher, type resolution.

Layout—the arrangement of graphics and text on a page. DTP programs provide the ability to do layout using a computer program.

Leading—the space between lines of type. Pronounced "ledding." Leading is measured in points, and is written as a fraction —10/12, but pronounced "ten on twelve." (In this example, the type is ten points high; the type size, plus two points of space between the rows of type equal twelve points or the measurement of the leading.)

Loren ipsum—dummy text used for examples in DTP. It is not Latin or any other language.

Mainframe—a large, central computer.

Megabyte—One million or actually 1,048,576 bytes; abbreviated MB.

Microprocessor—this is the heart of the computer on a single chip. Also known as the CPU or central processing unit.

Modem—an abbreviation of modulator-demodulator, a device that allows computers to communicate with each other over phone lines.

Monitor—the computer screen that looks like a TV screen. The monitor displays the work done on the computer. Monitors are available in a variety of sizes and either in monochrome or color.

Mouse—a small, palm-size device used to manipulate objects on a computer screen. It moves on a roller across a mouse pad and controls the moving cursor on the screen. A similar device is a trackball.

MS-DOS—Microsoft Disk Operating System. The operating system for PCs. Without an operating system, there is no way to tell the computer chip what tasks the software programs are to perform.

Nameplate—the graphic design and name of a newsletter as appears on the first page of the publication. Sometimes incorrectly referred to as the masthead.

Network—a connection of computers and software that enables users to share programs and projects.

Personal computer (PC)—a term that distinguishes a computer from one that is just a terminal tied into a mainframe. Both computers might look identical, but a PC can do all computing functions independent of any other machine.

Pica—primary measurement used in graphic arts and DTP. Much easier to use than inches because picas are always measured in whole numbers, never in fractions. Six picas equal an inch.

Pixel—shortened form of "picture element." Pixels are the square elements that make up the smallest unit on the computer screen. Characters and graphics are created and modified by turning the pixels on and off.

Points—measurement for type in DTP, graphic arts and printing—12 points to a pica, 6 picas to an inch and 72 points to an inch.

Program—a set of instructions, written in a language or code the computer can understand, that tells the computer what tasks to perform. The term "program" is often used interchangeably with software.

Programmer—a person who writes a computer program.

Public domain—graphic or written material that is not protected by a current copyright.

RAM—Random Access Memory—the computer's short-term memory. It is erased when the computer is turned off.

ROM—Read Only Memory. The internal memory storage of the computer, located on a chip on a board inside the computer.

Scanner—a machine linked to a computer that is similar to a miniature photocopy machine. Instead of the image coming out copied on paper, it is stored digitally on a hard drive or floppy disk.

Serif and sans serif—broadly defined, these terms refer to the two main categories of typefaces used in DTP. Specifically, a "serif" is the small stroke at the end of a letter. "Sans serif" means letters without serifs.

Sidebar—sections of text usually placed inside boxes. Often used for lists, tips, and schedules in publications.

SIG—special interest group. Within computer user groups, they are made up of people who share a common interest in a particular computer skill, such as DTP.

Software—computer programs designed to do specific type of task. For example, word processing software, spreadsheet software, and DTP software.

SPA—Software Publishers Association. A group of software publishers whose purpose is to monitor and prevent software piracy. Their hotline number for information and to report violations is 1-800-388-7478.

Spreadsheet—a specialized kind of software that primarily computes numbers.

Style guide—a sheet with actual examples and specific measurements for a publication; includes type sizes, leading and layout guidelines.

Subhead—words above a subdivision of text that summarize or label the text's content.

Subtitle or deck—a descriptive phrase below the headline that explains or expands the headline's meaning, shows its significance and encourages the reader to get into the text.

Template—the combination of a layout grid and the style sheet that forms an electronic prototype of a publication. The layout grid shows where blocks of text and graphics can be placed. The style sheet describes what type size, leading, style and indentation will be used in a publication.

Toolbox—a small box displayed on the screen within a computer program that has a selection of tools available in that program. Tools are selected by clicking them with the cursor.

Trackball—used to move the cursor and manipulate objects on the screen. Instead of moving the mouse on a pad, the user moves a ball in a plastic square.

Tracking—adjusting the overall spacing between letters. Some DTP programs allow users to do this manually.

Window—a separate viewing area of choices on your computer screen, such as the style palette or toolbox.

Windows—a graphics interface operating system developed by Microsoft that runs on PCs and is similar to the graphic interface of the Macintosh.

Word processing software—this software allows the user to enter, edit, move, and manipulate text in a variety of ways and print it.

World Wide Web or WWW—the graphical interface that has made the Internet accessible to everyone.

X-height—the size of the lower case letters of a typeface.

chapter 16

Resources

For additional training—Yvon Prehn's seminars

Yvon Prehn teaches seminars on a variety of topics in using technology in ministry today and in desktop publishing.

Some of the topics are:

- *Tap the Power of Desktop Publishing and the Internet for Your Church or Ministry*
- *Ministry Newsletters that Work—an overview of creating newsletters for churches and ministries using desktop publishing*
- *Advanced Newsletter Techniques in Writing and Design*
- *Writing to Reach Today's Audiences, a three-level approach that communicates to people today*
- *Technology Briefing—What You Need to Know About Technology to Minister Effectively in the Information Age.*

All except the Technology Briefing, these seminars are usually given as full-day training sessions. All topics can be given in one or more hour breakout sessions at conferences.

Topics relating specifically to technology and ministry can be used for keynote addresses at conferences and seminars.

Please call for information about having Yvon Prehn speak at national church and ministry conventions. In addition, Ministry Computing Resources has a very affordable plan for churches, camps or conference centers to sponsor a seminar on these topics. Publication consulting combined with the seminar is also available for churches, camps and conference centers who sponsor seminars at their locations.

For fees, details and to schedule Yvon Prehn for a seminar, please call: Ministry Computing Resources, phone (817) 861-9535 or E-mail: 75210.1600@compuserve.com.

Colorado Springs opportunities
Becky Towne, Colorado Springs Area Director

In Colorado Springs, Ministry Computing Resources offers a large variety of seminars on the above topics, plus training in computer hardware and software. Publication design services are also available.

For information, contact Becky Towne at phone (719) 632-5721 or E-mail: MinComp@kktv.com.

Ministry Computing Resources Newsletters

MCR publishes two great newsletters that will help you communicate effectively to your generation.

The book is an essential starter for anyone involved in DTP for ministry, but new products, ideas, resources and methods come out continuously and the first newsletter will keep you updated and informed.

The second newsletter, doesn't necessarily have anything to do with DTP, but it is for anyone wanting to be an informed witness for Jesus in the technological age.

#1—Desktop Publishing and New Media in Ministry, a bimonthly (6 issues per year) **newsletter** of ideas, inspiration, and information for Christian computer communicators—$36 per year.

#2—CYBERCHURCH UPDATE (10 issues per year) newsletter—$24 per year.

To order send check or MC/Visa information to: Ministry Computing Resources, P.O. Box 202730, Arlington, TX 76006, or phone (817) 861-9535 or E-mail at 75210.1600@compuserve.com.

Software discounts and deals

Consistent Computer Bargains
(800) 342-4222

***If you don't call anybody else, be sure to contact these folks! They have the best deals on software for ministries that have nonprofit status.

If you don't have nonprofit status, contact the mail order places listed below. Never pay full retail price for software, mail order will always have the best deals. In addition, stores rarely give software support, so you might as well save the money and buy mail order.

Surplus Direct
(800) 753-7877

A clearinghouse for previous version software, various closeouts, etc.—really good deals.

For PCs

MicroWarehouse
(800) 367-7080
Tiger Software
(800) 888-4437

For Macintoshes

Macs Place
(800) 367-4222
The Mac Zone
(800) 248-0800

Christian clip art

Proclaim Communications
(216) 888-7870
Fantastic stuff-photos, Christian Dingbats, templates

QuickArt
(800) 311-0869
Fun, upbeat images

Zondervan
(800) 727-7759
Great teen stuff, on CD

LOGOS
(800) 87-LOGOS
Classic, editable Bible art

Gospel Light
(805) 644-9721
Wonderful art for kids

Swan Lake Communications
(601) 372-7305
Words as art, unique

Pastoral Computer Services
(800) 272-2252
Beautiful Bible illustrations

Communication Resources
(800) 992-2144
Classy artwork, resources

Liguori Faithware
(800) 325-9521
Catholic artwork

Bible Study Software

Hyperbible
(800) 428-4385

Logos Research Systems
(800) 87-LOGOS

Online Bible
(908) 741-4298

NavPress Software
(800) 888-9898

Other software sources:

Call for the catalogs from the places below—they have a wide selection of Christian-related software, some of which is useful in DTP.

By the Numbers
(800) 554-9116

Ellis Enterprises
(800) 729-9500

Parsons Technology
(800) 223-6925

ByteSize Software
(800) 232-9837

On-line Providers

America Online
(800) 827-6364
Home of Christianity Online

CompuServe
(800) 848-8199
Home of Christian Interactive Network—Go CIN

Prodigy
(800) 776-3449

On-line recommended books

Christian Guide to Cyberspace
by Jason Baker

Internet for Christians, Everything You Need to Know to Start Cruising the Net Today
by Quentin J. Schultze

Christian Specialty Gifts Source

Dynamic Christian Concepts
(800) 432-1322

Other resources

One of the best places to check out the latest resource materials are the computer magazines at your public library. Occasionally go to the library and browse through the computer magazines taking special note of the ads. Most of these magazines have a card you can photocopy, fill out, and send in to find out more about advertised hardware and software.

Unless you know quite a bit about computer hardware, you may not want to purchase your hardware mail order. For hardware it helps to have a good computer store in town where you can go for advice and repairs. However, if you know someone who knows about computers, can repair them, and answer your hardware questions, there are significant savings for purchasing hardware by mail.

For software, unless you have a discount software outlet available, it's always cheapest and easiest to buy software by mail. You don't get any software support from most computer stores anyway and software savings through the mail can be several hundred dollars per program.

To find out about purchasing hardware through the mail, one of the best sources is the:

Computer Shopper
One Park Avenue, 11th Floor
New York, NY 10016
(800) 346-3247

This publication is available at most magazine stands, even ones in grocery stores. This "magazine" is about two inches thick and lists more mailorder sources for hardware and software in one issue than you can imagine.

The best resource of all

As you journey in this new land of desktop publishing, the best resources are your fellow pilgrims.

No matter where you are in the process, gather a group of fellow learners; get together each week; assign research projects to each other; bring your successes and tragedies; learn from and encourage each other.

Pray lots for each other and your projects; pray for insight and wisdom as you work. You are creating communication pieces that can change the destiny of souls for eternity—with the Lord's help your work can accomplish great things.

chapter 17

Index

help for Better Bulletins, Flyers & Newsletters

SAVE $5

ON AN INSPIRING VIDEO WORKSHOP

Here's a coupon for $5 off your purchase of the **How to Use Your Computer to Create Better Bulletins, Newsletters and More Video Training Seminar!** Improve your publications and save some money along the way.

This lively, easy-to-follow video seminar is like having three hours of personal training from a master instructor—any time you need it! **How to Use Your Computer to Create Better Bulletins, Newsletters and More** gives you plenty of advice, tips and insight to help you:

- Plan and produce great-looking publications
- Use typefaces to get maximum impact
- Create layouts and use pictures
- Work smarter, not harder
- And much more!

$5 off

Simply fill out this coupon, sign and return it to your favorite retailer and you'll receive $5 off the purchase price of **How to Use Your Computer to Create Better Bulletins, Newsletters and More Video Training Seminar** (UPC 6-07135-00066-2).

Name ______________________________

Address ______________________________

City ______________ State ________ Zip ________

Phone ______________________________

Signature ______________________________
(required for redemption)

Attention consumer: Redeemable only at participating retailers. Not redeemable through Gospel Light. You must pay applicable sales tax. LIMIT ONE COUPON PER CUSTOMER. NOT VALID WITH ANY OTHER OFFERS. Offer available while supplies last. Valid only if signed and phone number included for verification.

Attention Retailer: Customer is eligible for five dollars ($5.00) off the purchase of one copy of **How to Use Your Computer to Create Better Bulletins, Newsletters and More** (UPC 6-07135-00066-2) with this coupon, when completed and signed by customer. Please redeem coupon for $5 credit with your next Gospel Light payment. P.O. Box 3875, Ventura CA 93006-9891. Void where restricted or prohibited. This coupon has no cash value.

Priority Code 1551

Gospel Light